An Introduction to the History of America

Chittabrata Palit
Jenia Mukherjee

FOUNDATION®
BOOKS

Delhi • Bengaluru • Mumbai • Kolkata • Chennai • Hyderabad
Pune • Thiruvananthapuram

Published by
Cambridge University Press India Pvt Ltd
under the imprint of Foundation Books
Cambridge House, 4381/4 Ansari Road, Daryaganj, **New Delhi** 110 002

Cambridge University Press India Pvt Ltd
C-22, C-Block, Brigade M.M., K.R. Road, Jayanagar, **Bengaluru** 560 070
Plot No. 80, Service Industries, Shirvane, Sector-1, Nerul, **Navi Mumbai** 400 706
10 Raja Subodh Mullick Square, 2nd Floor, **Kolkata** 700 013
21/1 (New No. 49), 1st Floor, Model School Road, Thousand Lights, **Chennai** 600 006
House No. 3-5-874/6/4, (Near Apollo Hospital), Hyderguda, **Hyderabad** 500 029
Agarwal Pride, 'A' Wing, 1308 Kasba Peth, Near Surya Hospital, **Pune** 411 011
T.C. 25/ 2731 Lukes Lane, Ambujavilasam Road, **Thiruvananthapuram** 695 001

First Published 2014

ISBN 978-93-82993-18-6 (Paperback)

Published by Manas Saikia for Cambridge University Press India Pvt Ltd and printed at Akash Press, New Delhi 110 020

Contents

Preface

American History is the most widely explored area of research with numerous works getting added into the existing database on every particular topic every year. But all these include the work of American scholars and researchers. Though American History has been a constant part of post-graduate history syllabus of all Indian universities, no effective interpretative history, including wide range of topics from the birth of the nation to its emergence as the 'superpower hegemon' and its responses from other parts of the world, has been written historian by any Indian.

In this book, the authors have captured the historical sojourn of the American nation from pre-colonial to post-colonial times covering every important aspect that naturally flows from one to the other finally forming a cohesive whole. One interesting feature of this book is that the authors have provided historiography for every relevant theme with the understanding that as American History is such an emerging field, hence it is difficult for all to grab every book on a particular subject, posing the danger of making his/her knowledge incomplete. Hence, this book provides a brief synopsis of almost all major works till the recent times, also making the reader understand the immediate socio–economic and political trends that had shaped a particular research.

The authors have included two very interesting themes on American environmental history and American 'exceptionalism' to provide a critical analysis on the new range of evolving subjects. More such works should come up incorporating other socio–cultural perspectives.

The most significant contribution of this book is that it reveals the Southern perception and dissection of the North and brings out the often unaddressed tension between America's self-perception and the actual reality which can be mapped through crisis in the domestic front as well as impact on and response by 'others' (other peoples, nations, and cultures). Recently, American scholars are seeking for more comparative and transatlantic studies to break away from the isolationist and insular approach in American History. These studies will make proper sense when they also incorporate literature from non-American historians and researchers, who implement the comparative methodology in studying the American nation and the other (Southern) nations to underline what happened and is still happening in history, and radically explore the development of America as a 'Global Hegemon' at the cost of the underdevelopment of others. This kind of approach is also useful in eradicating the imitation model (where everything is viewed and understood from the Western/American prism, and non-Western countries seek to imitate the former forcibly following its 'developmentalist' path) and bringing out the particularities and potentialities of individual nations in the long course of human history.

Timeline of Events

Discoveries and Explorations

Year	Event(s)
1001	Leif Ericson explores North America
1492	Christopher Columbus discovers America
1497	John Cabot claims North America for England
1501	Amerigo Vespucci explores the coast of South America
1519	Ferdinand Magellan explores gulf Coast of America
1524	Giovanni Verrazano discovers New York Bay
1528	Panfilo de Narvaez conquers Cuba and explores Florida Alvar Cabeza de Vaca explores Texas, Arizona, and New Mexico
1534	Jacques Cartier explores the Great Lakes and the St. Lawrence River
1540	Garcia Lopez de Cardenas discovers the Grand Canyon
1541	Francisco Vásquez de Coronado explores Kansas
1542	Cabrillo explores and discovers the Californian coast Juan Rodriguez Cabrillo discovers San Diego Bay, California
1559	Tristan de Luna explores North America
1563	Francisco de Ibarra explores New Mexico
1576	Sir Martin Frobisher explores Baffin Bay and the Hudson Strait
1577	Sir Francis Drake circumnavigates the world – 13 December 1577 to 26 September 1580
1584	Philip Amadas and Arthur Barlowe (both in the service of Sir Walter Raleigh) explore the coast of North Carolina
1585	25 March: Walter Raleigh receives the patent to explore and settle in North America June: Walter Raleigh's fleet of seven vessels under Richard Grenville and Ralph Lane, with 108 men, reach Roanoke Island 4 June: Virginia colony of Roanoke Island established by Walter Raleigh
1598	Juan de Archuleta explores Colorado

1607	Captain John Smith explores Jamestown
1609	Henry Hudson explores Northeastern North America including the Hudson River

Anti-colonial Resistances and the War of Independence

1763	10 February: Treaty of Paris ends French and Indian War (1754–63) Canada east of the Mississippi River added to the British empire Pontiac's Rebellion against the British 7 October: The Proclamation of 1763 issued by King George III after the end of the French and Indian War/Seven Years' War to organize the new North American empire and stabilize relations with Native Americans No British settlements allowed west of the Appalachian mountains.
1764	February: James Otis urges a united response to the recent acts imposed by England. The phrase 'Taxation without Representation is Tyranny' is usually attributed to James Otis July: James Otis publishes 'The Rights of the British Colonies Asserted and Proved.' August: Boston merchants begin a boycott of British luxury goods
1765	22 March: The Stamp Act was passed by the British Parliament 24 March: The Quartering Act required American colonists to house British troops and supply them with food July: The Sons of Liberty is formed – a secret organization opposed to the Stamp Act December: Over 200 Boston merchants refuse to pay the Stamp Tax
1766	18 March: Stamp Act repealed January: New York assembly refuses to fully enforce the Quartering Act. August: Violence breaks out in New York between British soldiers and members of the Sons of Liberty
1768	July: Merchants in Boston and New York boycott British goods September: English warships sail into Boston Harbor leaving two regiments of English troops to keep order
1770	March: 'The Boston Massacre' – Four workers shot by British troops in Boston
1773	16 December: The Boston Tea Party – Massachusetts patriots dressed as Mohawk Indians protest against the British Tea Act by dumping crates of tea into Boston Harbor

1774	March: Passage of the Coercive/Intolerable Acts
1775	9 February: English Parliament declares Massachusetts to be in a state of rebellion 19 April: Shots fired at Lexington and Concord where weapons depot destroyed. 'Minute Men' force British troops back to Boston. George Washington takes command of the Continental Army. 15 June: George Washington appointed general and commander-in-chief of the new Continental Army 17 June: Battle of Bunker Hill 6 July: Declaration on the Causes and Necessity of Taking Up Arms stating that Americans are 'resolved to die free men rather than live as slaves.' Outbreak of the American Revolution
1776	2 May: The American Revolution gains support from King Louis XVI of France 4 July: Thomas Jefferson presents the United States Declaration of Independence
1777	15 November: Articles of Confederation – Congress is made sole authority of the new national government
1778	6 February: France signs a treaty of alliance with the United States and the American Revolution soon becomes a world war 14 September: Benjamin Franklin appointed American representative in France
1779	27 September: John Adams is appointed to negotiate peace with England
1782	27 February: English Parliament votes against further war in America. 10 November: The final battle of the Revolutionary War when Americans retaliate by attacking a Shawnee village in Ohio 30 November: Preliminary peace treaty signed in Paris recognizing American independence and the British withdrawal from America
1783	4 February: England officially declares an end to hostilities in America. 3 September: The Treaty of Paris is signed by the United States and Great Britain
1784	14 January: The Treaty of Paris is ratified by Congress and the American Revolutionary War officially ends
1789	First President George Washington elected The first 13 states were Delaware, Pennsylvania, New Jersey, Georgia, Connecticut, Massachusetts, Maryland, South Carolina, New Hampshire, Virginia, New York, North Carolina, and Rhode Island Judiciary Act passed

1791	Bill of Rights ratified
1797	Second President John Adams elected

The Formative Period (1800–1860)

1800	Library of Congress founded
1801	Third President Thomas Jefferson elected
1803	Louisiana Purchase Treaty
1807	Act Prohibiting Importation of Slaves
1808	US slave trade with Africa ends
1809	Fourth President James Madison elected
1812	War of 1812 begins
1817	Fifth President James Monroe elected
1818	Jackson Purchase in Kentucky
1819	Adams–Onis Treaty, including acquisition of Florida Illinois admission to the US
1820	Alabama and Maine admission to the US
1822	Missouri admission to the US
1825	Sixth President John Quincy Adams elected
1829	Seventh President Andrew Jackson elected
1835	Texas War for Independence begins
1836	Arkansas admission to the US
1837	Michigan admission to the US
1841	Ninth President William Henry Harrison elected Tenth President John Tyler elected
1845	Eleventh President James Knox Polk elected Texas admission to the US Florida admission to the US
1846	Mexican–American War begins Texas admission to the US Oregon Treaty signed
1847	Iowa admission to the US

1848	Gold discovered in California Wisconsin admission to the US Treaty of Guadalupe Hidalgo ends the Mexican–American War
1849	Twelfth President Zachary Taylor elected
1850	Thirteenth President Millard Fillmore elected
1851	California admission to the US
1853	Fourteenth President Franklin Pierce elected Gadsden Purchase
1857	Fifteenth President James Buchanan elected
1858	Minnesota admission to the US
1859	Oregon admission to the US
1860	Pony Express begins

Civil War and Civil Rights' Era

1861	Sixteenth President Abraham Lincoln elected Kansas admission to the US Confederate States of America (the Confederacy) established under President Jefferson Davis American Civil War begins
1863	West Virginia admission to the US
1865	April: Civil War ends with Northern victory Abraham Lincoln assassinated Seventeenth President Andrew Johnson elected Nevada admission to the US
1866	Civil Rights Act of 1866 Ku Klux Klan founded
1867	Nebraska admission to the US Alaska purchase from Russia
1869	Eighteenth President Ulysses Simpson elected
1871	Great Chicago Fire Treaty of Washington with Great Britain regarding the Dominion of Canada
1875	Civil Rights Act passed

1877 to the Pre-WWI Period

1877	Nineteenth President Rutherford Birchard Hayes elected Colorado admission to the US
1881	Twentieth President James Abram Garfield elected Twenty-First President Chester Alan Arthur elected
1885	Twenty-Second President Grover Cleveland elected
1889	Twenty-Third President Benjamin Harrison elected
1890	North Dakota, South Dakota, Montana, Washington, and Idaho admission to the US
1891	Wyoming admission to the US
1893	Twenty-Fourth President Grover Cleveland elected
1896	Utah admission to the US
1897	Twenty-Fifth President William McKinley elected
1898	Spanish-American War
1901	Twenty-Sixth President Theodore Roosevelt elected
1903	Ford Motor Company formed
1904	Panama Canal Zone acquired
1908	Oklahoma admission to the US
1909	Twenty-Seventh President William Howard Taft elected
1912	Arizona, Alaska, and New Mexico admission to the US
1913	Twenty-Eighth President Woodrow Wilson elected

WWI to the End of the WWII (1914–1945)

1914	The World War I begins
1917	US enters WWI
1919	The World War I comes to an end with the signing of the Treaty of Versailles
1921	Twenty-Ninth President Warren Gamaliel Harding elected
1923	Thirtieth President Calvin Coolidge elected
1924	Indian Reorganization Act
1929	Thirty-First President Herbert Clark Hoover elected Immigration Act Great Depression begins

1933	Thirty-Second President Franklin Delano Roosevelt elected Japan and Germany withdraw from League of Nations
1934	Dust Bowl begins
1935	Social Security Act
1939	Germany invades Poland; World War II begins
1941	Attack on Pearl Harbor US enters World War II
1945	Thirty-Third President Harry S. Truman elected US joins the United Nations Atomic bomb dropped on Hiroshima and Nagasaki Germany and Japan surrender World War II ends

The Cold War Period (1946–1991)

1946	The Cold War begins between the United States and the Soviet Union Atomic Energy Act
1948	Berlin Blockade
1949	North Atlantic Treaty Organization (NATO) formed Germany divided into East and West
1950	Senator Joseph McCarthy gains power and start Communist witch hunts (1950–54) Korean War begins
1953	Thirty-Fourth President Dwight David Eisenhower elected Armistice in Korea
1954	South East Asia Treaty Organization (SEATO) alliance
1955	Warsaw Pact
1956	Russians launch Sputnik
1958	National Aeronautics and Space Administration (NASA) formed
1959	Cuban Revolution
1961	Thirty-Fifth President John Fitzgerald Kennedy elected Vietnam War officially begins with 900 military advisors landing in Saigon Organization of the Petroleum Exporting Countries (OPEC) formed
1962	Cuban Missile Crisis

1963	President Kennedy assassinated Thirty-Sixth President Lyndon Baines Johnson elected
1969	Thirty-Seventh President Richard Milhous Nixon elected Neil Armstrong walks on the moon
1972	Anti-Ballistic Missile Treaty with USSR
1973	Vietnam War ends with US pulling out in 1973
1974	Thirty-Eighth President Gerald Rudolph Ford elected
1977	Thirty-Ninth President Jimmy Carter elected
1979	Three Mile Island nuclear accident 1979-Iran hostage crisis begins
1981	Fortieth President Ronald Wilson Reagan elected
1989	Fall of the socialist states allied to the Soviet Union
1990	Forty-First President George Herbert Walker Bush elected Iraq invades Kuwait leading to 1991 Gulf War
1991	Gulf War The Commonwealth of Independent States (CIS) formed 25 December: Gorbachev resigns from his office

Post-Cold War Period Till the Present Times (1992–2011)

1992	Los Angeles riots Hurricane Andrew causes devastation in Florida and Louisiana
1993	Forty-Second President William Jefferson Clinton elected World Trade Centre bombing
2001	Forty-Third President George Herbert Walker Bush elected 11 September: Terrorist (Al-Qaeda) attacks on the World Trade Centre and Pentagon Invasion of Afghanistan Operation 'Enduring Freedom'
2004	Occupation of Iraq, 2003–4
2005	Hurricane Katrina
2009	Forty-Fourth President Barack Obama, the first 'Black' President elected
2011	Assassination of Osama bin Laden (the founder of Al-Qaeda)

1

An Early History: From Settlement to Colonization

A prelude to the American Revolution, the chapter begins with a geological account of migration, spread and settlement of human population in the American continents in the Holocene period. The pre-colonial history of America is the history of efflorescence of several Native American cultures which is evident from archaeological excavations. The first section of the chapter sheds light on the economic, social, and cultural life of the Native Americans along with internal strife and conflicts between the native inhabitants and the Europeans. The discovery of America much before Amerigo Vespucci by the Norse (Vikings) is attested in the next section. The pre-Columbian expeditions were followed by Spanish, Portuguese, French, and later Dutch and English explorations. By explaining the reasons behind colonization in terms of god, glory, and gold, the final section provides detailed accounts of the exploration events and its impact on the indigenous communities and ecosystems of the continents.

a. Early Signs of Life and Native American Cultures

About 60,000–25,000 years ago, the Bering land bridge that joined Siberia to Alaska was created because of falling sea levels.[1] Migrations of humans from Eurasia to the Americas took place through this bridge till around 12,000 years ago. Linguistic and genetic data attest the fact that the early Paleo-Americans soon spread throughout the Americas and diversified into many hundreds of culturally distinct nations and tribes.[2] The North American climate stabilized by 8000 BCE, followed by widespread migration, cultivation of crops, and subsequently, a dramatic population spurt in the North and South Americas.

Archaeological excavations through the discovery of artefacts (the first discovery was conducted in 1932) in Clovis, New Mexico testify the existence of big-game hunting culture, labelled as the Clovis culture. It is primarily identified with the production of fluted projectile points. The culture is identified by the distinctive Clovis point, a flaked flint spear-point with a notched flute, by which it was inserted into a shaft. Archaeologists have dated the materials excavated from Clovis by establishing their association with animal bones and by the use of carbon-dating methods. Recent re-examinations of these materials using improved carbon-dating methods produced results of 11,050 and 10,800 radiocarbon years Before Present (BP), i.e., 9100 to 8850 BCE approximately.

Genetic and linguistic data connect the indigenous people of this continent with ancient northeast Asians. Numerous Paleo-Indian cultures migrated in North America and settled around the Great Plains and Great Lakes of the modern US and Canada and also in adjacent areas to the West and Southwest. The discovery of Folsom tools dated between 9000 and 8000 BCE reveal the presence of the Folsom Tradition (the term first used by J.D. Figgins, Director, Colorado Museum of Natural History) which was characterized by the use of Folsom points as projectile tips, and activities known from kill sites, where slaughter and butchering of bison took place. However, the Folsom diet apparently included mountain sheep, marmots, deer and cottontail rabbit. It occupied much of central North America.

Around 8000 BCE the Na-Dené-speaking peoples entered North America and reached the Pacific Northwest by 5000 BCE. From there they migrated along the Pacific Coast and further into the interior. Linguists, anthropologists and archaeologists believe that their ancestors comprised a separate migration into North America, later than the first Paleo-Indians, and they were the earliest ancestors of the Athabascan-speaking people, including the present-day and historical Navajo and Apache. They constructed large multi-family dwellings in their villages for seasonal use, especially in summer to hunt and fish and to gather food supplies for the winter. Evidences suggest the existence of the Oshara Tradition from 5500 BCE to 600 CE. It was a part of the Southwestern Archaic Tradition centred in North-central New Mexico, the San Juan Basin, the Rio Grande Valley, Southern Colorado, and Southeastern Utah.

Since 1990s, archaeologists have explored and dated 11 Middle Archaic sites in present-day Louisiana and Florida. In spite of being hunter-gatherers, these early culture people built complexes with multiple earthwork mounds. They were able to plan and organize large work forces over centuries to accomplish the complex mound and ridge constructions. The prime example is Watson Brake in northern Louisiana, whose 11 mound complex from three to 25 feet (7.6 m) in height, connected by ridges to form an oval nearly 900 feet (270 m) across, is dated to 3500 BCE. It is the oldest dated site in the Americas. The construction went on for 500 years and the site was abandoned around 2800 BCE, likely due to changing environmental conditions as Joe W. Saunders and Rolfe D. Mandel suggests in one of their articles entitled 'Watson Brake, a Middle Archaic Mound Complex in Northeast Louisiana' published in 2005 in *American Antiquity*.[3]

Evidence of a Late Archaic archaeological culture that inhabited the area of the Lower Mississippi Valley is the Poverty Point culture that thrived from 2200 BCE–700 BCE. Remains of this culture have been unearthed at more than 100 sites, from the major complex at Poverty Point, Louisiana across a 100-mile (160 km) range to the Jaketown Site near Belzoni, Mississippi. Poverty Point is a 1-square mile (2.6 square km) complex of six major earthwork concentric rings, with additional platform mounds at the site. Artefacts show that the people traded with other Native Americans located from Georgia to the Great Lakes region. This is one among numerous mound sites of complex indigenous cultures throughout the Mississippi and Ohio valleys. They were one of several succeeding cultures often described as mound builders.

The Woodland period of North American pre-Columbian cultures refers to the time period from roughly 1000 BCE to 1000 CE in the eastern part of North America. The term 'Woodland' was coined in the 1930s and refers to prehistoric sites dated between the Archaic period and the Mississippian cultures. This period is remarkable for having continuous development in stone and bone tools, leather crafting, textile manufacture, cultivation, and shelter construction. Pottery developed and reflected signs of sophistication and delicate decorations. Though there is no evidence of intensive agriculture during this period but the increasing use of agricultural tools and implements signify that people must have shifted from nomadic savagery to permanent settlement.

The Hopewell Tradition flourished along rivers in the Northeastern and Midwestern United States from 200 BCE to 500 CE. It was actually an integral part of the Woodland Period (Middle Woodland Period 1–500 CE) when patterns of migration and settlement could be noticed in the interior. By this time, a trade network developed in the Eastern United States with the increase of trade in exotic materials. The presence of remains of mortuary gifts in the burials of people with significant roles in the society, mostly in Illinois and Ohio, corroborates the fact. Thus, this tradition was actually a widely dispersed set of related populations, who were connected by a common network of trade routes, known as the Hopewell Exchange System. The system ran from the Southeastern United States into the Southeastern Canadian shores of Lake Ontario. Within this area, societies participated in a high degree of exchange. Waterways served as the major transportation routes.

Coles Creek culture developed between the Late Woodland Period (500–1000 CE) and the later Plaquemine culture period in the Lower Mississippi Valley (the present-day Southern United States). The period is marked with significant changes: there was a dramatic population spurt; other features of this culture are the increased use of flat-topped platform mounds arranged around central plazas, more complex political institutions, and a subsistence strategy still grounded in the Eastern Agricultural Complex and hunting. By 1000 CE, i.e., the end of this sequence, the formation of simple elite polities had begun. By the Coles Creek Period, the mounds also took on a newer shape and function. Instead of being only serving the burial purpose, mounds were constructed to support temples and other civic structures. Coles Creek sites are found in Arkansas, Louisiana, Oklahoma, Mississippi, and Texas. It is considered ancestral to the Plaquemine culture. The name appeared with James Ford's discovery of unique decoration on grog-tempered ceramic ware followed by his investigation of the site.

Hohokam is another major prehistoric archaeological tradition of the present-day American Southwest. This distinct culture was discovered by Harold S. Gladwin in the 2000s. This core area centred on the Phoenix basin, i.e., the Middle Gila River and Lower Salt River drainages. They constructed an assortment of simple canals combined with weirs;

and between the seventh and fourteenth centuries, they also built and maintained extensive irrigation networks along the core area that rivalled the complexity of those used in the ancient Near East, Egypt, and China. They cultivated varieties of cotton, tobacco, maize, beans, and squash and harvested a vast assortment of wild plants. Late in the Hohokam Chronological Sequence, they also used extensive dry-farming systems, primarily to grow agave. Their reliance on agricultural strategies based on canal irrigation, vital in their less than hospitable desert environment and arid climate, provided the basis for the aggregation of rural populations into stable urban centres.

The Mississippian culture (800 CE to 1500 CE approx) created the largest earthworks in North America, north of Mexico (most notably at Cahokia). It extended throughout the Ohio and Mississippi valleys and built sites throughout the Southeast. Its 10-story Monks Mound has a larger circumference than the Pyramid of the Sun at Teotihuacan or the Great Pyramid of Egypt. The 6-square miles (16 square km) city complex was based on the culture's cosmology and included more than 100 mounds, positioned to support their sophisticated knowledge of astronomy, and built with knowledge of varying soil types. It included a Woodhenge, whose sacred cedar poles were placed to mark the summer and winter solstices and fall and spring equinoxes. By 1250 CE it had 20,000–30,000 people. Several Mississippian chiefdoms flourished like Angel Mounds, Etowah, Moundville, the Parkin Site, Cahokia, etc. In the sixteenth century, the earliest Spanish explorers encountered Mississippian peoples in the interior of present-day North Carolina and the Southeast. Native Americans of the Mississippian culture interacted with Spanish explorers of the Juan Pardo expedition, who built a base there in 1567 called Fort San Juan. Expedition documentation and archaeological evidence of the fort and Native American culture both exist. The soldiers were at the fort for about 18 months (1567–68) before the natives killed them and destroyed the fort. They also killed soldiers stationed at five other forts; only one man out of 120 survived. Sixteenth-century Spanish artefacts have been recovered from the site, marking the first European colonization of what became the United States. The historic and modern day American Indian nations believed to have descended from the overarching Mississippian culture.

From the mid-fifteenth to sixteenth century, the distinct Iroquoian-speaking tribes came together to be known as the Iroquois League. They were also known as the Haudenosaunee (People of the Long House). Their system of affiliation was a kind of federation, different from the strong, centralized European monarchies. Leadership was restricted to a group of 50 sachem chiefs, each representing one clan within a tribe; the Oneida and Mohawk people had nine seats each; the Onondagas held 14; the Cayuga had 10 seats; and the Seneca had eight. Representation was not on the basis of population numbers, as the Seneca tribe greatly outnumbered the others. When a sachem chief died, his successor was chosen by the senior woman of his tribe in consultation with other female members of the clan. Property and hereditary leadership were passed matrilinally. Decisions were not made through voting but through consensus decision making with each sachem chief holding theoretical veto power. The Onondaga were the 'firekeepers', responsible for raising topics to be discussed. They occupied one side of a three-sided fire (the Mohawk and Seneca sat on one side of the fire and the Oneida and Cayuga sat on the third side). Historians believe that confederacy model contributed to the political thinking during the development of the later United States government. However, anthropologist Elizabeth Tooker has countered it and pointed out that it was unlikely that the US founding fathers were inspired by the confederacy, as it bears little resemblance to the system of governance which was based on inherited rather than elected leadership, selected by female members of the tribes, consensus decision-making regardless of population size of the tribes, and a single group capable of bringing matters before the legislative body.

From oral histories we come to know about numerous migrations to the historic territories where Europeans encountered them. The Iroquois invaded and attacked tribes in the Ohio River area of present-day Kentucky and claimed the hunting grounds. Historians have placed these events as occurring as early as the thirteenth century or in the seventeenth century Beaver Wars. Through warfare, the Iroquois drove several tribes to migrate west to what became known as their historically traditional lands west of the Mississippi River. Tribes originating in the Ohio Valley who moved west included the Osage, Kaw, Ponca, and Omaha people. By the mid-seventeenth century, they had resettled in their historical lands in present-day Kansas, Nebraska, Arkansas, and Oklahoma. The Osage warred with Caddo-speaking Native Americans, displacing them in turn by the mid-eighteenth century and dominating their new historical territories.

To know the history of America in the pre-colonial period one has to probe into these Native American traditions that sustained American economy and culture for a long period of time. In spite of severe internal strife, waves of external and internal (in the post-colonial times) colonization, exploitation, discrimination, and segregations, these communities still survive and sustain (though in very few numbers). To face current threats of social erosion and environmental degradation many Americans today look back and try to revive social cohesion and community management of natural resources practiced by the Native American communities.

Annotated Bibliography

- V. Deloria's *Red Earth White Lies: Native Americans and The Myth of Scientific Fact* (Golden, CO: Fulcrum Publishing, 1997) challenges scientific versions of evolution and creation and offers an alternative view of North American history.
- Brian M. Fagan's *Ancient North America: The Archaeology of a Continent*, 4th ed. (New York: Thames & Hudson Inc., 2005) provides a rich archaeological history of every major culture in North America with illustrations to the key sites and artefacts.
- The history of Hohokam culture is well illustrated in Mark Chenault Rick Ahlstrom and Tom Motsinger's *In the Shadow of South Mountain: The Pre-Classic Hohokam of 'La Ciudad de los Horno: 1991–1992*, 2 vols (Tuscon: SWCA Environmental Consultants Archaeological Report No. 93-30, 1993), and Emil Haury's *The Hohokam: Desert Farmers and Craftsmen: Excavations at Snaketown, 1964–1965* (Tuscon: The University of Arizona Press, 1978).
- E. Tooker's 'The United States Constitution and the Iroquois League' in J.A. Clifton, *The Invented Indian: Cultural Fictions and Government Policies* (New Brunswick: Transaction Publishers: 1990, pp. 107–28) offers a detailed account of the formation and functioning of the Iroquois League.

b. The Viking Conquest

The discovery of America by the Italian explorer Amerigo Vespucci is a very popular story; but centuries before that North Atlantic including the north-eastern fringes of North America was explored by the Norse (Vikings) which is testified by Norse sagas and later by more scientific historical sources.

According to the sagas of Icelanders, in 980s the Norsemen first settled in Greenland with the zeal and effort of Erik the Red. He issued tracts of land to his followers and led to the establishment of a colony which consisted of a population of 3,000–5,000 during its heyday. After few years of the establishment of this settlement, the Norse began explorations to the west of Greenland.

In 1001, Leif Ericson, the son of Erik the Red discovered this area and created a small settlement in the northeast coast of modern-day Canada. Leif sailed some 1,800 miles to the New World with a crew of 35. According to the Sagas of Icelanders, this exploration led to the discovery of three separate areas: *Helluland* (the land of the flat stones), *Markland* (the land of forests), and *Vinland* (the land of wine or meadows). He described Helluland as 'level and wooded, with broad white beaches wherever they went and a gently sloping shoreline.' The Vinland site on the northern tip of Newfoundland, known as L'Anse aux Meadows was discovered by Helge Ingstad and Anne Stine Ingstad in 1963.

Leif's exploration was followed by other Norse expeditions to this part of the world leading to an encounter between the Norse and the indigenous people. In 1004, Leif's brother, Thorvald Ericson sailed with a crew of 30 men to Newfoundland and attacked nine of the local people sleeping under three skin-covered canoes. The ninth victim escaped and came back to the Norse camp with a force. Thorvald died in the carnage. Another of their brothers, Thorstein, sailed to the New World to retrieve his dead brother's body and stayed there temporarily. In 1009 Thorfinn Karlsefni made his expedition with three ships carrying livestock and 160 men and women. Karlsefni's group also had conflicts with the indigenous people leading to wide-scale killings and making Nordic settlement temporary in North America. These settlements in continental North America actually aimed to exploit natural resources like furs, lumber, etc. which were scarce in Greenland. Though the Norse were killed by the native people and no Norse settlement could be permanently created in Vinland, Peter Schledermann has argued in *Voices in Stone: A Personal Journey into the Arctic Past* that sporadic voyages continued for many more centuries. Evidence of continuing trips includes the Maine Penny, a Norwegian coin from King Olaf Kyrre's reign (1067–93) allegedly found in a Native American archaeological site in the US state of Maine. This suggests an exchange between the Norse and the Native Americans after the eleventh century. The Icelandic Annals refers to a small Greenlandic vessel with a crew of 18 that arrived in Iceland while attempting to return to Greenland from Markland with a load of timber around the fourteenth century.

Interestingly enough, though these pre-Columbian voyages had not received greater significance, in his very recent work (2010) entitled *Icelanders in the Viking Age: The People of the Sagas*, William Short has mentioned of a letter by Christopher Columbus where he claimed that he had heard of these expeditions when he visited Iceland in 1477.

Annotated Bibliography

- Peter Schledermann's *Voices in Stone: A Personal Journey into the Arctic Past*, Komatik Series no. 5 (Calgary: The Arctic Institute of North America and the University of Calgary, 1996) is an adventurous personal sojourn of the discovery of human presence in the Arctic.
- In *The Vinland Sagas: The Norse Discovery of America* (Harmondsworth: Penguin Classics, 1965) Hermann Pálsson captures the coming of the Vikings and their discovery of the North American continent.
- William R. Short's *Icelanders in the Viking Age: The People of the Sagas* (USA: McFarland, 2010) is a companion and introduction to the daily lives and material culture of the Vikings. We get detailed accounts of the early history of Iceland relating to religion, housing, social customs, settlement of disputes, etc.
- In Robert Wernick's *The Seafarers: The Vikings* (Alexandria, Virginia: Time-Life Books, 1979) the commercial contributions of the Vikings have been well documented along with conventional narrative of invasion and pillaging.

c. In Search of God, Glory, and Gold

The late fifteenth and sixteenth centuries witnessed the beginning of a series of sea voyages when the great European maritime powers like Spain, Portugal and France, followed by England and Dutch joined the maritime race for fresh geographical discoveries. The motives of colonization can be explained in terms of the three G theory: God, Glory, and Gold.

Many groups of colonists came to the Americas searching for the right to practice their religion without persecution. Roman Catholics were the first major religious group to immigrate to the New World as settlers in the colonies of Portugal and Spain. The Protestant Reformation of the sixteenth century broke the unity of Western Christendom and led to the formation of numerous new religious sects. A strong believer in the notion of rule by divine right, England's Charles I persecuted religious dissenters. Waves of repression led to the migration of about 20,000 Puritans to New England between 1629 and 1642, where they founded multiple colonies. Later in the century, the new Pennsylvania colony was given to William Penn in settlement of a debt the king owed to his father. Its government was set up by William Penn around 1682 to become primarily a refuge for persecuted English Quakers; but others were welcomed. Baptists, Quakers, and German, and Swiss Protestants flocked to Pennsylvania. Hence, English and Dutch colonies tended to be more religiously diverse, and settlers to these colonies included Anglicans, Dutch Calvinists, English Puritans, English Catholics, Scottish Presbyterians, French Huguenots, German and Swedish Lutherans, as well as Quakers, Mennonites, Amish, Moravians, and Jews of various nationalities. The lure of cheap land, religious freedom and the right to improve themselves with their own hand was very attractive to those who wished to escape from persecution and poverty.

The Renaissance and the scientific discoveries like the invention of the mariner's compass, improvement in ship-building techniques and cartography, and the steady growth of nautical science created zeal of adventure among the Europeans to set sail for unknown lands. The pioneer in this field was the Portuguese monarch 'Henry the Navigator' and his laboratory. The spirit among the Europeans provoked them into explorations in search of new lands.

The economic or materialist considerations acted as the main motives behind American colonization. William Parry, J.S. Furnivall, and D.K. Fieldhouse have explained colonization by a rise in the exportable surplus of men, money, and material that created a need for geographical expansion eventually leading to the discovery or rather conquest of America. The colonies were founded as business ventures for investment of capital and extraction of surplus. The need for markets for Europe's surplus of manufactures paved towards the establishment of captured markets in the form of colonies. Wealthy businessmen sought opportunities to invest their money. The English joint-stock companies sold shares of stock to venturers and enabled them to share the great expense and risk of founding colonies as business enterprises. The prevailing economic theory of mercantilism stressed the need of a nation to accumulate precious metals – the English hoped to find gold in the colonies. And in spite of opposition and resistance, the profit-seeking goal came as a boost to colonize America. Richard Hakluyt wrote in *Pamphlet for the Virginia Enterprise* of 1585 that in the face of opposition from the Indians, 'we may, if we will proceed with extremity, conquer, fortify, and plant in soils most sweet, most pleasant, most strong, and most fertile, and in the end bring them all in subjection…'[4]

The Early Colonial Phase – Spain, Portugal, and France

Spain, eager to open trade relations with India, the proverbial land of spices, perfumes, and silks, sent Christopher Columbus during the reign of Ferdinand and Queen Isabella. He set sail across the Atlantic in search of a quicker route to Asia and reached unknowingly to the Caribbean islands which he mistook for India. This illusion persisted even when he returned to the same shores in 1496. It was left to another Spanish adventurer, Amerigo Vespucci to finally rectify this mistake. When he reached the shores of the new land, he knew for certain that it was a different continent altogether. Subsequently it acquired the new name America, after Amerigo Vespucci.

The Spanish and Portuguese colonization marked the first wave of European conquest of the Americas. The exploration of Columbus was followed by a number of other Spanish and Portuguese explorers like

John Cabot, Pedro Álvares Cabral, Amerigo Vespucci, and Vasco Núñez de Balboa. With Herman Cortes and Francisco Pizarro's conquest of the Aztec and the Inca Empires the Spanish colonization reached its climax with its autonomy over western South America, Central America, and southern North America, in addition to its earlier Caribbean conquests by the mid-sixteenth century. Colonization was not smooth and it had to encounter waves of resistances from the indigenous Americans who had to undergo through this forced conquest.[5] The Arauco and Chichimeca wars are evidences of the European and indigenous encounter.

Parts of South America, mainly Brazil, were colonized by Portugal. There were other explorations like that of Newfoundland by Corte-Real brothers in 1501–02, but severe indigenous uprisings were one of the major causes for which these efforts could not sustain. Pedro Álvares Cabral touched the soil of Brazil on 22 April 1500. Permanent settlement began with the foundation of São Vicente in 1532, followed by the establishment of sugar cane industry and its intensive labour demands met with native and African slaves in the later period. Salvador was established as the capital in 1549. The Dutch attempt to control the north-eastern part of Brazil between 1630 and 1654 was destroyed with the Portuguese victory in the Second Battle of Guararapes in 1649 leading to the returned control of all Brazilian land to the Portuguese by 1650s.

Unlike the Spanish, the Portuguese created captaincies and did not divide their colonial territory. The captaincies were ruled by centralized administration in Salvador which reported directly to the Crown in Lisbon. Unlike 'Spanish America', 'Dutch America', etc. the nomenclature 'Portuguese America' does not make sense as Brazil appeared to be a unified colony under Portugal.

Interestingly enough, the two early colonizers in America negotiated between themselves by the Treaty of Tordesillas (signed in 7 June 1484) that created the line of demarcation about halfway between the Portuguese-controlled Cape Verde Islands and those Spanish islands discovered by Columbus on his first voyage (named as Cipangu and Antilia, i.e., Cuba and Hispaniola in the treaty). Thus they reached a settlement by which they could establish their exclusive control over global territorial hemispheres. The impact of 'civilized' and 'rational' European could be felt at large that would take havoc pace in the subsequent centuries.

French colonization of America can be traced back to the early half of the sixteenth century when in 1524, the French king, Francis sent Giovanni da Verrazano to explore the region between Florida and Newfoundland for route to the Pacific Ocean. The land between New Spain and English Newfoundland was named Francesca and Nova Gallia by Verrazano. The French attempt to establish colony in Brazil and Rio de Janeiro failed due to Spanish and Portuguese vigilance. French colonies were mainly established in eastern North America, on a number of Caribbean islands, and in South America. However, France gradually lost its lands to British in a series of war fought between these inter-European powers, and New France[6] was taken by Britain.

The Later Phase – English and Dutch Colonization

Under the rule of Elizabeth I, England was rapidly growing more powerful and prosperous, and British mastery over the sea was acknowledged after the defeat of the Spanish Armada in 1588. This new-found confidence intensified British trade and commercial activities and generated enough surplus fund to set up a colony in America. Christopher Columbus had discovered the land of America but its mighty economic potential that could be commercially exploited was first realized by the two British adventurers, Walter Raleigh and Francis Drake. Besides, a thriving commercial agriculture, the existing Enclosure system, and the beginning of sheep farming and wool trade evicted a large number of peasants from the heartland home. The rural surplus labour was therefore forced to search for a new home. According to historian G.M. Trevelyan annually there was an exodus of 30,000 people from England to America during this time.

Apart from these individuals, a large number of companies also took part in the demographic transfer at different times. In 1607, the Virginia Company was founded and it had a charter which gave the company all business and trading rights in America from Virginia to Maine. The large number of settlers there grew tobacco that they could sell for a profit in England. Besides, there was the Massachusetts Bay Company with its target in North America and the Plymouth Company that was comparatively smaller in size.

On 11 December 1620, the ship, Mayflower transported the Pilgrim Fathers from the Plymouth harbour in England to the port of Provincetown in Massachusetts. Subsequently, after settling down, the Pilgrims made their own laws that collectively came to be known as the Mayflower Compact, and the history of the Massachusetts state began in this way.

Originally, the people from Britain had established 13 colonies in North America. Out of these, Massachusetts Bay owned five colonies in the north: Massachusetts, Connecticut, Rhodes Island, Delaware, and Maryland. Further down the territories previously known as New Netherland was taken away from the Dutch authority, and the new colonies of New York, New Jersey, and New Hampshire were created. Still further south, on the eastern coast, there were Pennsylvania and Virginia. Finally, through the Midlands to the South, North Carolina and South Carolina were established. The thirteenth colony in this chain was Georgia.

Table 1.1: The Thirteen Colonies of British America

Colony	**Year**	**Founded by**
Virginia	1607	London Company
Massachusetts	1620	Puritans
New Hampshire	1623	John Wheelwright
Maryland	1634	Lord Baltimore
Connecticut	1635	Thomas Hooker
Rhode Island	1636	Roger Williams
Delaware	1638	Peter Minuit and New Sweden Company
North Carolina	1653	Virginians
South Carolina	1663	Eight Nobles with a Royal Charter from Charles II
New Jersey	1664	Lord Berkeley and Sir George Carteret
New York	1664	Duke of York
Pennsylvania	1682	William Penn
Georgia	1732	James Edward Oglethorpe

Source: A.B. Hart, *American History Told by Contemporaries* (New York: The Macmillan Company, 1929), vol. 1.

The 13 colonies had well-established systems of self-government and elections based on the Rights of Englishmen, which they were determined to protect from imperial interference. The population mostly comprised of independent farmers, who owned their land and voted for their local and provincial government. In 1772, Benjamin Franklin made a comparison between the conditions of the people dwelling in the hovels of Scotland and the inhabitants of New England and found that in New England 'every man' was a property owner, had a vote in public affairs, lived in a tidy, warm house, had plenty of good food and fuel, with whole clothes from head to foot, the manufacture perhaps of his own family.[7]

There were three types of colonies in British America: the charter colonies where the King granted a charter to the colonial government establishing laws and rules under which the colony was to be governed; proprietary colonies where one or more individuals (mainly from the land-owning class) were subject to the parent state's sanctions; and royal colonies or the crown colonies which was a prototype of colonial administration of the English Empire. Apart from the 13 colonies, the British acquired other colonies that included seven colonies on the Atlantic coast of North America: Newfoundland, Rupert's Land (the area around the Hudson Bay), Nova Scotia, Prince Edward Island, East Florida, West Florida, and the Province of Quebec. There were few other colonies in British West Indies: Barbados, Antigua, Bahamas, Jamaica, Grenada, etc. which remained loyal to the Crown.

In 1602, the government of the Republic of the Seven United Netherlands chartered the Dutch East India Company with the mission of exploring it for a passage to the Indies and claiming any uncharted areas for the United Provinces. This was followed by several significant expeditions finally leading to the creation of the province of New Netherland. In 1609, i.e., two years after English establishment of Jamestown in Virginia, the Dutch East India Company hired the English sailor Henry Hudson who sailed into the mouth of the Hudson River and moved as far as present-day Albany. The first Dutch settlement in the Americas was founded in 1615 in Fort Nassau, on Castle Island in the Hudson. The settlement served mostly as trading port promoting fur trade with Native Americans and was later replaced by Fort Orange.

In 1621, the Dutch West India Company was established with a trading monopoly in the Americas and West Africa. It sought recognition for an area in the New World, between English Virginia and French Canada, which was called New Netherland.[8] The Dutch acquired exclusive trading rights in New Netherland by 1623. In 1624, the first colonists, mostly Walloons and company-owned slaves, arrived in the new province, and in 1626, Director of the Dutch West India Company, Peter Minuit purchased the island of Manhattan from the Lenape and started the construction of Fort Amsterdam, which later became the main port and capital, New Amsterdam. The colony gradually expanded to outlying areas of Pavonia, Brooklyn, Bronx, and Long Island. However, the settlement was short-lived, and the surrender of Fort Amsterdam to English control in 1664 was formalized in 1667, contributing to the Second Anglo-Dutch War. In 1673 the Dutch re-took the area, but later relinquished it under the 1674 Treaty of Westminster ending the Third Anglo-Dutch War.

Europeans and Native Americans: Response and Impact

There were several attempts on the part of the Native Americans to resist European colonization leading to violent skirmishes between them. Dee Brown's *Bury My Heart at Wounded Knee: An Indian History of the American West* provides a detailed depiction of the encounter between the Europeans and the Indian communities such as, the Apaches, the Nez Perces, the Utes, the Cheyennes, the Sioux, and the Navahos.[9] The Tainos and Arawaks resisted strongly against the Spanish 'when hordes of…bearded strangers began scouring their islands in search of gold and precious stones,'[10] followed by Powhatans' and Massasoits' resistance against the English. In Virginia, the English applied subtler strategies with the Powhatan. While the English put a gold crown on the head of Wahunsonacook and declared him the King of Powhatan, the later ensured steady supply of food to the white settlers. This alliance went as far as the marriage of John Rolfe and Pocahontas, the daughter of the King of Powhatan. But after the King's death, the Powhatans rose up in rebellion and were defeated by the English who reduced their number from 8,000 to less than 1,000.

In Plymouth, war broke out between the Indian confederacy under King Philip and the English in which the Indians attacked 52 settlements and destroyed 12 of them before they were defeated by the colonists and Philip was beheaded. The Mahicans and Ratirans rose up against the

Dutch colonizers in Manhattan Island, but they were ruthlessly exterminated when the Dutch soldiers opened fire and destroyed two entire villages at night, killing men, women, and children. Even the mightiest and most advanced of the eastern tribes, the Iroquois and their league (consisting of the five nations: Mohawk, Oneida, Onondaga, Cayuga, and Seneca) had to surrender before the British in their long struggle for political independence. During the 1760s when Pontiac of Ottawas united tribes in the Great Lakes country attempted to drive the British back across the Alleghenies, he did not succeed. His major error was an alliance with French-speaking white men who withdrew aid from the peaux-rouges during the siege of Detroit.[11]

The European colonization of Americas is a catastrophic chapter in human history bringing out the acute contradiction between two unequal powers: the colonizers and the natives. While the European fortune shone against the riches from the abundant new lands, the natives not only suffered from forced enslavement and butchery, their resistances were suppressed by colonial military and diplomatic techniques and strategies. Also, the colonizers created an artificial environment, much similar to Europe (Neo-Europe) that resulted in what was perhaps the greatest demographic disaster in history.

Alfred Crosby has written two fascinating treatises on the impact of the Old World colonization on the New World. From these two books, *Ecological Imperialism: The Biological Expansion of Europe, 900–1900* and *The Columbian Exchange: Biological and Cultural Consequences of 1492* we get a comprehensive view of ecological and social events in the post-Columbian period and how it altered entire landscapes of the two continents: the Americas. In the first book he also looked into some other parts of the world including New Zealand and Australia 'and argued for a systematic, asymmetrical impact of biological exchange which helped Europeans dominate much of the world in recent centuries.'[12] Colonization brought in the greatest biological transfer that the world had ever seen, and the successful exploitation of the Americans depended on the ability of the Europeans to 'Europeanize' American flora and fauna. The biological transfer or exchange followed some of these following trends:

- American plants and seeds were distributed extensively in areas where they were unknown in the pre-Columbian times to feed the Europeans in the American continents. Example: the cultivation of white potato spread to North America in the seventeenth century.

- American plants and other native products were raised on extensive plantations and exported across the Atlantic. Example: tobacco, paprika, cocoa, rice, sugar, indigo, guaiacum, sassafras, etc.
- There was huge-scale importation of plant and animal sources of food from the eastern hemisphere. Example: banana was brought in to Antilles from the Canaries in 1516; the first contingent of horses, cattle, chickens, sheep, goats, pigs, and dogs arrived with Columbus on his second voyage in 1493; in 1540 Gonzalo Pizarro was accompanied by more than 2,000 pigs along with horses, dogs, and llamas in one of his expeditions on the east of Andes.

Table 1.2: The Columbian Exchange

From New World to Old World	From Old World to New World
Corn, potatoes, sweet potatoes, manioc, coffee, vanilla, tobacco, chocolate, pumpkins, squash, beans, sunflowers, tomatoes, wild rice, quinine, avocados, bell and chilli peppers, blueberries, pineapples, pecans, cashews, peanuts, petunias, dahlias, marigolds	Horses, cattle, pigs, sheep, goats, chickens, rats, honeybees, wheat, barley, oats, yams, lettuce, okra, peaches, pears, watermelons, citrus fruit, bananas, olives, lilacs, daffodils, tulips, crabgrass, dandelions, smallpox, measles, malaria, influenza, amoebic dysentery, diphtheria, chicken pox, typhus, whooping cough, bubonic plague

Source: William J. Rorabaugh, Donald T. Critchlow and Paula Baker, *America's Promise: A Concise History of the United States*, vol. I (USA: Rowman and Littlefield Publishers, INC., 2004), p. 3.

The European mission was to transform the New World into the Old World as much as possible leading to 'the greatest biological revolution in the Americas since the end of the Pleistocene era.'[13] The impact was two-fold. While the burgeoning number of the new livestock led to the extinction of native plants, animals, and Indian themselves, for the colonizers there was a colossal increase in the quantity of American protein. America provided the best feeding option which might have been a more important factor behind European migration in the New World than other ideological and religious factors.[14]

The history of American colonization is also the history of disease, death, and pestilence. Mutation, ecological alterations, and migration caused epidemics like small pox, typhus, measles, etc., which were previously unknown to the isolated Americas. The fatal diseases entered the New World with the Old World explorers and conquistadors. Crosby argues that, disease, ably assisted by Spanish brutality, had killed off most of the peoples of the Antilles and the lowlands of New Spain, Peru, and the Caribbean by 1580s. There is a debate on the disappearance of the Arawaks of the Greater Antilles and Bahamas. Some argue that they deceased due to Spanish brutality, others point out that they died out of diseases. The second argument seems logical as the Spaniards required labour and subjected the Arawaks for that purpose. During the initial phase of contact with the Europeans and Africans (who worked as slaves in the plantations) the Mexicans and Peruvians died because of series of epidemics that broke out between 1520 and 1600.[15] The little immunity among the natives can be explained by the long isolation of the American continents from the other parts of the world. From the accounts of Bartholome de las Casa, William Bradford, Francis Drake, Thomas Harriot, and others we get detailed narratives of the death of the native population once they came in touch with the Europeans. The Europeans were also responsible for the spread of diseases from South to North America.

Crosby's outstanding research has brought into limelight how epidemics changed the course of history.

> The triumphant Aztecs had not expected the Spaniards to return after their expulsion from Tenochtitlan. The sixty days during which the epidemic lasted in the city, however, gave Cortes and his troops a desperately needed respite to reorganize and prepare a counter attack. When the epidemic subsided, the siege of the Aztec capital began. Had there been no epidemic, the Aztecs, their war-making potential unimpaired and their warriors fired with victory, could have pursued the Spaniards, and Cortes might have ended his life spread-eagled beneath the obsidian blade of a priest of Huitzilopochtli.[16]

Depopulation of the original inhabitants from epidemics and diseases seemed to be a boon for the Europeans left with abundant lands to settle, colonize, and exploit to accomplish the European purpose.

Finally, it is important to look into the process and impact of colonization from the spatial–temporal context. The colonial motives in the initial phase was different (though similar also) from the later phases. James Lang in *Conquest and Commerce: Spain and England in the Americas* has pointed out the contrasts between Spanish America and British America. He argues that Spain's empire in America was the 'empire of conquest' while Britain's America was the 'empire of commerce'. As the colonization processes differed hence the impact of colonization was different in Hispanic America from British America. However, following the universal law of colonization, the impact of European colonization was immensely beneficial for the European continent and certainly harmful for the exploited and subjugated natives and their environment.

Annotated Bibliography

- While A.B. Hart's *American History Told by Contemporaries*, Volume I, Era of Colonization, 1492–1689 (New York: The Macmillan Company, 1929) contains the political history of colonization of Americas, In *Empires of the Atlantic World: Britain and Spain in America, 1492–1830* (USA: Yale University Press, 2007), J.H. Elliot specifically focuses on British and Spanish moves.
- Nicholas P. Canny's *The Ideology of English Colonization: From Ireland to America, The William and Mary Quarterly,* Third Series, Vol. 30, No. 4 (October, 1973), pp. 575–98 is an interesting exploration of ideological understanding of British motives behind colonization.
- Dee Brown's *Bury My Heart at Wounded Knee: An Indian History of the American West, The Illustrated Edition* (New York: Sterling Publishing Co., Inc., 2009) is a brilliant portrayal of the encounter between Indians and Europeans in which the author rejects the Eurocentric view and tells the story from the vantage point of those who lost the battles – the Indian tribes and communities.
- Victor Bulmer-Thomas, John H. Coatsworth and Roberto Cortés Conde, eds, *The Cambridge Economic History of Latin America*, volume 1 (New York: Cambridge University Press, 2006, Chapter 5: 'The Demographic Impact of Colonization' by Linda A. Newson) narrate the severe demographic impact of colonization on the native inhabitants of Latin America.
- In *The Columbian Exchange: Biological and Cultural Consequences of 1492* (USA: Praeger Publishers, 2003) and *Ecological Imperialism: The Biological Expansion of Europe, 900–1900* (Cambridge: Cambridge University Press, 2004), 2nd edition, Alfred Crosby has bring out the severe consequences of Old World colonization on the New World. In these two books, we get a

comprehensive account of how entire landscapes of the two continents were altered through a systematic, asymmetrical impact of biological exchange between Europe and Americas.

Notes

1. J. Ehlers and P.L. Gibbard, *Quaternary Glaciations: Extent and Chronology 2* (Amsterdam: Elsevier, 2004), Part II, North America.
2. Olive Dickason, *Canada's First Nations: A History of the Founding Peoples from the Earliest Times* (Toronto: Oxford University Press, 1997), 2nd edition.
3. Joe W. Saunders, Rolfe D. Mandel, et al., 'Watson Brake, a Middle Archaic Mound Complex in Northeast Louisiana', *American Antiquity*, Vol. 70, No. 4 (October 2005), pp. 631–668.
4. Quoted in J.H. Elliot, *Empires of the Atlantic World: Britain and Spain in America, 1492–1830* (Yale: Yale University Press, 2007), p. 9.
5. Recent archaeological excavations have also induced the notion of a vast Spanish-Indian alliance against the control of the Inca Empire; Rick Vecchio, *Discovery: The Inca Rebellion of 1536* (Available online at: http://www.fertur-travel.com/blog/2009/discovery-the-inca-rebellion-of-1536/728/#_ftn3 date of access: 26.03.2012).
6. New France was the area colonized by France in North America during a period beginning with the exploration of the Saint Lawrence River by Jacques Cartier in 1534 and ending with the cession of New France to Spain and Great Britain in 1763.
7. Claude H. Van Tine, *The Causes of the War of Independence* (New York, 1922), p. 318.
8. Returning from his expedition of 1614, Adriaen Block compiled a map where he first applied the name 'New Netherland' to the area between English Virginia and French Canada.
9. Dee Brown, *Bury My Heart at Wounded Knee: An Indian History of the American West, The Illustrated Edition* (New York: Sterling Publishing Co., Inc., 2009).
10. Ibid., p. 2.
11. Ibid., p. 4.
12. Alfred Crosby, *The Columbian Exchange: Biological and Cultural Consequences of 1492* (USA: Praeger Publishers, 2003), J.R. McNeill, Foreword, p. xiii.
13. Alfred Crosby, *The Columbian Exchange: Biological and Cultural Consequences of 1492*, p. 66.
14. Ibid., p. 108.

15. Charles Gibson, *The Aztecs under Spanish rule: A History of the Indians of the Valley of Mexico, 1519–1810* (Stanford: Stanford University Press, 1976), pp. 448–51, revised edition, Henry F. Dobyns, *An Outline of Andean Epidemic History to 1720* (Baltimore: John Hopkin University, Institute of History of Medicine, 1963).
16. Alfred Crosby, *The Columbian Exchange*, p. 49.

2

The American War of Independence

The chapter explores the causes behind the outbreak of the American Revolution from economic and ideological perspectives. It provides an account of the various events that sketched the final transition to the American War of Independence culminating in the making of the US constitution. The nature of the Revolution has been variously interpreted by various scholars belonging to different generations. A historiographical approach has been used covering the main arguments and interpretations from the Whig historians, Progressive school to the New Social historians to show the changing trends in history writing incorporating latest research methodologies.

a. The American Revolution: Causes and Events

Causes of the Origins of the American Revolution

The origins of the American Revolution can be explained mainly from the economic and ideological points of view. The crystallization of a wealthy, influential and a powerful class of American bourgeoisie who made their fortunes mostly in the plantation sector led inevitably in the long run to a growing conflict between them and Great Britain. The rising class of businessmen began to bitterly resent the mercantilist economic policy of the British government that was essentially concerned with the welfare of the mother-country. Louis Hacker thus argues that the American Revolution was a clash of conflict between British mercantilism and American capitalism. That Great Britain was trying to thwart colonial economy was evident in colonial restrictions in many instances.

The primary objective of mercantile Britain was the prosperity of the mother country at the cost of her colonies. Though the colonies were allowed to send raw materials but they were restricted to export manufactured products to the mother-country. Great Britain absorbed the major part of the raw materials for their factories, mills, and other areas and retailed major parts of it in the continent itself. Forced to import the manufactured goods only from the mother-country at prices fixed by the latter, the colonies were prohibited to enter into any cheaper deal with France, Holland, or any other country. Further, the manufacture of any kind of finished product was forbidden in the colonies where abundance of natural resources, labour and talent were readily available. America's industrial potential was sought to be restricted in the same way the British government scotched the industrial development in colonial India later.

Various acts were passed to have control over the colonial empire. As early as 1651, a series of laws were passed that obstructed the use of foreign shipping for trade between England and her colonies. The colonies obeyed these laws until and unless the enactment of the Molasses Act of 1733 that imposed a tax of six pence per gallon on imports of molasses (used to make rum) from non-British colonies. The Act provided:

> ... there shall be raised, levied, collected and paid, unto and for the use of his Majesty ..., upon all rum or spirits of the produce or manufacture of any of the colonies or plantations in America, not in the possession or under the dominion of his Majesty ..., which at any time or times within or during the continuance of this act, shall be imported or brought into any of the colonies or plantations in America, which now are or hereafter may be in the possession or under the dominion of his Majesty ..., the sum of nine pence, money of Great Britain, ... for every gallon thereof, and after that rate for any greater or lesser quantity: and upon all molasses or syrups of such foreign produce or manufacture as aforesaid, which shall be imported or brought into any of the said colonies or plantations ..., the sum of six pence of like money for every gallon thereof ...; and upon all sugars and paneles of such foreign growth, produce or manufacture as aforesaid, which shall be imported into any of the said colonies or plantations ... a duty after the rate of five shillings of like money, for every hundred weight Avoirdupoize....

The provisions clearly show the colonial motive of regulating trade between New England and Middle Colonies and the French, Dutch, and

Spanish West Indian possessions by making British products cheaper than those from the French West Indies. John C. Miller argues that the tax '...threatened New England with ruin, struck a blow at the economic foundations of the Middle colonies, and at the same time opened the way for the British West Indians – whom the continental colonists regarded as their worst enemies – to wax rich at the expense of their fellow subjects on the mainland.'[1]

In 1764 the Sugar and Currency Acts were passed. The first direct act, the Stamp Act was passed by British Prime Minister George Grenville and the Parliament in 1765. By the provision of this act, all official documents, newspapers, almanacs, and pamphlets – decks of playing cards – were required to have the stamps. In 1767 the Parliament passed the Townshend Acts which placed a levy on numerous essential goods like paper, glass, and tea.

Other restrictions were also imposed to check the power and prosperity of the American new bourgeoisie. In 1763 Great Britain took control of the French holdings in North America outside the Caribbean after its victory in the French and Indian War. To keep the Indian tribes separated from the American frontiersmen, the Royal Proclamation of 1763 was enacted that restricted settlement west of the Appalachian Mountains and designated the area as an Indian Reserve.[2] The proclamation was soon modified (as the Americans disregarded it and continued to settle in the prohibited area) and was no longer a hindrance to settlement, but the fact that it had been promulgated without their prior consultation angered the colonists.[3]

Finally the Quebec Act[4] of 1774 and the series of Intolerable Acts[5] enraged the Americans, the latter being prepared to contest the overbearing economic domination of Great Britain.

While the economic rift theory emphasizes on these economic restrictions, there is the ideological rift theory also that projects the American Revolution as an ideological conflict between the colonizers and the colonized. The most significant profounder of this theory is Bernard Bailyn (*The Ideological Origins of the American Revolution*). The revolutionary situation was created because of the ideological differences regarding the justifiability of the laws through which Britain was maintaining its hold over the 13 colonies. Professor Hari S. Vasudevan states that in Britain there was an aristocracy, a well-ordered government, and social mobility was much slower than it was in the United States. White male Americans enjoyed more political rights than the English. Property was the yardstick for both America and Britain, but abundant land provided the colonist the opportunity to gain the real estate. In England there was the tradition of the landed aristocracy with dukes, earls and lords entitlement to huge wealth and privileges and hence they did not become a part of the emigrant community to Americas. Thus, America lacked titled nobles and many of them were born middle class. William J. Rorabaugh, Donald T. Critchlow, and Paula Baker argue in *America's Promise: A Concise History of the United States*: 'From the viewpoint of an English duke, colonial society lacked leadership provided by aristocrats. From the viewpoint of a colonist, America offered a unique possibility for ordinary people to develop their own political leadership.'[6] To Bailyn it was a fight between liberty and authority.

The Americans were open to the radical ideas of Enlightenment and had interest in the notions regarding voting pattern, representation, and equality, ideas which were actually considered in Britain to be unacceptable. Before 1776, much ideological inspiration was provided through the circulation of pamphlets, a major medium of popular propaganda. The principles of basic freedom which included life, liberty, and pursuit of happiness, later on clarified in the *Declaration of Independence*, were sought to be disseminated. In this respect Tom Paine's pamphlet *Common Sense* created a great stir. He argued that independence was the only remedy, and it would be more difficult to win the longer it was delayed.

Again, there is a religious dimension to the origins of the American Revolution. The dissenting, i.e., Protestant churches of the day were the schools of democracy. President John Witherspoon of the College of New Jersey wrote widely circulated sermons linking the American Revolution to the teachings of the Hebrew Bible. Bernard Bailyn argues that the evangelism of the era challenged traditional notions of natural hierarchy by teaching that the Bible taught all men are equal, so that the true value of a man lies in his moral behaviour, not his class.[7] Throughout the colonies dissenting Protestant congregations like the Congregationalist, Baptist, and Presbyterian preached revolutionary themes in their sermons while most Church of England ministers preached loyalty to the King.[8] The religious motivation to fight against tyranny reached across socio-economic lines to encompass rich and poor, men and women, frontiersmen and townsmen, and farmers and merchants. In his most recent work *God of Liberty: A Religious History of the American Revolution* published in 2010, Thomas Kidd argues that religious disestablishment, belief in God as the guarantor of human rights, and shared convictions about sin, virtue, and divine providence worked together to unite rationalists and evangelicals encouraging American defiance of the Empire. Emphasizing intense opposition to sending an Anglican bishop to the colonies and anger at the pro-Catholic Quebec Act[9] of 1774, Kidd argues that these reflected the long-term impact of the Great Awakening, in terms of apocalyptic warnings, religious egalitarianism, and anti-Catholicism. When battles over taxation without representation escalated by 1773, Patriots were prepared to defy British administrators.

Events Leading to the Revolution

The passage of the various acts could not impose much control over the colonists and rather generated a chain of negative consequences for the fate of the Empire. They hardly obeyed the Molasses Act and moreover, smuggling, bribery, or intimidation of customs officials effectively nullified the law. Miller writes, 'Against the Molasses Act, Americans had only their smugglers to depend upon – but these redoubtable gentry proved more than a match for the British. After a brief effort to enforce the act in Massachusetts in the 1740s, the English government tacitly accepted defeat and foreign molasses was smuggled into the Northern colonies in an ever-increasing quantity. Thus the New England merchants survived – but only by nullifying an act of Parliament.'[10] Other acts were also looked with disrespect and led to corruption of the local officials.

The colonists considered themselves loyal subjects of the British Crown, with the same historic rights and obligations as subjects in Britain. The colonists had not much objection to be taxed to incur the British expenses of defending the continental colonies and the British West Indies, but they wanted representation in the Parliament. While the American slogan was 'No taxation without representation', London responded that the colonists were 'virtually represented' and the Americans rejected it.

In Boston on 5 March 1770, a large mob gathered around a group of British soldiers and started throwing snowballs, rocks, and debris at them.

All but one of the soldiers fired into the crowd; 11 people were hit and three civilians were killed at the scene of the shooting; two died after the incident. The event came to be called the **Boston Massacre**, and the widespread descriptions of the event soon became propaganda to turn colonial sentiment against the British. The downward spiral in the relationship between Britain and the Province of Massachusetts began.

The **Gaspée Affair** of June 1772 added more elements to the anti-colonial cause and sentiments when the British warship that had been vigorously enforcing unpopular trade regulations was burned by American patriots including John Brown. In 1773, private letters were published in which Massachusetts Governor Thomas Hutchinson called for the abridgement of colonial rights, and Lieutenant Governor Andrew Oliver called for the direct payment of colonial officials (until then it was under the purview of the colonial assembly). The furore over the affair contributed to Hutchinson's recall and brought a conciliatory Benjamin Franklin who was firmly to the side of the colonists.

This was followed by the most dramatic incident known as the **Boston Tea Party** when on 16 December 1773, a group of men, led by Samuel Adams and dressed to evoke American Indians, boarded the ships of the government-favoured British East India Company and dumped an estimated £10,000 worth of tea from its holds into the harbour.

Patrick Henry in Virginia and James Otis in Massachusetts rallied the people in opposition. The secret group called the *Sons of Liberty* got involved in the various violent actions. In 1772, groups of colonists began to create the *Committees of Correspondence*, which would lead to their own Provincial Congresses in most of the colonies. In the course of two years, the Provincial Congresses or their equivalents rejected the Parliament and effectively replaced the British ruling apparatus in the former colonies, leading to the birth of the First Continental Congress in 1774. In response to protests in Boston over Parliament's attempts to assert authority, the British sent combat troops, dissolved local governments, and imposed direct rule by the royal officials. This called for an open carnage and the colonies mobilized their militias in 1775. First ostensibly loyal to King George III and desiring to govern themselves while remaining in the empire, the repeated pleas by the First Continental Congress for royal intervention on their behalf with Parliament resulted in the declaration by the King that the states were 'in rebellion', and the members of the

Congress were traitors. In 1776, representatives from each of the original 13 states voted unanimously in the Second Continental Congress to adopt a *Declaration of Independence*, which then rejected the British monarchy and the Parliament and established the sovereignty of the new nation external to the British Empire. The *Declaration* established the United States, which was originally governed as a loose confederation through a representative democracy selected by state legislatures.

It was mainly the class of lawyers that included men like James Otis, Patrick Henry, L. Franklin, and John Adam who provided the ideological leadership and were the chief spokespersons of the revolution. The only exceptions were George Washington, a military commander and Thomas Jefferson, a gentleman farmer. Nevertheless, they had close connections with the lawyers. The merchant class and the professional lawyers emerged as avant-gardes of the Revolution. There was also French influence to some extent. Lafayette, a gallant military man who had come on his own to America trained the American fighters for freedom. So, a multiplicity of groups including the merchants, the lawyers, the planters, the farmers, the mechanics, and the labourers took part in the Revolution.

Conclusion: How Revolutionary was the American Revolution?

The most significant result of the Revolution was the creation of a democratically elected representative government responsible to the will of the people. However, sharp political debates erupted over the appropriate scale of democracy desirable in the new government, with a number of founders fearing mob rule. According to Jameson, who belongs to the New Left School of historians, the American Revolution was basically a bourgeois democratic revolution. It was a revolution of the bourgeoisie, by the bourgeoisie, and for the bourgeoisie. They fought in the battlefields of Boston, Massachusetts, Concord, or Lexington thereby moving from north to west, and the common people participated only as canon fighters but actually having no place in the decision-making exercise. There was a major fight at Camp Valley Forge where the British army was finally defeated.

To sum up, the American Revolution can be described as a **White Revolution** since neither the African slaves nor the Red Indians who were the aborigines of the United States were to be found in the mainstream of the movement. Completely marginalized, they throughout remained outside the purview of the newly formed 'democratic' constitution and the main scenes of activity. This argument seems truthful enough when one takes into account the new constitution that was to be established soon afterwards.

Annotated Bibliography

- In *The Triumph of American Capitalism* (London: Columbia University Press, 1946), Louis Hacker provides an economic interpretation to the American Revolution and argues that it was the inevitable result of conflict between British mercantilism and American capitalism.
- Bernard Bailyn's *The Ideological Origins of the American Revolution* (Cambridge, Massachusetts: Belknap Press of Harvard University Press, 1992) is an exploration of the ideological environment that paved the American War of Independence.
- In *From Resistance to Revolution: Colonial Radicals and the Development of American Opposition to Britain, 1765–1776* (New York: W.W. Norton and Company, 1991), Pauline Maier provides an intellectual interpretation of the American Revolution and traces the process through which the extra-legal institutions of the colonial resistance movement assumed authority from the British.
- J.C. Miller's *Origins of the American Revolution* (Stanford, California: Stanford University Press, 1959; revised edition) is a collection of the various interpretations of the American Revolution.
- William J. Rorabaugh, Donald T. Critchlow and Paula Baker's *America's Promise: A Concise History of the United States*, vol. I (USA: Rowman and Littlefield Publishers, 2004) is a balanced portrait of America's past with an effective blending of political, social, and cultural history.

b. Nature of the Revolution: A Brief Historiography

The American Revolution was an event of vast magnitude. Like a gigantic volcanic disturbance it spewed forth its hot lava great distances from the crater. Richard. B. Morris argues in *The American Revolution Re-considered*, 'It may have started at Lexington, but it continues in

Birmingham, and Saigon and Lagos.'[11] The nature of the Revolution has been variously interpreted by various scholars belonging to different generations.

The **Whig Historians** were the eyewitnesses of the Revolution and used Dodley's *Annual Register* (a British news summary) as the primary source. Edmund Burke, William Gordon, and David Ramsay are the Whig scholars who mainly borrowed facts from the register and did not provide detailed interpretation. Burke could hardly conceal their sympathies for the American cause but Ramsay in *History of the American Revolution* had a didactic purpose – it was designed to awaken Americans to their responsibilities as citizens under the new government. His evaluation of causation is profound than the others, and he viewed it as more than a response to a catalogue of grievances accumulating shortly before the outbreak of the Revolution. He recognized the importance of distance, dissenting tradition in religion, intellectual currents of the Enlightenment and the English Whig tradition, the relative degree of social equality prevailing in the colonies, and the long established constitutional liberties exercised there in, along with the gradual erosion among successive generation of colonists of the bonds of affection for the mother country as the causes of the Revolution.

Most of the **nineteenth-century historians** reflected that the main theme of American History was the quest for liberty; and within this context the Revolution was viewed in black-and-white terms as a struggle of liberty versus tyranny between America and Britain. George Bancroft in his 10-volume *History of the United States*, published between 1830s and 1870s pointed out that it represented one phase of a master plan by God for the march of mankind towards a golden age of greater human freedom. America symbolized the forces of liberty and progress and Britain that of tyranny and reaction.

The scholars who revised Bancroft's interpretation between 1890s and 1940s and regarded it as ultra-nationalist and patriotic, fell into two broad schools – the imperial and the progressive school. George Louis Beer, Charles M. Andrews, Herbert L. Osgood, and Lawrence H. Gipson were the **imperial historians** whose writings provided a reappraisal of the origins of the Revolution. Beer wrote four monographs between 1893 and 1912 on Britain's commercial policies in the seventeenth and eighteenth centuries and claimed that the colonists prospered under a system that was both liberal and enlightened. He argued that independence was the logical consequence, not of British oppression, but of a long period of evolution of uniquely American institutions and tendencies. The Andrews thesis pointed out about the two movements working at cross purposes in the British Empire in America since its beginning up to the Revolution. The colonies kept moving steadily in the direction of greater self-government and the mother country towards greater control over the empire. By the eve of the Revolution, the colonists arrived at a new concept of empire – colonies as self-governing units within an empire held together only by a common allegiance to the king; but the British, clinging to their traditional ideas of dependent colonies, considered this idea both radical and dangerous. The dispute was the very essence of the American Revolution and it represented a deep-seated conflict between two incompatible societies. Gipson in *The British Empire before the American Revolution* revealed light on the need of the British government to streamline colonial administration after the last inter-colonial war and assembled detailed statistics to prove that the colonists were not paying their share of the costs of empire and were under-taxed as compared to George III's subjects in Great Britain.

The emergence of the **progressive school** during the Progressive Era between 1900 and 1920 paved the way towards an economic interpretation of history. Carl. L. Becker provided the 'dual revolution' thesis in *The History of Political Parties in the Province of New York, 1760–1776*. He argued that there were not one Revolution, but two Revolutions – the external one, the colonial rebellion against Britain caused by clash of economic interests between the colonies and the mother country and the internal one, a conflict between America's social classes to determine whether there would be elite or non-elite takeover followed by the British departure. Charles Beard's *An Economic Interpretation of the Constitution* also saw the period between 1760s and 1780s as one of continuous conflicts between social classes in America over economic matters. In *The Colonial Merchants and the American Revolution*, Arthur M. Schlesinger studied the merchant class in all the colonies between 1763 and 1776 and noted that this usually conservative group played a leading role. Disenchantment of the merchants with the British rule arose from economic reverses that they suffered as a result of the strict policy of imperial control enacted by the mother country after the French and

Indian wars. However, resistance among the merchants grew less intense after 1770 out of fear of what might happen to their position and property if the more radical social classes should gain the upper hand.

The progressive historians were challenged by the **neo-conservative school**. They argued that the colonial society was an open society which was characterized by high degree of social mobility. The American Revolution was a conservative movement and was fought to preserve a social order that was already democratic in colonial days. Instead of class conflict, they put forward the theory of general consensus among the American people in the revolutionary era. In *The Genius of American Politics*, Daniel J. Boorstein pointed out that the Revolution was a conservative movement on the imperial as well as the local level because Americans were fighting to retain traditional rights and liberties granted to them under the British constitution. The colonists rebelled to maintain the status quo and not to initiate a new order. The patriots were insisting upon an old liberty and not a new right. There was resistance when the Americans felt that they were being denied their rights as Englishmen by a misguided Parliament. Edmund S. Morgan in *The Birth of the Republic, 1763–1789* focussed on two themes – the consensus among Americans on principles and the continuity of ideas. From the passage of the Stamp Act in 1765 to the writing of the Constitution in 1787, most of the Americans consistently sought to realize three principles – the protection of property and liberty, the achievement of human equality, and a form of American nationalism that would embrace the ideas of both liberty and equality. Morgan concluded that the progressive historians grossly exaggerated the divisions among the American people during the revolutionary era and that the most remarkable and exciting fact was union.

The **intellectual historians**, contrary to the progressive historians, emphasized the primacy of ideas in the Revolution. Bernard Bailyn in *The Ideological Origins of the American Revolution* viewed it as a radical intellectual movement. The Revolution was in the minds of the people; the radical change in principles, opinions, sentiments and affections of the Americans was the real Revolution. Before the Revolution the Americans saw their divergences from the norms of European society as shortcomings, they felt a sense of inferiority because they lacked a titled aristocracy, cosmopolitan culture, and a stratified society. After the Revolution they looked upon the differences as good, not bad, virtues, not vices, and advantages rather defects. Gordon Wood's *Creation of the American Republic* was an extension of the Bailyn thesis where he explains how the dissenting tradition was transformed during the years following independence into a distinctive American republican ideology and how, under the forcing pressure of the revolutionary events, that ideology evolved from its original, utopian formulation of 1776–78 into the quite different federalist republicanism of the late 1780s.

The trends that emerged between mid-1960s and 1990s and contradicted the neo-conservative school were the **neo-progressive** and **loyalist interpretations**. The leading neo-progressive historian to inherit the mantle of Beard was Merill Jensen who viewed the Revolution in terms of conflict, particularly political and economic clashes between both the colonies and the mother country and within the colonies themselves. Jensen's *The Founding of a Nation* focussed on the political instability in Britain and the American provinces and the tensions that arose as a result of these differences. James K. Martin argued in *Men in Rebellion* that the transfer of political power occurred mainly among elites and that this process from which the people ultimately benefitted came about through chance rather than through the actions of revolutionary leaders. The loyalist interpretation has been provided by William H. Nelson in *The American Tory*. According to him, the loyalists comprised of a collection of isolated cultural minorities and social groups who were acutely aware that they had never been assimilated into American society. These cultural enclaves therefore looked to Britain for protection against the threatening Whig majorities that surrounded them. Mary Beth Norton in *The British Americans* pointed out that the loyalist recognized how much American they were when they felt ill at ease and out of place in the English society.

The protest movements in the US in the 1960s, 70s and 80s by the poor, blacks, ethnic minorities, and women led to the rise of the new social historians, loosely united by their desire to examine American social structure and changes within that. Mary B. Norton's *Liberty's Daughters: The Revolutionary Experience of American Women, 1750–1800* (1980) and Judith S. Murray's *On the Equality of the Sexes* (1998) have captured the role of women in the revolutionary period. Barbara Graymount (*The Iroquis in the American Revolution,* 1972) and Benjamin Quarles (*The Negroes in the American Revolution,* 1976) have reflected on the Indian tribes. Psycho history emerged between 1970s and 1990s in which the scholars suggested that the Americans might have been caught up in a serious identity crisis on the eve of the Revolution which might be a possible explanation of the colonists' rebellious behaviour. Jack P. Greene, John M. Murrin, and Robert M. Weir are renowned scholars in this trend.

There has been a revolution itself in this field of historiography with the new methodological innovations, quantitative techniques, and research in non-traditional sources (wills, deeds and tax lists) to explore the inner lives of the inarticulate masses who had left few personal memoirs. In this context, mention may be made of the community case-studies by Robert Gross (*The Minutemen and their World*, 1976) and Richard Bushman (*From Puritan to Yankee*, 1967).

There have been new and newer ways of looking into the American Revolution. Now the greatest challenge before us is how to put the story together again from these various perceptions and draw from the information available (quantitative, qualitative, statistical, literary, visual, and oral) into readable accounts of the Revolution.

Annotated Bibliography

- Gwenda Morgan's *The Debate on the American Revolution (Issues in Historiography)* (Manchester: University Press, 2008) is the first in-depth study of the way in which historians dealt with the coming of the American Revolution and the formation of the US Constitution from the first generation of writers, whose ideas about history were shaped by the Enlightenment to those of the twenty-first century, who drew on the rich legacy provided by black studies, gender studies, cultural studies, and ethno-history.
- Richard Morris's *The American Revolution Reconsidered* (New York: Harper and Row, 1967) is a critical analysis of the great revolutionary struggle that gave birth to America. It offers a new conservative interpretation of the American Revolution.
- Roy Lokken's 'The Political Theory of the American Revolution: Changing Interpretations' (*The History Teacher*, Vol. 8, No. 1 (November, 1974), pp. 81–95), Nelson Paul David, 'British Conduct of the American Revolutionary War: A Review of Interpretations', (*The Journal of American History*, Vol. 65, No. 3 (1978), pp. 623–53) and Murray Rothbard's *Modern Historians Confront the American Revolution* (available at: http://www.lewrockwell.com/rothbard/rothbard153.html, date of access: 16 July 2012) are about how past and present historians have interpreted the political theory and other causes of the Revolutionary War.

c. The Making of the American Constitution

The Revolution of 1776 finally severed America from its colonial ties with Great Britain and the most immediate and imperative task appeared to be the framing of a new constitution based on the new needs and exigencies of the situation. The Revolution was a matter of joy but it had also created anarchy. Apart from the law-and order-situation, partly created by the disbandment of the Revolutionary forces and the retreat of the British army, there were new political, financial, and legal challenges that had to be addressed.

America's first constitution, the *Articles of Confederation*, had been written soon after the Declaration of Independence by the Second Continental Congress. At the outset only there was an apple of discord between John Dickinson, who was in favour of a strong central government, and his fellow Revolutionaries, who wanted each state to retain its sovereignty and freedom. It was finally clear that the Confederation would not enjoy any real power over the states; it would have any separate executive branch, independent judiciary, and upper chamber in the legislature and would also have no independent source of income. The *Articles* called for a unicameral representative assembly that would conduct the government's business in the main three sectors. The *Articles of Confederation* was finally ratified five years later in 1781.[12] The renowned historian on American constitution, Carol Berkin argues,

> The Articles...reflected the ardent desire of the Revolutionary leaders to prevent the rise of tyranny from the ashes of an older one. To insure that the government they created would not, could not, become oppressive, they did more than drastically limit the scope of its authority.[13]

The Confederation, however, proved to be inadequate and unsatisfactory. The restrictions and injustices suffered in the colonial era ended but many advantages of the British period could not be reaped. Though the New England fishermen owned the right to fish off Newfoundland, they lost the British Caribbean markets. The Chesapeake tobacco planters lost their most reliable sources of credit. While an independent American merchant marine was free to carry American products to various ports of their own choice, the protection of British navy in the high seas was no longer there; American vessels carrying wheat and flour to southern European markets became easy prey to pirates in the Barbary Coast. When the ruler of Tripoli offered to insure safe passage to American ships for a price, the Congress failed to raise the money. America suffered a series of humiliations from western countries. The American ambassadors could not properly negotiate with Spain to reopen the port of New Orleans, a gateway to the ocean. When the British violated the Paris Treaty and refused to evacuate the Ohio Valley forts, and Spain continuously aided the Indian tribes like Choctaw, Creek, and Cherokee against American migration along the southern frontier, the Confederation could do little against these. When Britain assured to give up the forts on the ground of repayment of personal debts by American planters to British creditors and compensation to Loyalists for confiscated property, the Congress failed to take steps as it had neither money nor military strength to fight against its rivals.

The volatile diplomatic and external situation was combined with internal conflicts and competition among states. Economic problems in post-war depression mainly in the South and New England created divisions and competitions among states in spite of bringing the Americans together. The competing interests of creditors and debtors, rural farmers and urban merchants, and artisans and importers acted as centrifugal forces dividing the nation. While real political power remained in the hands of the state government, relationships among states were not good. The British restrictions were replaced by internal restrictions as state legislators enacted tariffs and trade barriers, missing no opportunity to exploit their neighbouring states. New Jersey created its own customs service; Virginia imposed penalties for avoiding its interstate import duties; and Virginia and South Carolina squeezed hapless North Carolina, New York, and Pennsylvania with locational (ports) advantages by imposing steep duties on all goods for neighbouring states.[14] All these had negative impact on domestic trade. Further, the scramble for land in the Wild West and a fierce competition to gain territories there embittered inter-state relationships. The Americans also lacked well-trained and well-equipped army to protect them from Indian attacks in their migration towards west. Virginia and Maryland fought bitterly over river navigation of River Potomac in the northeast. It was clear that these crucial issues could not be solved by the individual states on their own. All the 13 colonies were now autonomous and independent to retain their political autonomy, fiscal rights, and also some right over the border of the West. But as George Washington pointed out, the states were united by a rope of sand, and the lack of unanimity among the states on a number of issues deterred the smooth functioning of government. The Revolutionary strategist Henry Knox from Massachusetts declared that the present federal government was a name, a shadow, without power or effect.

At this critical juncture, the protection of a federal government against Great Britain, an amicable settlement of river navigation, a satisfactory solution to the scramble for land in the west, and the establishment of a universally acceptable legal tender seemed to be the requirements of the time. The Americans realized their new dilemma: Who would provide the protection colonists once found in the sheltering arms of their mother country?[15] Who would protect the interest of the nation as a whole in place of parochialism? The solution was in the hands of the national government.

Men like George Washington, Edmund Randolph, Henry Knox, James Madison, and most importantly, Alexander Hamilton supported the cause of a federal government. Under their initiative, Virginia appointed commissioners to negotiate with Maryland over the navigation of River Potomac. The problem resolved and with this amicable agreement Maryland proposed that a meeting on inter-state commerce can be held involving other states. Patrick Henry, the Governor of Virginia, called for a convention in Annapolis and asked all his fellow governors to send representatives at the Annapolis Convention which was organized in September 1783. Though only five states were represented, this convention was a landmark event with most of the delegates being ardent supporters of the nationalist cause.

When the convention was going on in Annapolis, around 600 farmers were involved in a rebellion called Shay's Rebellion (named after Daniel Shays), storming the courthouse at Springfield, Massachusetts. Rising property taxes, declining profits, and inaction on the part of state government, dominated by mortgage holders, forced the farmers to take up arms. The rebellion spread rapidly and took violent and radical turns when farmers started blocking and occupying courthouses. Shay's Rebellion shocked and injected fears among planters and wealthy merchants and it was gradually getting clear that only a strong government was the need of the hour.

The Congress, meeting in New York planned for another convention in Philadelphia in May 1787. Very few of the selected delegates were present on the designated day of 14 May, and it was not until 25 May that a quorum of seven states was secured. Between May and September 1787, representatives from all 13 states joined the convention, though the number ranged from minimum two to maximum five delegates, from each state. There were uneven representations not only in numbers but they were from different professions. Apart from such stalwarts including George Washington, Benjamin Franklin, Alexander Hamilton, James Madison, John Jay, Willis and Morris, there were some lawyers, politicians, businessmen, and also a few soldiers. Some of the leaders who were active in bringing about the Revolution were not present in the convention. Jefferson was in France; John Adams in England. However, the Philadelphia Convention was probably the most nearly representative political assemblage to be found anywhere in the western world at that time as A. Nevins and H.S. Commager pointed out in *A Short History of the United States.*[16] The number of delegates was 55.

On 25 May 1787 delegates from the various states met in the Pennsylvania State House in Philadelphia and the first orders of business included the election of George Washington as the President of the Convention. The rules were soon established including complete secrecy concerning its deliberations that would guide the proceedings later.[17]

Four days later, Governor Edmund Randolph of Virginia presented and defended a plan for new structure of government (called the *Virginia Plan*) that had been chiefly drafted by fellow Virginia delegate, James Madison. The Virginia Plan called for a strong national government with both branches of the legislative branch apportioned by population and gave the national government the power to legislate in all cases in which the separate States would be incompetent. It even gave a proposed National Council of Revision a veto power over state legislatures.

Delegates from smaller states and states less sympathetic to broad federal powers opposed many of the provisions in the Virginia Plan. Charles Pinckney of South Carolina reflected his anxiety asking whether proponents of the plan meant to abolish the State Governments altogether. On 14 June a competing plan, called the *New Jersey Plan* was presented by delegate William Paterson of New Jersey which kept federal powers rather limited and created no new Congress. Instead, the plan enlarged some of the powers then held by the Continental Congress. Paterson made plain the adamant opposition of delegates from many of the smaller states to any new plan that would deprive them of equal voting power ('equal suffrage') in the legislative branch.

Over the course of the next three months, a series of compromises between the competing plans were worked out by delegates. It was agreed that foreign policy, defence, issues related to land acquisition in the West, and coins and currency would be left to federal government, but provisions which would give the national government a veto power over new state laws were rejected. Under a plan put forward by delegate Roger Sherman of Connecticut (*the Connecticut Compromise*) on 11 June representation in the House of Representatives would be on the basis of population while each state would be guaranteed an equal two senators in the new Senate. In a sense, it blended the Virginia (large-state) and New Jersey (small-state) proposals, and what was ultimately included in the constitution was a modified form of this plan. In the Committee of Detail, Benjamin Franklin added the requirement that revenue bills would originate in the house, and rather than the state delegations voting as a block as instructed by their state legislatures, Franklin's modification made them free agents.[18]

David Stewart rightly argues that among the most controversial issues confronting the delegates was the issue of slavery.[19] At the insistence of delegates from southern states, the Congress was denied the power to limit the slave trade for a minimum of 20 years (that is, not until after 1808). In exchange for this concession, the federal government's power to regulate foreign commerce would be strengthened by provisions that allowed for taxation of slave trades in the international market and that reduced the requirement for passage of navigation acts from two-thirds majorities of both the houses of the Congress to simple majorities. Slaves, although denied the vote and not recognized as citizens by those states were however, allowed to be counted as three-fifth persons for the purpose of apportioning representatives and determining electoral votes.

By September 1787, the final compromises were made. Each state, regardless of its number of delegates, had one vote, so a state evenly split could not register a vote for adoption. Thirty-nine of the 55 delegates supported adoption of the new Constitution and it was executed by 11 states and Colonel Hamilton.[20] The success of the Philadelphia Convention was obvious. The state rights were preserved and simultaneously the federal rights were asserted too. The inalienable natural rights of man were also enshrined. Above all, a new-found idealism that comes from a great sense of freedom seems to have permeated the minds of all the members of the convention after long debates between the Federalists and the Anti-federalists.[21] As the final delegates were signing the document on 17 September, Franklin commented on the painting of a sun behind Washington's chair at the front of the room. He said he often looked at the painting, 'without being able to tell, whether it was rising or setting. But now at length, I have the happiness to know it is a rising, and not a setting sun.' The Constitution was submitted to the states for ratification, pursuant to its own Article VII.

d. Nature of the American Constitution

A 'Conflict vs. Consensus' debate revolves around relating to the nature of the American Constitution.[22] While the Americans entered the twentieth century, convinced by George Bancroft and others that the Convention portrayed the ongoing battle between liberty and tyranny, in which 'the statesman who were to create a new constitution...knew themselves to be forerunners of reform for the civilized world,'[23] by 1913 came out the path-breaking study of the Marxist historian Charles A. Beard entitled *An Economic Interpretation of the Constitution of the United States*[24] which brought a halt to Americans' uncritical reverence for the revolutionary past of their nation, questioned the Founding Fathers' motivations in drafting the Constitution, and viewed it as a product of economic self-interest. Investigating and analyzing the original sources, he situated the constitutional convention in the great social struggles in the immediate post-Revolutionary period. The farmers, workers, and small tradesmen who had been the bulwark of the revolutionary struggle were suffering from economic crisis in the aftermath of the Declaration of Independence. The power of the state governments, squarely in the hands of the merchants and planters, stood behind the seizure of the lands of farmers who could no longer pay the banks and merchants. Sporadic rebellions broke out and threatened the propertied class and the law-and-order mechanism. This led to the call for the Constitutional Conventions where the wealthier class, who had profited from the Revolution and by the economic disaster farmers and tradesmen faced by buying up certificates for land in compensation for services to the Revolution, met to chalk out Constitutional provisions for a secure state that could safeguard their economic interests. Extensively researching through the primary documents such as the Federalist Papers, early Treasury Department records, and Madison's convention notes, Beard asserted that the Constitution was enacted to protect the interests of the rich moneyed classes, the bond and stock holding classes or the rich speculators, the manufacturing/rich capitalists, and those who had trade and shipping interests. And these were the men who were the representatives in the Philadelphia Convention. The slaves, indented servants who could not qualify the property tests and disfranchised women did not represent in the Convention. The composition clearly shows that the great body of representatives came mostly from the propertied elite group of men and the 'Founding Fathers' deliberately excluded the subaltern classes.

In the ratification of the Constitution, three-fourth of the qualified voters were excluded by some means or another, aiding the one-fourth who benefited from the passage of the constitution. The ratification of the Constitution was further narrowed down to where only one-sixth of the qualified voters participated in its passing. The one-sixth of the qualified voters came from the same minority who held large holdings in money, bonds and stocks, manufacturing, and trade and shipping. Thus, the main societal divisions in the ratification were among the propertied class on the one hand and the farming and debtor class one the other. This materialist argument was put forward by Beard only when he succeeded to test his hypothesis imperative for such an economic interpretation of the framing and adoption of the Constitution. His work involved the laudable task of sketching an economic biography (a list of the real and personal property owned: land and houses, with encumbrances, money at interest, slaves, capital invested in shipping and manufacturing, and in state and continental securities) of all those associated with the Constitution's framing and adoption. Based on these detailed data, Beard finally concluded that the 'Founding Fathers' included a clear strategy for colonial economics in the writing of the Constitution and in essence, 'it was an economic document drawn with superb skill by men whose property interests were immediately at stake; and as such it appealed directly and unerringly to identical interests in the country at large.'[25] It was based 'upon the concept that the fundamental private rights of property are anterior to government and morally beyond the reach of popular majorities.'[26]

Beard's thesis was countered by Charles Warren, Robert E. Thomas and others who argued that the thesis was too simple, lacking an increasingly complicated and sophisticated differentiation of groups and interests.[27] Forrest McDonald in *We the People: The Economic Origins of the Constitution* applied Beard's methodology with increasing thoroughness and concluded that Beard's interpretation cannot be justified as factors other than economic interests also had strong influences.[28] With few exceptions like Gerry, King, Sherman, and Ellsworth, who wanted to advance their private investments through decisions at the Convention, to most of the delegates, however, public interest transcended private gains. The conflict has to be understood in terms of dichotomies such as: large states versus small, northern versus southern states, commercial versus staple states, and the naturally bounded states versus those still claiming unsettled land in the west.

Again, in defence of the 'Founding Fathers' and their high ideals, came out the works of Walter Lippmann and Martin Diamond.[29] The conflict versus consensus debate rolled on until the publication of recent works[30] with alternative methodologies that steadily moved toward an interpretation of the Convention that sees 'a congeries of conflicting, competitive interests, underlain by a basic agreement on the fundamental principles of government.'[31] The various collections in Stephen Botein, Edward C. Carter, and Richard R. Beeman edited *Beyond Confederation: Origins of the Constitution and American National Identity* is an attempt in this direction that challenge many of the traditional generalizations and raise fresh questions about the Constitution as it enters its third century.[32]

Annotated Bibliography

- A detailed analysis of the *Articles of Confederation* and the Constitutional Conventions can be found in the classic books on American History including A. Nevins and H.S. Commager, *A Short History of the United States* (New York: Random House, 1945), Henry B. Parks, *The United States of America* (New York: Alfred Knopf, 1959, 2nd edition), Richard N. Current, T.H. Williams, and Frank Friedel, *American History: A Survey* (New York: Alfred Knopf, 1966).

- Merill Jensen's *The New Nation: A History of the United States during the Confederation, 1781–1789* (Boston: Northeastern University Press, 1981) is an interpretative discussion of the period between independence and the drafting of the Constitution, often christened as the 'critical period' by American scholars.
- Stephen Botein, Edward C. Carter, and Richard R. Beeman, eds *Beyond Confederation: Origins of the Constitution and American National Identity* (USA: The University of North Carolina Press, 1987) consists of a number of essays that shed light on various issues from federalist political economy to Shay's Rebellion to slavery.
- Calvin C. Jillson's *Constitution Making: Conflict and Consensus in the Federal Convention of 1787* (New York: Agathon Press, 2002), along with a detailed sketch of the temporal context of the Constitution, covers a comprehensive historiography on the subject and makes a sophisticated handling of the debate on the nature of the Constitution.
- Carol Berkin's *Brilliant Solution: Inventing the American Constitution* (USA: First Harvest, 2003) takes a fresh look at the delegates who framed the Constitution and portrays the hearts and minds of the founders, exposing their fears, anxieties, yet, commitment and dedication at the same time.

Annexure: The American Constitution of 1787

Source: The Pennsylvania Packet, September 19, 1787
available at: http://msc-inc.net/documents/usa_constitution.html
(date of access: 11.11.2012)
(*The original spelling and capitalization has been retained*)

We the People of the United States, in Order to form a more perfect Union, establish Justice, insure domestic Tranquility, provide for the common defence, promote the general Welfare, and secure the Blessings of Liberty to ourselves and our Posterity, do ordain and establish this Constitution for the United States of America.

Article I

Section 1. All legislative Powers herein granted shall be vested in a Congress of the United States, which shall consist of a Senate and House of Representatives.

Section 2. The House of Representatives shall be composed of Members chosen every second Year by the People of the several States, and the Electors in each

State shall have the Qualifications requisite for Electors of the most numerous Branch of the State Legislature.

No Person shall be a Representative who shall not have attained to the age of twenty five Years, and been seven Years a Citizen of the United States, and who shall not, when elected, be an Inhabitant of that State in which he shall be chosen.

Representatives and direct Taxes shall be apportioned among the several States which may be included within this Union, according to their respective Numbers, which shall be determined by adding to the whole Number of free Persons, including those bound to Service for a Term of Years, and excluding Indians not taxed, three fifths of all other Persons. The actual Enumeration shall be made within three Years after the first Meeting of the Congress of the United States, and within every subsequent Term of ten Years, in such Manner as they shall by Law direct. The Number of Representatives shall not exceed one for every thirty Thousand, but each State shall have at Least one Representative; and until such enumeration shall be made, the State of New Hampshire shall be entitled to chuse three, Massachusetts eight, Rhode Island and Providence Plantations one, Connecticut five, New-York six, New Jersey four, Pennsylvania eight, Delaware one, Maryland six, Virginia ten, North Carolina five, South Carolina five, and Georgia three.

When vacancies happen in the Representation from any State, the Executive Authority thereof shall issue Writs of Election to fill such Vacancies.

The House of Representatives shall chuse their Speaker and other Officers; and shall have the sole Power of Impeachment.

Section 3. The Senate of the United States shall be composed of two Senators from each State, chosen by the Legislature thereof, for six Years; and each Senator shall have one Vote.

Immediately after they shall be assembled in Consequence of the first Election, they shall be divided as equally as may be into three Classes. The Seats of the Senators of the first Class shall be vacated at the Expiration of the second Year, of the second Class at the Expiration of the fourth Year, and the third Class at the Expiration of the sixth Year, so that one third may be chosen every second Year; and if Vacancies happen by Resignation, or otherwise, during the Recess of the Legislature of any State, the Executive thereof may make temporary Appointments until the next Meeting of the Legislature, which shall then fill such Vacancies.

No Person shall be a Senator who shall not have attained to the Age of thirty Years, and been nine Years a Citizen of the United States and who shall not, when elected, be an Inhabitant of that State for which he shall be chosen.

The Vice President of the United States shall be President of the Senate, but shall have no Vote, unless they be equally divided.

The Senate shall chuse their other Officers, and also a President pro tempore, in the Absence of the Vice President, or when he shall exercise the Office of President of the United States.

The Senate shall have the sole Power to try all Impeachments. When sitting for that Purpose, they shall be on Oath or Affirmation. When the President of the United States is tried, the Chief Justice shall preside: And no Person shall be convicted without the Concurrence of two thirds of the Members present.

Judgment in Cases of Impeachment shall not extend further than to removal from Office, and disqualification to hold and enjoy any Office of Honor, Trust or Profit under the United States: but the Party convicted shall nevertheless be liable and subject to Indictment, Trial, Judgment and Punishment, according to Law.

Section 4. The Times, Places and Manner of holding Elections for Senators and Representatives, shall be prescribed in each State by the Legislature thereof; but the Congress may at any time by Law make or alter such Regulations, except as to the Places of chusing Senators.

The Congress shall assemble at least once in every Year, and such Meeting shall be on the first Monday in December, unless they shall by Law appoint a different Day.

Section 5. Each House shall be the Judge of the Elections, Returns and Qualifications of its own Members, and a Majority of each shall constitute a Quorum to do Business; but a smaller Number may adjourn from day to day, and may be authorized to compel the Attendance of absent Members, in such Manner, and under such Penalties as each House may provide.

Each House may determine the Rules of its Proceedings, punish its Members for disorderly Behaviour, and, with the Concurrence of two thirds, expel a Member.

Each House shall keep a Journal of its Proceedings, and from time to time publish the same, excepting such Parts as may in their Judgment require Secrecy; and the Yeas and Nays of the Members of either House on any question shall, at the Desire of one fifth of those Present, be entered on the Journal.

Neither House, during the Session of Congress, shall, without the Consent of the other, adjourn for more than three days, nor to any other Place than that in which the two Houses shall be sitting.

Section 6. The Senators and Representatives shall receive a Compensation for their Services, to be ascertained by Law, and paid out of the Treasury of the United States. They shall in all Cases, except Treason, Felony and Breach of the Peace, be privileged from Arrest during their Attendance at the Session of their respective Houses, and in going to and returning from the same; and for any Speech or Debate in either House, they shall not be questioned in any other Place.

No Senator or Representative shall, during the Time for which he was elected, be appointed to any civil Office under the Authority of the United States, which shall have been created, or the Emoluments whereof shall have been encreased during such time: and no Person holding any Office under the United States, shall be a Member of either House during his Continuance in Office.

Section 7. All Bills for raising Revenue shall originate in the House of Representatives; but the Senate may propose or concur with Amendments as on other Bills.

Every Bill which shall have passed the House of Representatives and the Senate, shall, before it become a Law, be presented to the President of the United States; if he approve he shall sign it, but if not he shall return it, with his Objections to that House in which it shall have originated, who shall enter the Objections at large on their Journal, and proceed to reconsider it. If after such Reconsideration two thirds of that House shall agree to pass the Bill, it shall be sent, together with the Objections, to the other House, by which it shall likewise be reconsidered, and if approved by two thirds of that House, it shall become a Law. But in all such Cases the Votes of both Houses shall be determined by Yeas and Nays, and the Names of the Persons voting for and against the Bill shall be entered on the Journal of each House respectively. If any Bill shall not be returned by the President within ten Days (Sundays excepted) after it shall have been presented to him, the Same shall be a Law, in like Manner as if he had signed it, unless the Congress by their Adjournment prevent its Return, in which Case it shall not be a Law.

Every Order, Resolution, or Vote to which the Concurrence of the Senate and House of Representatives may be necessary (except on a question of Adjournment) shall be presented to the President of the United States; and before the Same shall take Effect, shall be approved by him, or being disapproved by him, shall be repassed by two thirds of the Senate and House of Representatives, according to the Rules and Limitations prescribed in the Case of a Bill.

Section 8. The Congress shall have Power To lay and collect Taxes, Duties, Imposts and Excises, to pay the Debts and provide for the common Defence and general Welfare of the United States; but all Duties, Imposts and Excises shall be uniform throughout the United States;

To borrow Money on the credit of the United States;

To regulate Commerce with foreign Nations, and among the several States, and with the Indian Tribes;

To establish an uniform Rule of Naturalization, and uniform Laws on the subject of Bankruptcies throughout the United States;

To coin Money, regulate the Value thereof, and of foreign Coin, and fix the Standard of Weights and Measures;

To provide for the Punishment of counterfeiting the Securities and current Coin of the United States;

To establish Post Offices and post Roads;

To promote the Progress of Science and useful Arts, by securing for limited Times to Authors and Inventors the exclusive Right to their respective Writings and Discoveries;

To constitute Tribunals inferior to the supreme Court;

To define and punish Piracies and Felonies committed on the high Seas, and Offences against the Law of Nations;

To declare War, grant Letters of Marque and Reprisal, and make Rules concerning Captures on Land and Water;

To raise and support Armies, but no Appropriation of Money to that Use shall be for a longer Term than two Years;

To provide and maintain a Navy;

To make Rules for the Government and Regulation of the land and naval Forces;

To provide for calling forth the Militia to execute the Laws of the Union, suppress Insurrections and repel Invasions;

To provide for organizing, arming, and disciplining, the Militia, and for governing such Part of them as may be employed in the Service of the United States, reserving to the States respectively, the Appointment of the Officers, and the Authority of training the Militia according to the discipline prescribed by Congress;

To exercise exclusive Legislation in all Cases whatsoever, over such District (not exceeding ten Miles square) as may, by Cession of particular States, and the Acceptance of Congress, become the Seat of the Government of the United States, and to exercise like Authority over all Places purchased by the Consent of the Legislature of the State in which the Same shall be, for the Erection of Forts, Magazines, Arsenals, dock-Yards, and other needful Buildings; And

To make all Laws which shall be necessary and proper for carrying into Execution the foregoing Powers, and all other Powers vested by this Constitution in the Government of the United States, or in any Department or Officer thereof.

Section 9. The Migration or Importation of such Persons as any of the States now existing shall think proper to admit, shall not be prohibited by the Congress prior to the Year one thousand eight hundred and eight, but a Tax or duty may be imposed on such Importation, not exceeding ten dollars for each Person.

The Privilege of the Writ of Habeas Corpus shall not be suspended, unless when in Cases of Rebellion or Invasion the public Safety may require it.

No Bill of Attainder or ex post facto Law shall be passed.

No Capitation, or other direct, Tax shall be laid, unless in Proportion to the Census or Enumeration herein before directed to be taken.

No Tax or Duty shall be laid on Articles exported from any State.

No Preference shall be given by any Regulation of Commerce or Revenue to the Ports of one State over those of another: nor shall Vessels bound to, or from, one State, be obliged to enter, clear or pay Duties in another.

No Money shall be drawn from the Treasury, but in Consequence of Appropriations made by Law; and a regular Statement and Account of Receipts and Expenditures of all public Money shall be published from time to time.

No Title of Nobility shall be granted by the United States: And no Person holding any Office of Profit or Trust under them, shall, without the Consent of the Congress, accept of any present, Emolument, Office, or Title, of any kind whatever, from any King, Prince, or foreign State.

Section 10. No State shall enter into any Treaty, Alliance, or Confederation; grant Letters of Marque and Reprisal; coin Money; emit Bills of Credit; make any Thing but gold and silver Coin a Tender in Payment of Debts; pass any Bill of Attainder, ex post facto Law, or Law impairing the Obligation of Contracts, or grant any Title of Nobility.

No State shall, without the Consent of the Congress, lay any Imposts or Duties on Imports or Exports, except what may be absolutely necessary for executing it's inspection Laws: and the net Produce of all Duties and Imposts, laid by any State on Imports or Exports, shall be for the Use of the Treasury of the United States; and all such Laws shall be subject to the Revision and Control of the Congress.

No State shall, without the Consent of Congress, lay any Duty of Tonnage, keep Troops, or Ships of War in time of Peace, enter into any Agreement or Compact with another State, or with a foreign Power, or engage in War, unless actually invaded, or in such imminent Danger as will not admit of delay.

Article II

Section 1. The executive Power shall be vested in a President of the United States of America. He shall hold his Office during the Term of four Years, and, together with the Vice President, chosen for the same Term, be elected, as follows:

Each State shall appoint, in such Manner as the Legislature thereof may direct, a Number of Electors, equal to the whole Number of Senators and Representatives to which the State may be entitled in the Congress: but no Senator or Representative, or Person holding an Office of Trust or Profit under the United States, shall be appointed an Elector.

The Electors shall meet in their respective States, and vote by Ballot for two Persons, of whom one at least shall not be an Inhabitant of the same State with themselves. And they shall make a List of all the Persons voted for, and of the Number of Votes for each; which List they shall sign and certify, and transmit sealed to the Seat of the Government of the United States, directed to the President of the Senate. The President of the Senate shall, in the Presence of the Senate and House of Representatives, open all the Certificates, and the Votes shall then be counted. The Person having the greatest Number of Votes shall be the President, if such Number be a Majority of the whole Number of Electors appointed; and if there be more than one who have such Majority, and have an equal Number of Votes, then the House of Representatives shall immediately choose by Ballot one of them for President; and if no Person have a Majority, then from the five highest on the List the said House shall in like Manner choose the President. But in choosing the President, the Votes shall be taken by States, the Representation from each State having one Vote; A quorum for this Purpose shall consist of a Member or Members from two thirds of the States, and a Majority of all the States shall be necessary to a Choice. In every Case, after the Choice of the President, the Person having the greatest Number of Votes of the Electors shall be the Vice President. But if there should remain two or more who have equal Votes, the Senate shall choose from them by Ballot the Vice President.

The Congress may determine the Time of choosing the Electors, and the Day on which they shall give their Votes; which Day shall be the same throughout the United States.

No Person except a natural born Citizen, or a Citizen of the United States, at the time of the Adoption of this Constitution, shall be eligible to the Office of President; neither shall any Person be eligible to that Office who shall not have attained to the Age of thirty five Years, and been fourteen Years a Resident within the United States.

In Case of the Removal of the President from Office, or of his Death, Resignation, or Inability to discharge the Powers and Duties of the said Office, the Same shall devolve on the Vice President, and the Congress may by Law provide for the Case of Removal, Death, Resignation or Inability, both of the President and Vice President, declaring what Officer shall then act as President, and such Officer shall act accordingly, until the Disability be removed, or a President shall be elected.

The President shall, at stated Times, receive for his Services, a Compensation, which shall neither be increased nor diminished during the Period for which he shall have been elected, and he shall not receive within that Period any other Emolument from the United States, or any of them.

Before he enter on the Execution of his Office, he shall take the following Oath or Affirmation:—"I do solemnly swear (or affirm) that I will faithfully execute the Office of President of the United States, and will to the best of my Ability, preserve, protect and defend the Constitution of the United States."

Section 2. The President shall be Commander in Chief of the Army and Navy of the United States, and of the Militia of the several States, when called into the actual Service of the United States; he may require the Opinion, in writing, of the principal Officer in each of the executive Departments, upon any Subject relating to the Duties of their respective Offices, and he shall have Power to grant Reprieves and Pardons for Offences against the United States, except in Cases of Impeachment.

He shall have Power, by and with the Advice and Consent of the Senate, to make Treaties, provided two thirds of the Senators present concur; and he shall nominate, and by and with the Advice and Consent of the Senate, shall appoint Ambassadors, other public Ministers and Consuls, Judges of the supreme Court, and all other Officers of the United States, whose Appointments are not herein otherwise provided for, and which shall be established by Law: but the Congress may by Law vest the Appointment of such inferior Officers, as they think proper, in the President alone, in the Courts of Law, or in the Heads of Departments.

The President shall have Power to fill up all Vacancies that may happen during the Recess of the Senate, by granting Commissions which shall expire at the End of their next Session.

Section 3. He shall from time to time give to the Congress Information of the State of the Union, and recommend to their Consideration such Measures as he shall judge necessary and expedient; he may, on extraordinary Occasions, convene both Houses, or either of them, and in Case of Disagreement between them, with Respect to the Time of Adjournment, he may adjourn them to such Time as he shall think proper; he shall receive Ambassadors and other public Ministers; he shall take Care that the Laws be faithfully executed, and shall Commission all the Officers of the United States.

Section 4. The President, Vice President and all civil Officers of the United States, shall be removed from Office on Impeachment for, and Conviction of, Treason, Bribery, or other high Crimes and Misdemeanors.

Article III

Section 1. The judicial Power of the United States, shall be vested in one supreme Court, and in such inferior Courts as the Congress may from time to time ordain and establish. The Judges, both of the supreme and inferior Courts, shall hold their Offices during good Behaviour, and shall, at stated Times, receive for their Services, a Compensation, which shall not be diminished during their Continuance in Office.

Section 2. The judicial Power shall extend to all Cases, in Law and Equity, arising under this Constitution, the Laws of the United States, and Treaties made, or which shall be made, under their Authority;—to all Cases affecting Ambassadors, other public Ministers and Consuls;—to all Cases of admiralty and maritime Jurisdiction;—to Controversies to which the United States shall be a Party;—to Controversies between two or more States;—between a State and Citizens of another State;—between Citizens of different States;—between Citizens of the same State claiming Lands under Grants of different States, and between a State, or the Citizens thereof, and foreign States, Citizens or Subjects.

In all Cases affecting Ambassadors, other public Ministers and Consuls, and those in which a State shall be Party, the supreme Court shall have original Jurisdiction. In all the other Cases before mentioned, the supreme Court shall have appellate Jurisdiction, both as to Law and Fact, with such Exceptions, and under such Regulations as the Congress shall make.

The Trial of all Crimes, except in Cases of Impeachment, shall be by Jury; and such Trial shall be held in the State where the said Crimes shall have been committed; but when not committed within any State, the Trial shall be at such Place or Places as the Congress may by Law have directed.

Section 3. Treason against the United States, shall consist only in levying War against them, or in adhering to their Enemies, giving them Aid and Comfort. No Person shall be convicted of Treason unless on the Testimony of two Witnesses to the same overt Act, or on Confession in open Court.

The Congress shall have Power to declare the Punishment of Treason, but no Attainder of Treason shall work Corruption of Blood, or Forfeiture except during the Life of the Person attainted.

Article IV

Section 1. Full Faith and Credit shall be given in each State to the public Acts, Records, and judicial Proceedings of every other State. And the Congress may by general Laws prescribe the Manner in which such Acts, Records, and Proceedings shall be proved, and the Effect thereof.

Section 2. The Citizens of each State shall be entitled to all Privileges and Immunities of Citizens in the several States.

A Person charged in any State with Treason, Felony, or other Crime, who shall flee from Justice, and be found in another State, shall on Demand of the executive Authority of the State from which he fled, be delivered up, to be removed to the State having Jurisdiction of the Crime.

No Person held to Service or Labour in one State, under the Laws thereof, escaping into another, shall, in Consequence of any Law or Regulation therein, be discharged from such Service or Labour, but shall be delivered up on Claim of the Party to whom such Service or Labour may be due.

Section 3. New States may be admitted by the Congress into this Union; but no new States shall be formed or erected within the Jurisdiction of any other State; nor any State be formed by the Junction of two or more States, or Parts of States, without the Consent of the Legislatures of the States concerned as well as of the Congress.

The Congress shall have Power to dispose of and make all needful Rules and Regulations respecting the Territory or other Property belonging to the United States; and nothing in this Constitution shall be so construed as to Prejudice any Claims of the United States, or of any particular State.

Section 4. The United States shall guarantee to every State in this Union a Republican Form of Government, and shall protect each of them against Invasion; and on Application of the Legislature, or of the Executive (when the Legislature cannot be convened) against domestic Violence.

Article V

The Congress, whenever two thirds of both Houses shall deem it necessary, shall propose Amendments to this Constitution, or, on the Application of the Legislatures of two thirds of the several States, shall call a Convention for proposing Amendments, which, in either Case, shall be valid to all Intents and Purposes, as Part of this Constitution, when ratified by the Legislatures of three fourths of the several States, or by Conventions in three fourths thereof, as the one or the other Mode of Ratification may be proposed by the Congress; Provided that no Amendment which may be made prior to the Year One thousand eight hundred and eight shall in any Manner affect the first and fourth Clauses in the Ninth Section of the first Article; and that no State, without its Consent, shall be deprived of its equal Suffrage in the Senate.

Article VI

All Debts contracted and Engagements entered into, before the Adoption of this Constitution, shall be as valid against the United States under this Constitution, as under the Confederation.

This Constitution, and the Laws of the United States which shall be made in Pursuance thereof; and all Treaties made, or which shall be made, under the Authority of the United States, shall be the supreme Law of the Land; and the Judges in every State shall be bound thereby, any Thing in the Constitution or Laws of any State to the Contrary notwith-standing.

The Senators and Representatives before mentioned, and the Members of the several State Legislatures, and all executive and judicial Officers, both of the United States and of the several States, shall be bound by Oath or Affirmation, to support this Constitution; but no religious Test shall ever be required as a Qualification to any Office or public Trust under the United States.

Article VII

The Ratification of the Conventions of nine States, shall be sufficient for the Establishment of this Constitution between the States so ratifying the Same.

Done in Convention by the Unanimous Consent of the States present the Seventeenth Day of September in the Year of our Lord one thousand seven hundred and Eighty seven and of the Independence of the United States of America the Twelfth

In witness whereof We have hereunto subscribed our Names,

- George Washington—President and deputy from Virginia
- New Hampshire: John Langdon, Nicholas Gilman
- Massachusetts: Nathaniel Gorham, Rufus King
- Connecticut: William Samuel Johnson, Roger Sherman
- New York: Alexander Hamilton
- New Jersey: William Livingston, David Brearly, William Paterson, Jonathan Dayton
- Pennsylvania: Benjamin Franklin, Thomas Mifflin, Robert Morris, George Clymer, Thomas FitzSimons, Jared Ingersoll, James Wilson, Gouverneur Morris
- Delaware: George Read, Gunning Bedford, Jr., John Dickinson, Richard Bassett, Jacob Broom
- Maryland: James McHenry, Daniel of Saint Thomas Jenifer, Daniel Carroll
- Virginia: John Blair, James Madison, Jr.
- North Carolina: William Blount, Richard Dobbs Spaight, Hugh Williamson

- South Carolina: John Rutledge, Charles Cotesworth Pinckney, Charles Pinckney, Pierce Butler
- Georgia: William Few, Abraham Baldwin

Notes

1. J.C. Miller, *Origins of the American Revolution* (Stanford: Stanford University Press, 1959) revised edition, p. 95.
2. Colin G. Calloway, *The Scratch of a Pen: 1763 and the Transformation of North America* (Oxford: Oxford University Press, 2006), pp. 92–98.
3. Woody Holton, 'The Ohio Indians and the coming of the American Revolution in Virginia', *Journal of Southern History,* (Aug. 1994), Vol. 60, No. 3, pp. 453–78.
4. It had certain implications for the Quebec Province, the most important being the expansion of its territory to take over part of the Indian Reserve, including much of what was then Southern Ontario, plus Illinois, Indiana, Michigan, Ohio, Wisconsin, and parts of Minnesota.
5. These included four acts: the Massachusetts Government Act, which altered the Massachusetts charter and restricted town meetings; the Administration of Justice Act, which ordered that all British soldiers who were to be tried were to be arraigned in Britain and not in the colonies; the Boston Port Act, which closed the port of Boston until the British had been compensated for the tea lost in the Boston Tea Party; and the Quartering Acts of 1774, which allowed royal governors to house British troops in the homes of citizens without requiring permission of the owner.
6. William J. Rorabaugh, Donald T. Critchlow and Paula Baker, *America's Promise: A Concise History of the United States*, vol. I (New York: Rowman and Littlefield Publishers, 2004), p. 87.
7. Bernard Bailyn, *The Ideological Origins of the American Revolution* (Cambridge, Massachusetts: Belknap Press of Harvard University Press, 1992), p. 303.
8. William H. Nelson, *The American Tory* (New York: Oxford University Press, 1961), p. 186.
9. It guaranteed free practice of the Catholic faith.
10. Miller, *Origins of the American Revolution*, p. 99.
11. Richard. B. Morris, *The American Revolution Re-considered* (New York: Harper and Row, 1967), p. 1.
12. The disputes among states over claims to western lands delayed the ratification process.
13. Carol Berkin, *Brilliant Solution: Inventing the American Constitution* (USA: First Harvest, 2003), p. 19.

14. Ibid., p. 15.
15. Ibid., pp. 13, 22.
16. A. Nevins and H.S. Commager, *A Short History of the United States* (New York: Random House, 1945).
17. Edward J. Larson and Michael P. Winship, *The Constitutional Convention: A Narrative History from the Notes of James Madison* (New York: The Modern Library, 2005), p. 11.
18. Richard Beeman, *Plain Honest Men: The Making of the American Constitution* (New York: Random House, 2009), p. 199.
19. David O. Stewart, *The Summer of 1787* (New York: Simon & Schuster, 2007), p. 68.
20. Rhode Island did not send delegates, and two of New York's three delegates did not stay at the Convention for long.
21. Merrill Jensen, *The New Nation: A History of the United States during the Confederation, 1781–1789* (New York: Vintage Books, 1950).
22. Calvin C. Jillson, *Constitution Making: Conflict and Consensus in the Federal Convention of 1787* (USA: Agathon Press, 2002).
23. George Bancroft, *History of the United States: From the Discovery of the American Continent* (New York: D. Appleton and Co. 1882), vol. 1, pp. 207–8.
24. Charles A. Beard, *An Economic Interpretation of the Constitution of the United States* (New York: Macmillan Co., 1913).
25. Ibid., p. 188.
26. Ibid., p. 324.
27. Charles Warren, *The Making of the Constitution* (Boston: Little, Brown and Co., 1928); Robert E. Thomas, 'A Reappraisal of Charles A. Beard's An Economic Interpretation of the Constitution of the United States', *American Historical Review*, Vol. 57, No. 2 (Jan., 1952), pp. 370–5.
28. Forrest McDonald, *We the People: The Economic Origins of the Constitution* (Chicago: University of Chicago Press, 1958).
29. Walter Lippman, *The Public Philosophy* (New York: New American Library, 1955); Martin Diamond, 'The Declaration and the Constitution: Liberty, Democracy, and the Founders', Nathan Glazer and Irving Kristol, eds, *The American Commonwealth* (New York: Basic Books, 1976).
30. Martin Diamond, *The Founding of the Democratic Republic* (Itasca, IL: F.E. Peacock Press, 1981).
31. Calvin C. Jillson, *Constitution Making*, p. 6.
32. Stephen Botein, Edward C. Carter, and Richard R. Beeman, eds *Beyond Confederation: Origins of the Constitution and American National Identity* (North Carolina: The University of North Carolina Press, 1987).

3

The Formative Period: The Era of Solidarity and Expansion

This chapter is on the political evolution of the newly born American nation. From the history of the election of the first President of the United States and the establishment of the Supreme Court in 1789, we enter into the more complicated and intriguing Jefferson-Hamilton debates in several matters like finance, war, foreign policy, etc. The chapter provides an account of the War of 1812, also known as the 'second revolutionary war'. American policy towards other states and especially Britain was most important during its 'formative period'. It concentrated more on the principle of solidarity and internal expansion, and the Monroe Doctrine was the most important contribution to that. Along with the political details of the doctrine, there is a critical interpretation to what it actually meant and the internal and external impact of the reiteration of its principles for the later centuries. American expansion corroborated to the westward movement which determined the very essence of American uniqueness, democracy, and development as Frederick Jackson Turner pointed out. The section on westward expansion is on Turner's 'frontier thesis' and how other scholars had responded to it. The chapter ends with detailed narrative of the evolution of judiciary and political parties, the two pillars of American democracy between 1840 and 1860.

a. George Washington and the Jefferson-Hamilton Debate

George Washington, the most powerful military and political leader of America between 1775 and 1799, was born in an affluent, well-connected family of tobacco planters in Virginia that used slave labour. He showed his military prowess early in life when he joined the colonial forces as a senior officer between 1754 and 1758 during the war between France and

Great Britain in North America which ultimately led to the beginning of the Seven Years War (1756–63) in Europe.

A born leader, Washington came to the forefront of the American Revolutionary war in the capacity of the Commander-in-Chief of the Continental army against the British between 1775 and 1783. In spite of his many defeats, he never surrendered to his enemies and fought against the British with great tenacity and military valour singularly that finally brought him victory. Truly the success of the American Revolution was to a large extent due to Washington's military genius.

In 1787, when the Convention of Constitution began in Philadelphia, Washington was elected unanimously to preside over it. His overarching personality and support inspired great confidence among the delegates; and after the convention was over all the 13 states were moved to ratify the new constitution. In 1789, Washington was unanimously chosen by the Electoral College as the first President of the United States, a position that he held for two consecutive terms till 1793. He took the oath of office as the first President under the Constitution on 30 April 1789 at the Federal Hall in New York. The Residence Act of 1790 authorised the President to select a permanent seat of government along River Potomac. Subsequently in 1791, the capital was selected in the city of Washington in the territory of Columbia.

When Washington assumed office, the newly established government was in a rudimentary state. Through the Judiciary Act of 1789, the President established the Supreme Court. He also began the cabinet system which included a team of brilliant supporters and policy makers to help in the running of day-to-day administration. During the entire period of his presidency, he was able to create a strong national government through strict discipline, able administration, and relentless hard work. An excellent judge of character and talent, he was always solicitous of opinions of others. His first concern after becoming the President was to bring all the rival factions together to keep the nation united.

Washington was not a member of any political party, nor was he in favour of the party system; but the two of his most distinguished cabinet members Alexander Hamilton, the Secretary of Treasury and Thomas Jefferson, the Secretary of State, belonged to two different schools of political thought. Whereas Hamilton believed in a strong centre, diminution of state rights, a strong federal structure, and a pro-British foreign policy,

Jefferson believed in a soft centre, preservation of state rights, and a pro-French foreign policy. Washington however counted on the huge experiences of both these remarkable men who were a part of his cabinet. Their constant debates over every important issue connected with the nation-building process became famous as the Jefferson-Hamilton Debate, which according to D.W. Brogan contained seeds of the party system in America.

The first basic point of difference between the two ministers veered round the question of state rights versus federal rights. In view of the fluid political situation in the country, Washington supported Hamilton on the question of a strong centre. A strong assertion of state rights could endanger the bond of unity in the new nation. However, he gave as much allowance as possible to Jefferson's view that state rights should also be preserved. A harmony was struck between federal rights and state rights. The second issue was concerned with financial network. Hamilton believed in a centralized federal bank of United States, a strong tariff policy for import and export of goods to and from America, and suitable excise duties. Jefferson stoutly resisted the idea of too much concentration of power in the Bank of United States or the Secretary of Treasury. He opposed high tariffs and local duties of any kind. He felt that interference of the centre should be kept at minimum and the states should have some concurrent rights in matters related to taxation.

Washington accommodated the divergent views of the two cabinet ministers by establishing a strong federal centre with provisions for state rights as well. In matters relating to questions of finance, Washington supported Hamilton's programme of establishing the Bank of United States but it was put under restraint by Jefferson's interventions. Tariff policies and excise duties were created according to Hamilton's guidelines. In 1791, Hamilton also proposed a tax on liquor which was accepted by the government and made into a law. But it immediately sparked off a bitter protest by the farmers in the frontier districts of Pennsylvania, Virginia, Maryland, and New Jersey, who traditionally had a profitable earning by making whiskey from the excess grain they produced. By 1794, the resistance assumed the shape of the armed Whiskey Rebellion. However, with the help of a strong federal militia it was eventually crushed and the rebels were imprisoned. The incident revealed the military strength of the new government and its ability to protect itself. It was also the first instance of the constitutional federal government using strong military force to exert authority over the states.

When the French Revolution erupted in 1789, there was a strong undercurrent sympathy within America for the revolutionary ideals in view of the earlier support given by France during the American War of Independence; but Washington felt that America as a new nation was still unprepared to get involved in continental politics. After the Revolution ended in 1792, the same year when Washington started his second term, the new French Republic declared war on many European nations including Great Britain. Once again Jefferson and his supporters wanted to help France but Washington adhered to a strict policy of neutrality. On 22 April 1793 he declared the Policy of Neutrality, thereby reiterating America's neutrality in the war between France and Great Britain. Later, Washington sent Chief justice John Jay to London to negotiate a commercial treaty (thereafter known as the Jay's Treaty) in 1795, thereby winning some profitable trade rights and establishing a close economic bond between the two countries.

The architect and founding father of the American nation, Washington proved to be one of its most discerning, persevering, and pragmatic statesmen. His Farewell Address issued on 17 September 1796 encapsulates advice and guidelines for a young state that influenced American history more than probably Washington could have himself anticipated. The valedictory touches upon the importance of national union, warnings against party strife and factionalism, the danger of foreign entanglements, proper virtues of a republican people, and a passionate plea for morality and good faith in all public affairs. Dr Henry Steele Commager writes that no man was ever revered and admired more by the people than Washington. He came to be looked upon truly as the Father of his country.

Annotated Bibliography

- Richard Brookhiser's *Founding Father: Rediscovering George Washington* (New York: Free Press, 1996) traces the astonishing achievements of Washington's career and illuminates how his character and his values shaped the beginnings of American politics.

- In *Washington: A Life* (New York: Penguin Press, 2010), the biographer Ron Chernow provides a rich portrait of the father of the nation and gives a detailed account of his troubled boyhood, precocious feats in the French and Indian War, creation of Mount Vernon, heroic exploits with the Continental Army, presiding over the Constitutional Convention, and magnificent performance as America's first president.
- Don Higginbotham, ed., *George Washington Reconsidered* (Charlottesville: University Press of Virginia, 2001) is a rich collection of 13 essays by leading scholars striking a balance between Washington's personal life and character and his public life as a soldier and political figure.
- K. Anthony Scott's *Thomas Jefferson and Alexander Hamilton: A Defining Political Debate* (Boca Raton, Florida, USA: Universal Publishers, 2008) shows how the political philosophy of Jefferson and Hamilton came together to affect their perception of the common law and the federal judiciary and in turn shaped the action they took either supporting or opposing federal common law jurisdiction.

b. Life and Times of Thomas Jefferson

Another founding figure of the American Republic and the third President of America, Thomas Jefferson was born in one of the richest gentleman farmer families of Virginia. His father, Peter Jefferson was a generous and liberal man who owned 2,500 acres of land and 150 slaves. After completing his study in the best possible school and William and Mary College in Virginia, Thomas was drawn to the American War of Independence. He turned out to be one of its best theoreticians and was given the task of actually writing the text of the *Declaration of Independence* which had been conceptualised by a committee of five. It was adopted by the American Congress on 2 July and proclaimed on 4 July 1776. This epoch-making document and his *Notes on Virginia* are clear indices of his political ideology.

The key-words enshrined in the *Declaration of Independence* are life, liberty, and pursuit of happiness borrowed largely from Locke's *Two treatises on Civil Government*. These three 'unalienable' rights actually are the bases of the philosophy of democracy. The root idea is that these rights are not granted by any benevolent government but these are rights that are inherent in all men since birth and which can never be lost.

In his *Notes on Virginia* the same emphasis is placed on democracy and 'natural rights' of men as also on the concept of 'individualism' side by side with state rights. Not only was he a supporter of democracy, but he also suggested the promotion of higher education in order to safeguard a democratic government. He considered education to be really a part and parcel of democracy. He is credited with the foundation of the University of Virginia. Another important point of discussion in this book is on agriculture which he believed was crucial for making a society stable. He favoured expansion of agriculture and taming of the Wild West, thereby bringing more land under the plough.

Jefferson was thought to be influenced by the Physiocrats because of his strong faith in the agrarian democratic system of government. Having been an ambassador in France, his link with France further deepened through his admiration of Rousseau and the French revolutionary ideals. In fact, a contemporary text also described him as a Francophile. Richard Hofstadter reflects that he was an aristocrat turned democrat.

After the war, when Jefferson was appointed the Secretary of State in the cabinet of George Washington, he played a significant role in the birth and formation of the party system in America. In the free and liberal ambience of Washington's cabinet, all his ministers could freely speak on important state matters ranging from foreign policy, forms of government, or westward movement; and from these discussions and debates there gradually emerged two distinct political parties as we have already seen in the previous section.

With the help of his Secretary of Treasury, Albert Gallatin, tax-burden on people was reduced from 80 million dollars to 45 million dollars. The much-hated high tax on whisky and liquor that had led to the 'Whisky Rebellion' during George Washington's presidency was now repealed.

The **Louisiana Accord** was a very important achievement of his administration. He sent a proposal to the French for the purchase of Louisiana in New Orleans, the only navigable port in the south. Napoleon favoured the idea since he was planning to go to Egypt rather than retain any foothold in the New World. After some negotiations Napoleon agreed to sell Louisiana to the United States for 670 million francs. Possession of this free port of New Orleans added a vast amount of arable land to the Republic and enhanced Jefferson's popularity giving a boost to his party.

The administrative set-up was significantly economized with unnecessary and excess posts in the government being abolished. This helped to save a considerable amount of revenue. His immensely successful first regime of presidency created great public confidence and paved the path for his re-election as the president from 1805–09. Jefferson's achievements in the field of home administration has been pithily summarized by one of his colleagues, John Randolph, who wrote, that no other administration was more brilliant than that of Mr Jefferson; it was marked with numerous successful experiments that included the availability of public debt for both principal and interest, the implementation of Louisiana Accord, the abolition of sine quos, etc.

Whereas his first presidency had witnessed far-reaching and successful administrative reforms at home, his second term of office was mostly taken up with foreign policy matters. America's erstwhile master, Great Britain still remained a source of threat, especially in the region of New Orleans as well as in Central America. Besides, relations between the two countries were further embittered by Jefferson's pro-French leanings. By way of military development, Jefferson established a military academy where there would be kept ready a 25,000 strong army and 7000 warships to be deployed for any possible military encounter. There was also the problem of 'impressments', i.e., the illegal capture of American ships in the high seas by British vessels, followed by loot and illegal arrest of American sailors who were taken as prisoners of war. This was a matter of national dishonour and Jefferson had to fight to show his protest. This conflict ultimately culminated in the War of 1812 which broke out during the presidency of Madison.

On the whole, Jefferson remains one of the greatest presidents of the United States. A founding father of the American Republic, he showed great constructive genius that helped to strengthen the roots of democracy and build a strong nation. His tolerant temperament and his ability to accommodate all shades of opinion made him truly the representative of the people. But the Native Americans and the African Blacks continued to be excluded from the mainstream. America also remained a nation of agrarian democrats only. Industrial America was a distant dream. It was left for Andrew Jackson, the seventh president of America (1828–36), who in his manifesto stated that his government would not only be for the planters and the farmer, but also for the mechanic and the labourer.

Jackson's success as a president would be in a large measure due to his inheritance of a strong and stable government left behind by Jefferson in the early years of the nineteenth century.

Annotated Bibliography

- R.B. Bernstein's *Thomas Jefferson* (New York: Oxford University Press, 2003; first edition), Victoria Sherrow's *Thomas Jefferson* (USA: Lerner Publications Company, 2002), and Norman K. Risjord's, *Thomas Jefferson* (Boston, Lanham, Maryland: Rowman and Littlefield Publishers, 2002) discuss the private life and public career of the fifth president of the United States.

c. War of 1812

The War of 1812, often called the 'second revolutionary war', after two-and-a-half decades of the outbreak of the American Revolution and fought between Great Britain and the United States had long-term consequences not only for these two powers but also for the Native Indian tribes. It is interesting to look into this military conflict between the newly independent US and the former colonizer Great Britain to understand the dynamics of power-relationship between these western blocks on one hand and also the use of diplomacy that actually decided the fate of these countries (and also other countries who were tied to them politically and economically) in the subsequent decades. Donald R. Hickey remarks in *The War of 1812: A Forgotten Conflict*, 'Although looking into the past, the war was fraught with consequences for the future, and for this reason it is worth studying today.'[1]

Causes of the Conflict

There were several causes of the war which can be categorized mainly into maritime and non-maritime causes. As 'a large section of influential British opinion, both in the government and in the country, thought that

America presented a threat to British maritime supremacy,'[2] Britain tried to impose naval and commercial restrictions on America. Harry L. Coles rightly argues in *The War of 1812* that the concept of right versus right is applicable for the war.[3] While Britain was portraying herself as the protector of liberties of the entire world by resisting Napoleon and regarding its each and every step as righteous, America also talked of their rights in the domestic and foreign sectors.

In 1807, Britain introduced a series of **trade restrictions** via a series of **Orders in Council** to impede American trade with France with whom it was engaged in a long and protracted war. Between 1802 and 1810, the American merchant marine had come close to doubling, making it by far the largest neutral fleet. Britain was the largest trading partner, receiving 80 per cent of US cotton and 50 per cent of other US exports. The British public and press were resentful of the growing mercantile and commercial competition. Thus, while the British tried to prevent the flourishing American trade with France, regardless of their theoretical right as neutrals to do so, the United States contested these restrictions as illegal under international law.[4]

Then there was the question of '**search and seizure**'[5] when desperate British captains acted as customs inspectors turning everything inside out of an American ship. **Impressment** provided not only the right to search for deserters, but by this any officer of the Royal Navy could make an on-spot decision. Many British sailors deserted because of poor food, hard work, and harsh discipline and sought for protection under American flag. They did that legitimately by the process of naturalization. Sometimes mistakes were made when native-born Americans were impressed. The United States believed in the right of the British deserters to become United States citizens. However, Britain did not recognize naturalized United States citizenship. So, in addition to recovering deserters, it considered United States citizens born British liable for impressment. This situation was aggravated by the widespread use of forged identity papers by sailors.[6] This made the matter worse and more difficult for the Royal Navy to distinguish Americans from non-Americans and led it to impress some Americans who had never been British. Men were also impressed in the US territorial waters itself. 'Free trade and sailors' rights' was a rallying cry for the United States throughout the conflict.[7] The impressment and ship seizures caused serious diplomatic tension and played an important role in turning American public opinion against Britain. Impressment became a cause of national dishonour to the Americans.

The westward expansion of America (the details of which is covered in the next section) and its impact on the Indian tribes was an important element in the War of 1812. Recent works [Richard White, *The Middle Ground: Indians, Empires, and Republics in the Great Lakes Region, 1650–1815* (New York: Cambridge University Press, 1991); Carl Benn, *The Iroquois in the War of 1812* (Toronto: University of Toronto Press, 1998)] have reflected on this dimension attributing its significance in determining historical events. The British Empire had ceded the **Northwest Territory**, comprising the modern states of Ohio, Indiana, Illinois, Michigan, and Wisconsin, and this territory had been an area of dispute between the Indian Nations and the United States since the passage of the Northwest Ordinance in 1787.[8] Richard White calls the Old Northwest, 'the middle ground,' a no-man's land where Indians and whites interacted in an extraordinary variety of ways, most of which had very little to do with imperial or tribal policy.[9] The Indian Nations followed *Tenskwatawa*, the Shawnee Prophet and the brother of Tecumseh who formed a confederation of numerous tribes to block American expansion. Having the long-standing aim of creating a large 'neutral' Indian state covering much of Ohio, Indiana, and Michigan, the British saw the Indian nations as valuable allies and a buffer to its Canadian colonies. Hence, the British supported the Indian cause and provided them with arms. Attacks on American settlers in the Northwest aggravated tensions between Britain and the United States.

With this issue was incorporated the **Canada question**. Historian Paul Johnson states that the 'South and the burgeoning West favored war for imperial reasons…they thought of appropriating…British Canada.'[10] Albert Weinberg writes, 'It has been plausibly argued by Professor Pratt [1925] that this war, long explained by reference to impressments and commercial restrictions, was caused fundamentally by the desire of Western States for the annexation of Canada.'[11] John Randolph remarks in his 16 December 1811 speech, 'Agrarian cupidity not maritime right, urges war. Ever since the report of the Committee of Foreign Relations came into the House, we have heard but one word…Canada! Canada! Canada!'[12] Canada would be the appropriate reparation for the economic ills suffered because of British policies such as the Orders in Council; it also fell within the natural and inevitable expansionist mode that had been a part of American land lust since the first days of colonization. Hence, geographic pre-destination was included in the expansionist factor. On one hand expansion in the frontier and on the other, permanent expulsion of the British played an important role in the Canada issue. Former President Thomas Jefferson rightly argues that the acquisition of Canada, as far as Quebec, would not only be a mere matter of marching but also provide the Americans the experience for the attack on Halifax, an attempt which would finally expel the English from the American continent.

Finally, at the home front, the US was in a period of significant **political tussle between the Federalist Party** (based mainly in the Northeast) **and the Democratic-Republican Party** (with its greatest power base in the South and West). While the former favoured a strong central government and closer ties to Britain, the later was sided with a weak central government, preservation of slavery, expansion into Indian land, and a stronger break with Britain. By 1812, the Democratic-Republicans, with James Madison completing his first term of office and control of the Congress, was in a very strong position to pursue its more aggressive agenda against Britain and attempted to further weaken its Federalist rivals as evident from Alan Taylor's *The Civil War of 1812: American Citizens, British Subjects, Irish Rebels and Indian Allies.*[13] Though support for the US cause was weak or sometimes non-existent in Federalist areas of the Northeast, throughout the war, and after the war, there was support towards the aspirations of the Democratic-Republicans from all parts of the country.

Events and Course of the War

It was a protracted war. The first two years marked the British victory when US soldiers under General William Hull retreated to Detroit and surrendered before the British, Canadian, and Native Indian militia, led by British Major General Isaac Brock and Shawnee leader Tecumseh. On 13 October US forces were again defeated at the Battle of Queenston Heights. After these initial defeats, the US started a rapidly expanded programme of building warships at Sackets Harbor on Lake Ontario as a decisive use of naval power came on the Great Lakes. In 1813, the Americans won control of Lake Erie in the Battle of Lake Erie and cut off British and Native American forces in the west from their supply base. Tecumseh was killed leading to the disintegration of his Indian coalition. The Americans controlled Western Ontario and permanently ended the threat of Indian raids based in Canada into the American Midwest.

At sea, the powerful Royal Navy blockaded much of the coastline, and the American strategy of using small gunboats to defend ports was a fiasco as the British raided the coast at will. The most dramatic episodes were a series of British raids on the shores of Chesapeake Bay, including an attack on Washington that resulted in the British burning of the White House, the Capitol, and the Navy Yard. The Americans sent out several hundred privateers to attack British merchant ships and in the first four months of war they captured 219 British merchant ships.[14] British commercial interests were damaged in the West Indies.

After the abdication of Napoleon in 1814, veteran armies were sent to the US. A major invasion was launched by British General Prevost in the New York State with the veteran soldiers, but the American fleet under Thomas Macdonough gained control of Lake Champlain and the British lost the Battle of Plattsburgh in September 1814.

Britain ended the trade restrictions and the impressment of American sailors, removing two more causes of the war once Britain and France became allies after Napoleon's defeat. The Treaty of Ghent was signed on 24 December 1814. A British invasion of Louisiana (after the Treaty of Ghent) was met with very heavy British losses by General Andrew Jackson at the Battle of New Orleans in January 1815. The victory made Jackson a national hero, restored the American sense of honour, and ruined the efforts of the Federalist Party to condemn the war as a failure. Finally, the peace treaty was ratified in February 1815.

Consequences

David and Jeanne Heidler in *The War of 1812* (Westport, London: Greenwood Press, 2002) and Daniel Walker Howe in *What Hath God Wrought: The Transformation of America, 1815–1848* (New York: Oxford University Press, 2007) argue that **all three nations were the real winners of the War of 1812**. The war could have been avoided in the first place by better diplomacy, and it was a mistake for everyone concerned because it was badly planned and marked by multiple fiascos and failures on both sides, as especially evident by the repeated American failure to seize parts of Canada and the failed British invasions of New Orleans and upstate New York.

Carl Benn in *The War of 1812* (Oxford: Osprey Publishing, 2002) and Jon Latimer in *1812: War with America* (Cambridge: Belknap Press, 2007) however take another stance and argue that the war constituted **a British victory and an American defeat**. The British achieved their military objectives in 1812 by stopping the repeated American invasions of Canada and Canada retained her independence of the United States. Thus, the Americans suffered a defeat when their armies failed to achieve their war goal of seizing part or all of Canada. Additionally, the US lost as it failed to stop impressment, which the British refused to repeal until the end of the Napoleonic Wars, and the US actions had no effect on the Orders in Council, which were rescinded before the war started.

Wesley Turner argue in *The War of 1812: The War That Both Sides Won* (Toronto: Dundurn Press, 2000) that both the US and Britain won the war and achieved their main objectives, while the **Indians were the losing party**. And this area has become a very important theme of research in the current decades. Finally, it can be concluded by saying that throughout the war the British had played on American soldiers' terror of the tomahawks and scalping knives of their Indian allies; and by its end American fear and hatred escalated into a merciless determination to exterminate all Indians and seize their lands. The withdrawal of British protection gave the Americans a free hand. The War of 1812 gave the Americans continental predominance and left the Indians dispossessed, powerless, and vulnerable.

Annotated Bibliography

- Donald R. Hickey's *The War of 1812: A Forgotten Conflict* (Illinois: The University of Illinois, 2012; Bicentennial Edition) is a comprehensive history of the War of 1812 with an exploration of the military, diplomatic, and domestic history of America's second war with Great Britain. It is an

up-to-date book covering recent scholarship on all aspects of the war, from the Gulf of Mexico to Canada.
- Alan Taylor's *The Civil War of 1812: American Citizens, British Subjects, Irish Rebels and Indian Allies* (New York: Alfred A. Knopf, 2010) is a thoughtful treatise covering all aspects of the war and the role played by American Citizens, British Subjects, Irish Rebels and Native Indians, and the impact of the war on these different groups and communities.
- At the beginning of the War of 1812 Captain David Porter flew from his mast a banner with the phrase 'Free Trade and Sailors' Rights'. This slogan reflected ideas that derived from the Age of Revolution combining patrician interest in free trade with more plebeian concerns about rights and the protection of seamen from impressment. In 'Free Trade and Sailors' Rights: The Rhetoric of the War of 1812' (*Journal of the Early Republic*, Spring 2010, vol. 30, issue 1, pp. 1–23), Paul A. Gilje shows how Americans used the phrase to explain their support for the war, and how the phrase continued to be used in a wide variety of relevant and irrelevant contexts.
- In *What Hath God Wrought: The Transformation of America, 1815–1848* (New York: Oxford University Press, 2007), Daniel Walker Howe illuminates the period from the battle of New Orleans to the end of the Mexican-American War, an era when the United States expanded to the Pacific and won control over the richest part of the North American continent. It touches upon the rapidly expanding economy, foreign relations, and social structures of America along with an exploration of social issues like race, gender, and ethnicity, and also include the history of religious revivals and the evolution of moral consciousness, reform movements, and political institutions.
- Including an overview essay providing historical background, seven essays on specific topics related to the war, biographies of the major players, 10 important primary documents, and a timeline, David and Jeanne Heidler's *The War of 1812* (Westport, London: Greenwood Press, 2002) provides major historical interpretations of the causes, progress, and consequences of the War of 1812.
- In *The War of 1812* (Oxford: Osprey Publishing, 2002), Carl Benn examines the events leading up to the War of 1812 and describes the views of all parties, the Indians, the Canadians, the United States, and the Great Britain.

d. The Monroe Doctrine

The Monroe Doctrine formulated by the fifth President of America James Monroe on 2 December 1823, was one of its longest-standing tenets that dominated the American and international scene for the subsequent decades. It has left one of the permanent imprints on US policy at the external front. The doctrine had been modified, re-interpreted, and invoked by many US statesmen and several US presidents, including Theodore Roosevelt, John F. Kennedy, Ronald Reagan, and others and implemented to suit the immediate needs and interests of the country. Noam Chomsky[15] has argued that in practice the Monroe Doctrine has functioned as a declaration of the right of unilateral intervention over the Americas: a sphere of influence 'to leave America for the Americans' that grew stronger in the later centuries along with the additional element of US control and hegemony veiled under its 'Big Brother' attitude for the other nations.

With the end of the War of 1812, the United States concentrated all its energies to domestic issues, its primary concern being the protection of democracy and strengthening of home administration. Matters of foreign policy were shelved for the time being. By the time James Monroe became the president in 1817, there were certain significant political developments in the international scene that seemed to threaten the internal peace and security of the American nation.

Historian George C. Herring has pointed out in *From Colony to Superpower: U.S. Foreign Relations Since 1776* that as the Napoleonic Wars ended by 1815, Prussia, Austria, and Russia formed the Holy Alliance to defend monarchism.[16] On the other hand, there was a series of successful revolts in the South American Spanish colonies including Bolivia, Peru, Argentina, and Chile under their able leaders San Martin and Bolivar. The situation prompted the Quadruple Alliance in the continent to despatch a joint contingent of troops to the New World to suppress the rebellious forces and support their ally Spain in maintaining its hold over the Latin American countries. The Holy Alliance authorized military incursions to re-establish Bourbon rule over Spain and its colonies, which were establishing their independence. Dexter Perkins argues that the Monroe Doctrine was inspired by the Napoleonic Wars. The American government feared that the victorious European powers would revive the monarchical government.[17]

Allowing Spain to re-establish control of its former colonies would have cut Great Britain from its profitable trade with the region. Thus, the British Foreign Minister, George Canning proposed to the United States that it was time for them to mutually declare and enforce a policy of separating the New World from the Old. The United States resisted a joint statement because of the recent memory of the War of 1812, leading to unilateral statement. The provocation also came from the Czarist Russia's annexationist move from the northern border of Canada to Alaska and Russian proclamation of territorial sovereignty over Northwestern America forbidding non-Russian ships from approaching the coast.

These new turn of events in continental politics that certainly jeopardized the safety and security of the United States propelled the latter to re-orient its earlier foreign policy. James Monroe realized that in spite of its military and naval weaknesses, it was imperative for America to make a bold counter-offensive to the outside world so as to keep the Old world rivals at a distance.

The policy was introduced by James Monroe on 2 December 1823. President James Monroe first stated the doctrine during his seventh annual State of the Union Address to the Congress (**annexure**). The policy was initially called Monroe's message; it gradually came to be known as the Monroe Doctrine towards the end of the nineteenth century. The policy was drafted by John Quincy Adams, the Secretary of the State. It sharply noted that further efforts by European nations to colonize land or interfere with states in North or South America would be viewed as acts of aggression calling for US intervention. It also stated that the United States would neither interfere with existing European colonies nor meddle in the internal concerns of European countries.

Dexter Perkins writes in *The Monroe Doctrine, 1823–1826* that Monroe's message had two parts – the first two provisions can be called 'affirmative' and the second two may be called 'negative' provisions. The first 'affirmative' provision was non-colonization, i.e., European powers would be forbidden to establish any new dependencies within America. The second positive statement was that America would not allow any transplantation of the continental political system into the New World. On the negative side a milder attitude was revealed. The third provision laid down that with regard to continental politics, as United States had always believed in the past, its future policy would also be one of 'non-interference'. The fourth and the last provision was that America, being a democracy, cherished no desire of colonization in any part of the Old World. The first two affirmative proposals were supported by a strong assertiveness. The second two provisions, in a way smacked of a kind of surrender and submission to the Old World. However, the idea that America required a long period of 'splendid isolation' and 'salutary neglect' by the continental powers to nurture its democratic set-up came out loud through Monroe's message. Notwithstanding Dexter Perkins' thesis, one can be led to conclude that on the whole it was a positive statement of America's foreign policy from which the nation could reap fruits.

The reaction to the Monroe Doctrine was a mixed one as per the political and economic interests of the states. Latin America accepted and revered it. John Crow, author of *The Epic of Latin America*, states, 'Simón Bolívar himself, still in the midst of his last campaign against the Spaniards, Santander in Colombia, Rivadavia in Argentina, Victoria in Mexico–leaders of the emancipation movement everywhere–received Monroe's words with sincerest gratitude'.[18] Though they appreciated and praised their support in the North, the Latin American realist leaders knew well that their future of independence was in the hands of the British and their powerful navy. To them the Monroe Doctrine was to become nothing more than a tool of national policy, 'It was not meant to be, and was never intended to be a charter for concerted hemispheric action'.[19] In 1826, Bolivar called upon his Congress of Panama to host the first Pan-American meeting.

So far as Great Britain was concerned, the doctrine met with tacit British approval; the Royal Navy enforced it tacitly as part of the wider *Pax Britannica* which enforced the neutrality of the seas. Rolf Hobson argues in *Imperialism at Sea* that Britain knew that if the newly independent Latin American states would become Spanish colonies again, its access to these markets would be cut off by Spanish mercantilist policy. The British approval to the doctrine was in line with British commercial interests.

The immediate impact of Monroe's message was astounding. It successfully deterred the aggressive policy of the continental powers; the Quadruple Alliance was thwarted in its move to help Spain and meddle into Latin American politics; and Russia was forced to withdraw from the Alaskan border. In 1836, the US government objected to Britain's alliance with the newly created Republic of Texas on the principle of the Monroe Doctrine. In the entire period from John Quincy Adams, who succeeded Monroe as the President in 1826, till 1848 when America was almost on the brink of war with the Mexican government, the Monroe Doctrine was kept in abeyance. With no intervention from the continental powers America could rapidly develop from within and steadily follow a policy of expansion towards the Southwest, mid-west, and also northwest, if possible. It ushered in 'an era of good feelings' inaugurated by President Andrew Jackson who held two terms of office from 1828–32 and from 1832–36.

In the subsequent decades the Monroe doctrine had been re-interpreted and applied in a variety of instances from US President James Polk, John Tyler, Grover Cleveland to Theodore Roosevelt (Roosevelt Corollary). It was no longer proclaiming simply protection and defence for America, but trying to ascertain the new status of America as the protector of democracy, peace, and prosperity all over the New World. In other words, America became a 'big brother' to all neighbouring countries, whether in Latin America or Canada or Alaska. This was the 'New American Zone'. Whittaker writes that there was the dawn of a New World philosophy and a Western Hemisphere idea. All these were extensions of the original Monroe message.

The re-iteration of the principles of the Monroe Doctrine had successful results as the continental powers desisted from any kind of intervention and America won a resounding victory, and its claim over Texas and control over the mineral-rich Latin American states brought in abundance of wealth for the country. In this way the Monroe message slowly evolved into a pragmatic and powerful doctrine that could be periodically put into practice to suit the exigencies of the situations. A remarkable feature was that it was never backed by any strong military or naval power. The Monroe Doctrine followed a long legacy, the spirit and essence of the doctrine being modified from 'splendid isolation' to 'manifest destiny' to suit the politico-economic framework of the American nation (**chapter** 7).

Annotated Bibliography

- George Dangerfield's *Defiance to the Old World: The Story Behind the Monroe Doctrine* (New York: Putnam, 1970) and Ernest R. May's *The Making of the Monroe Doctrine* (Cambridge: Belknap Press of Harvard

University Press, 1975) contain descriptions of the political events that led to the formation and implementation of the doctrine by President Monroe.

- Donald Marquand Dozer, ed. *The Monroe Doctrine, Its Modern Significance* (Tempe: Center for Latin American Studies, Arizona State University, 1976) and Charles Morrow Wilson's *The Monroe Doctrine: An American Frame of Mind* (Princeton: Auerbach, 1971) explore the significance of the doctrine in the foreign relations of the United States and the rise 'pan-Americanism' in the twentieth century.
- In his three volumes, *The Monroe Doctrine, 1823–1826* (Gloucester: P. Smith, 1966, vol. 1), *The Monroe Doctrine, 1826–1867* (Gloucester: P. Smith, 1966, vol. 2), and *The Monroe Doctrine, 1867–1907* (Gloucester: P. Smith, 1966 vol. 3), Dexter Perkins illustrates the history of formation, modification, and re-interpretation of the Monroe Doctrine between 1823 and 1907 to suit the immediate needs and interests of the country.

Annexure: President James Monroe's seventh annual message to Congress, 2 December 1823[20]

Fellow-Citizens of the Senate and House of Representatives:

Many important subjects will claim your attention during the present session, of which I shall endeavor to give, in aid of your deliberations, a just idea in this communication. I undertake this duty with diffidence, from the vast extent of the interests on which I have to treat and of their great importance to every portion of our Union. I enter on it with zeal from a thorough conviction that there never was a period since the establishment of our Revolution when, regarding the condition of the civilized world and its bearing on us, there was greater necessity for devotion in the public servants to their respective duties, or for virtue, patriotism, and union in our constituents.

Meeting in you a new Congress, I deem it proper to present this view of public affairs in greater detail than might otherwise be necessary. I do it, however, with peculiar satisfaction, from a knowledge that in this respect I shall comply more fully with the sound principles of our Government.

The people being with us exclusively the sovereign, it is indispensable that full information be laid before them on all important subjects, to enable them to exercise that high power with complete effect. If kept in the dark, they must be incompetent to it. We are all liable to error, and those who are engaged in the management of public affairs are more subject to excitement and to be led astray by their particular interests and passions than the great body of our constituents, who, living at home in the pursuit of their ordinary avocations, are calm but deeply interested spectators of events and of the conduct of those who are parties to them.

To the people every department of the Government and every individual in each are responsible, and the more full their information the better they can judge of the wisdom of the policy pursued and of the conduct of each in regard to it. From their dispassionate judgment much aid may always be obtained, while their approbation will form the greatest incentive and most gratifying reward for virtuous actions, and the dread of their censure the best security against the abuse of their confidence. Their interests in all vital questions are the same, and the bond, by sentiment as well as by interest, will be proportionably strengthened as they are better informed of the real state of public affairs, especially in difficult conjunctures. It is by such knowledge that local prejudices and jealousies are surmounted, and that a national policy extending its fostering care and protection to all the great interests of our Union, is formed and steadily adhered to.

A precise knowledge of our relations with foreign powers as respects our negotiations and transactions with each is thought to be particularly necessary. Equally necessary is it that we should for a just estimate of our resources, revenue, and progress in every kind of improvement connected with the national prosperity and public defense. It is by rendering justice to other nations that we may expect it from them. It is by our ability to resent injuries and redress wrongs that we may avoid them.

The commissioners under the 5th article of the treaty of Ghent, having disagreed in their opinions respecting that portion of the boundary between the Territories of the United States and of Great Britain the establishment of which had been submitted to them, have made their respective reports in compliance with that article, that the same might be referred to the decision of a friendly power. It being manifest, however, that it would be difficult, if not impossible, for any power to perform that office without great delay and much inconvenience to itself, a proposal has been made by this Government, and acceded to by that of Great Britain, to endeavor to establish that boundary by amicable negotiation.

It appearing from long experience that no satisfactory arrangement could be formed of the commercial intercourse between the United States and the British colonies in this hemisphere by legislative acts while each party pursued its own course without agreement or concert with the other, a proposal has been made to the British Government to regulate this commerce by treaty, as it has been to arrange in like manner the just claim of the citizens of the United States inhabiting the States and Territories bordering on the lakes and rivers which empty into the St. Lawrence to the navigation of that river to the ocean. For these and other objects of high importance to the interests of both parties a negotiation has been opened with the British Government which it is hoped will have a satisfactory result.

The commissioners under the 6th and 7th articles of the treaty of Ghent having successfully closed their labors in relation to the 6th, have proceeded to the discharge of those relating to the 7th. Their progress in the extensive survey required for the performance of their duties justifies the presumption that it will be completed in the ensuing year.

The negotiation which had been long depending with the French Government on several important subjects, and particularly for a just indemnity for losses sustained in the late wars by the citizens of the United States under unjustifiable seizures and confiscations of their property, has not as yet had the desired effect. As this claim rests on the same principle with others which have been admitted by the French Government, it is not perceived on what just ground it can be rejected. A minister will be immediately appointed to proceed to France and resume the negotiation on this and other subjects which may arise between the two nations.

At the proposal of the Russian Imperial Government, made through the minister of the Emperor residing here, a full power and instructions have been transmitted to the minister of the United States at St. Petersburg to arrange by amicable negotiation the respective rights and interests of the two nations on the North West coast of this continent. A similar proposal had been made by His Imperial Majesty to the Government of Great Britain, which has likewise been acceded to. The Government of the United States has been desirous by this friendly proceeding of manifesting the great value which they have invariably attached to the friendship of the Emperor and their solicitude to cultivate the best understanding with his Government. In the discussions to which this interest has given rise and in the arrangements by which they may terminate the occasion has been judged proper for asserting, as a principle in which the rights and interests of the United States are involved, that the American continents, by the free and independent condition which they have assumed and maintain, are henceforth not to be considered as subjects for future colonization by any European powers.

Since the close of the last session of Congress the commissioners and arbitrators for ascertaining and determining the amount of indemnification which may be due to citizens of the United States under the decision of His Imperial Majesty the Emperor of Russia, in conformity to the convention concluded at St. Petersburg on [1822-07-12], have assembled in this city, and organized themselves as a board for the performance of the duties assigned to them by that treaty. The commission constituted under the 11th article of the treaty of [1819-02-22], between the United States and Spain is also in session here, and as the term of three years limited by the treaty for the execution of the trust will expire before the period of the next regular meeting of Congress, the attention of the Legislature will be drawn to the measures which may be necessary to accomplish the objects for which the commission was instituted.

In compliance with a resolution of the House of Representatives adopted at their last session, instructions have been given to all the ministers of the United States accredited to the powers of Europe and America to propose the proscription of the African slave trade by classing it under the denomination, and inflicting on its perpetrators the punishment, of piracy. Should this proposal be acceded to, it is not doubted that this odious and criminal practice will be promptly and entirely suppressed. It is earnestly hoped that it will be acceded to, from the firm belief that it is the most effectual expedient that can be adopted for the purpose.

At the commencement of the recent war between France and Spain it was declared by the French Government that it would grant no commissions to privateers, and that neither the commerce of Spain herself nor of neutral nations should be molested by the naval force of France, except in the breach of a lawful blockade. This declaration, which appears to have been faithfully carried into effect, concurring with principles proclaimed and cherished by the United States from the first establishment of their independence, suggested the hope that the time had arrived when the proposal for adopting it as a permanent and invariable rule in all future maritime wars might meet the favorable consideration of the great European powers. Instructions have accordingly been given to our ministers with France, Russia, and Great Britain to make those proposals to their respective Governments, and when the friends of humanity reflect on the essential amelioration to the condition of the human race which would result from the abolition of private war on the sea and on the great facility by which it might be accomplished, requiring only the consent of a few sovereigns, an earnest hope is indulged that these overtures will meet with an attention animated by the spirit in which they were made, and that they will ultimately be successful.

The ministers who were appointed to the Republics of Colombia and Buenos Ayres during the last session of Congress proceeded shortly afterwards to their destinations. Of their arrival there official intelligence has not yet been received. The minister appointed to the Republic of Chile will sail in a few days. An early appointment will also be made to Mexico. A minister has been received from Colombia, and the other Governments have been informed that ministers, or diplomatic agents of inferior grade, would be received from each, accordingly as they might prefer the one or the other.

The minister appointed to Spain proceeded soon after his appointment for Cadiz, the residence of the Sovereign to whom he was accredited. In approaching that port the frigate which conveyed him was warned off by the commander of the

French squadron by which it was blockaded and not permitted to enter, although apprised by the captain of the frigate of the public character of the person whom he had on board, the landing of whom was the sole object of his proposed entry. This act, being considered an infringement of the rights of ambassadors and of nations, will form a just cause of complaint to the Government of France against the officer by whom it was committed.

The actual condition of the public finances more than realizes the favorable anticipations that were entertained of it at the opening of the last session of Congress. On the first of January there was a balance in the Treasury of $4,237,427.55. From that time to the 30th of September the receipts amounted to upward of $16.1M, and the expenditures to $11.4M. During the 4th quarter of the year it is estimated that the receipts will at least equal the expenditures, and that there will remain in the Treasury on the first day of January next a surplus of nearly $9M.

On [1825-01-01], a large amount of the war debt and a part of the Revolutionary debt become redeemable. Additional portions of the former will continue to become redeemable annually until the year 1835. It is believed, however, that if the United States remain at peace the whole of that debt may be redeemed by the ordinary revenue of those years during that period under the provision of the act of [1817-03-03], creating the sinking fund, and in that case the only part of the debt that will remain after the year 1835 will be the $7M of 5% stock subscribed to the Bank of the United States, and the 3% Revolutionary debt, amounting to $13,296,099.06, both of which are redeemable at the pleasure of the Government.

The state of the Army in its organization and discipline has been gradually improving for several years, and has now attained a high degree of perfection. The military disbursements have been regularly made and the accounts regularly and promptly rendered for settlement. The supplies of various descriptions have been of good quality, and regularly issued at all of the posts. A system of economy and accountability has been introduced into every branch of the service which admits of little additional improvement. This desirable state has been attained by the act reorganizing the staff of the Army, passed on [1818-04-14].

The moneys appropriated for fortifications have been regularly and economically applied, and all the works advanced as rapidly as the amount appropriated would admit. Three important works will be completed in the course of this year–that is, Fort Washington, Fort Delaware, and the fort at the Rigolets, in Louisiana.

The Board of Engineers and the Topographical Corps have been in constant and active service in surveying the coast and projecting the works necessary for its defense.

The Military Academy has attained a degree of perfection in its discipline and instruction equal, as is believed, to any institution of its kind in any country.

The money appropriated for the use of the Ordnance Department has been regularly and economically applied. The fabrication of arms at the national armories and by contract with the Department has been gradually improving in quality and cheapness. It is believed that their quality is now such as to admit of but little improvement.

The completion of the fortifications renders it necessary that there should be a suitable appropriation for the purpose of fabricating the cannon and carriages necessary for those works.

Under the appropriation of $5,000 for exploring the Western waters for the location of a site for a Western armory, a commission was constituted, consisting of Colonel McRee, Colonel Lee, and Captain Talcott, who have been engaged in exploring the country. They have not yet reported the result of their labors, but it is believed that they will be prepared to do it at an early part of the session of Congress.

During the month of June last General Ashley and his party, who were trading under a license from the Government, were attacked by the Ricarees while peaceably trading with the Indians at their request. Several of the party were killed and wounded and their property taken or destroyed.

Colonel Leavenworth, who commanded Fort Atkinson, at the Council Bluffs, the most western post, apprehending that the hostile spirit of the Ricarees would extend to other tribes in that quarter, and that thereby the lives of the traders on the Missouri and the peace of the frontier would be endangered, took immediate measures to check the evil.

With a detachment of the regiment stationed at the Bluffs he successfully attacked the Ricaree village, and it is hoped that such an impression has been made on them as well as on the other tribes on the Missouri as will prevent a recurrence of future hostility.

The report of the Secretary of War, which is herewith transmitted, will exhibit in greater detail the condition of the Department in its various branches, and the progress which has been made in its administration during the three first quarters of the year.

I transmit a return of the militia of the several States according to the last reports which have been made by the proper officers in each to the Department of War. by reference to this return it will be seen that it is not complete, although great exertions have been made to make it so. As the defense and even the liberties of the country must depend in times of imminent danger on the militia, it is of the highest importance that it be well organized, armed, and disciplined throughout the Union.

The report of the Secretary of War shews the progress made during the three first quarters of the present year by the application of the fund appropriated for arming the militia. Much difficulty is found in distributing the arms according to the act of Congress providing for it from the failure of the proper departments in many of the States to make regular returns. The act of [1820-05-12] provides that the system of tactics and regulations of the various corps of the Regular Army shall be extended to the militia. This act has been very imperfectly executed from the want of uniformity in the organization of the militia, proceeding from the defects of the system itself, and especially in its application to that main arm of the public defense. It is thought that this important subject in all its branches merits the attention of Congress.

The report of the Secretary of the Navy, which is now communicated, furnishes an account of the administration of that Department for the three first quarters of the present year, with the progress made in augmenting the Navy, and the manner in which the vessels in commission have been employed.

The usual force has been maintained in the Mediterranean Sea, the Pacific Ocean, and along the Atlantic coast, and has afforded the necessary protection to our commerce in those seas.

In the West Indies and the Gulf of Mexico our naval force has been augmented by the addition of several small vessels provided for by the "act authorizing an additional naval force for the suppression of piracy", passed by Congress at their last session. That armament has been eminently successful in the accomplishment of its object. The piracies by which our commerce in the neighborhood of the island of Cuba had been afflicted have been repressed and the confidence of our merchants in a great measure restored.

The patriotic zeal and enterprise of Commodore Porter, to whom the command of the expedition was confided, has been fully seconded by the officers and men under his command. And in reflecting with high satisfaction on the honorable manner in which they have sustained the reputation of their country and its Navy, the sentiment is alloyed only by a concern that in the fulfillment of that arduous service the diseases incident to the season and to the climate in which it was discharged have deprived the nation of many useful lives, and among them of several officers of great promise.

In the month of August a very malignant fever made its appearance at Thompsons Island, which threatened the destruction of our station there. Many perished, and the commanding officer was severely attacked. Uncertain as to his fate and knowing that most of the medical officers had been rendered incapable of discharging their duties, it was thought expedient to send to that post an officer of rank and experience, with several skilled surgeons, to ascertain the origin of the fever and the probability of its recurrence there in future seasons; to furnish every assistance to those who were suffering, and, if practicable, to avoid the necessity of abandoning so important a station. Commodore Rodgers, with a promptitude which did him honor, cheerfully accepted that trust, and has discharged it in the manner anticipated from his skill and patriotism. Before his arrival Commodore Porter, with the greater part of the squadron, had removed from the island and returned to the United States in consequence of the prevailing sickness. Much useful information has, however, been obtained as to the state of the island and great relief afforded to those who had been necessarily left there.

Although our expedition, cooperating with an invigorated administration of the government of the island of Cuba, and with the corresponding active exertions of a British naval force in the same seas, have almost entirely destroyed the unlicensed piracies from that island, the success of our exertions has not been equally effectual to suppress the same crime, under other pretenses and colors, in the neighboring island of Porto Rico. They have been committed there under the abusive issue of Spanish commissions.

At an early period of the present year remonstrances were made to the governor of that island, by an agent who was sent for the purpose, against those outrages on the peaceful commerce of the United States, of which many had occurred. That officer, professing his own want of authority to make satisfaction for our just complaints, answered only by a reference of them to the Government of Spain. The minister of the United States to that court was specially instructed to urge the necessity of immediate and effectual interposition of that Government, directing restitution and indemnity for wrongs already committed and interdicting the repetition of them. The minister, as has been seen, was debarred access to the Spanish Government, and in the mean time several new cases of flagrant outrage have occurred, and citizens of the United States in the island of Porto Rico have suffered, and others been threatened with assassination for asserting their unquestionable rights even before the lawful tribunals of the country.

The usual orders have been given to all our public ships to seize American vessels in the slave trade and bring them in for adjudication, and I have the gratification to state that not one so employed has been discovered, and there is good reason to believe that our flag is now seldom, if at all, disgraced by that traffic.

It is a source of great satisfaction that we are always enabled to recur to the conduct of our Navy with price and commendation. As a means of national defense it enjoys the public confidence, and is steadily assuming additional importance. It is submitted whether a more efficient and equally economical organization of it might not in several respects be effected. It is supposed that higher grades than now exist by law would be useful. They would afford well-merited rewards to those who have long and faithfully served their country, present the best incentives to good conduct, and the best means of insuring a proper discipline; destroy the inequality in that respect between military and naval services, and relieve our officers from many inconveniences and mortifications which occur when our vessels meet those of other nations, ours being the only service in which such grades do not exist.

A report of the PostMaster-General, which accompanies this communication, will shew the present state of the Post-Office Department and its general operations for some years past.

There is established by law 88,600 miles of post roads, on which the mail is now transported 85,700 miles, and contracts have been made for its transportation on all the established routes, with one or 2 exceptions. There are 5,240 post offices in the Union, and as many post masters. The gross amount of postage which accrued from [1822-07-01] to [1823-07-01] was $1,114,345.12. During the same period the expenditures of the Post-Office Department amounted to $1,169,885.51 and consisted of the following items, viz:

- Compensation to post masters, $353,995.98;
- incidental expenses, $30,866.37;
- transportation of the mail, $784,600.08;
- payments into the Treasury, $423.08.
- On the first of July last there was due to the Department from post masters $135,245.28;
- from late post masters and contractors, $256,749.31;
- making a total amount of balances due to the Department of $391,994.59.

These balances embrace all delinquencies of post masters and contractors which have taken place since the organization of the Department. There was due by the Department to contractors on the first of July last $26,548.64.

The transportation of the mail within five years past has been greatly extended, and the expenditures of the Department proportionably increased. Although the postage which has accrued within the last three years has fallen short of the expenditures $262,821.46, it appears that collections have been made from the outstanding balances to meet the principal part of the current demands.

It is estimated that not more than $250,000 of the above balances can be collected, and that a considerable part of this sum can only be realized by a resort to legal process. Some improvements in the receipts for postage is expected. A prompt attention to the collection of moneys received by post masters, it is believed, will enable the Department to continue its operations without aid from the Treasury, unless the expenditures shall be increased by the establishment of new mail routes.

A revision of some parts of the post office law may be necessary; and it is submitted whether it would not be proper to provide for the appointment of post masters, where the compensation exceeds a certain amount, by nomination to the Senate, as other officers of the General Government are appointed.

Having communicated my views to Congress at the commencement of the last session respecting the encouragement which ought to be given to our manufactures and the principle on which it should be founded, I have only to add that those views remain unchanged, and that the present state of those countries with which we have the most immediate political relations and greatest commercial intercourse tends to confirm them. Under this impression I recommend a review of the tariff for the purpose of affording such additional protection to those articles which we are prepared to manufacture, or which are more immediately connected with the defense and independence of the country.

The actual state of the public accounts furnishes additional evidence of the efficiency of the present system of accountability in relation to the public expenditure. Of the moneys drawn from the Treasury since [1817-03-04], the sum remaining unaccounted for on the 30th of September last is more than $1.5M less than on the 30th of September preceding; and during the same period a reduction of nearly $1M has been made in the amount of the unsettled accounts for moneys advanced previously to [1817-03-04]. It will be obvious that in proportion as the mass of accounts of the latter description is diminished by settlement the difficulty of settling the residue is increased from the consideration that in many instances it can be obtained only by legal process. For more precise details on this subject I refer to a report from the first Comptroller of the Treasury.

The sum which was appropriated at the last session for the repairs of the Cumberland road has been applied with good effect to that object. A final report has not been received from the agent who was appointed to superintend it. As soon as it is received it shall be communicated to Congress.

Many patriotic and enlightened citizens who have made the subject an object of particular investigation have suggested an improvement of still greater importance. They are of the opinion that the waters of the Chesapeake and Ohio may be connected together by one continued canal, and at an expense far short of the value and importance of the object to be obtained. If this could be accomplished it is impossible to calculate the beneficial consequences which would result from it.

A great portion of the produce of the very fertile country through which it would pass would find a market through that channel. Troops might be moved with great facility in war, with cannon and every kind of munition, and in either direction. Connecting the Atlantic with the Western country in a line passing through the seat of the National Government, it would contribute essentially to strengthen the bond of union itself.

Believing as I do that Congress possess the right to appropriate money for such a national object (the jurisdiction remaining to the States through which the canal would pass), I submit it to your consideration whether it may not be advisable to authorize by an adequate appropriation the employment of a suitable number of the officers of the Corps of Engineers to examine the unexplored ground during the next season and to report their opinion thereon. It will likewise be proper to extend their examination to the several routes through which the waters of the Ohio may be connected by canals with those of Lake Erie.

As the Cumberland road will require annual repairs, and Congress have not thought it expedient to recommend to the States an amendment to the Constitution for the purpose of vesting in the United States a power to adopt and execute a system of internal improvement, it is also submitted to your consideration whether it may not be expedient to authorize the Executive to enter into an arrangement with the several States through which the road passes to establish tolls, each within its limits, for the purpose of defraying the expense of future repairs and of providing also by suitable penalties for its protection against future injuries.

The act of Congress of [1822-05-07], appropriated the sum of $22,700 for the purpose of erecting two piers as a shelter for vessels from ice near Cape Henlopen, Delaware Bay. To effect the object of the act the officers of the Board of Engineers, with Commodore Bainbridge, were directed to prepare plans and estimates of piers sufficient to answer the purpose intended by the act. It appears by their report, which accompanies the documents from the War Department, that the appropriation is not adequate to the purpose intended; and as the piers would be of great service both to the navigation of the Delaware Bay and the protection of vessels on the adjacent parts of the coast, I submit for the consideration of Congress whether additional and sufficient appropriations should not be made.

The Board of Engineers were also directed to examine and survey the entrance of the harbor of the port of Presquille, in PA, in order to make an estimate of the expense of removing the obstructions to the entrance, with a plan of the best mode of effecting the same, under the appropriation for that purpose by act of Congress passed 3rd of March last. The report of the Board accompanies the papers from the War Department, and is submitted for the consideration of Congress.

A strong hope has been long entertained, founded on the heroic struggle of the Greeks, that they would succeed in their contest and resume their equal station among the nations of the earth. It is believed that the whole civilized world take a deep interest in their welfare. Although no power has declared in their favor, yet none according to our information, has taken part against them. Their cause and their name have protected them from dangers which might ere this have overwhelmed any other people. The ordinary calculations of interest and of acquisition with a view to aggrandizement, which mingles so much in the transactions of nations, seem to have had no effect in regard to them. From the facts which have come to our knowledge there is good cause to believe that their enemy has lost forever all dominion over them; that Greece will become again an independent nation. That she may obtain that rank is the object of our most ardent wishes.

It was stated at the commencement of the last session that a great effort was then making in Spain and Portugal to improve the condition of the people of those countries, and that it appeared to be conducted with extraordinary moderation. It need scarcely be remarked that the result has been so far very different from what was then anticipated. Of events in that quarter of the globe, with which we have so much intercourse and from which we derive our origin, we have always been anxious and interested spectators.

The citizens of the United States cherish sentiments the most friendly in favor of the liberty and happiness of their fellow men on that side of the Atlantic. In the wars of the European powers in matters relating to themselves we have never taken any part, nor does it comport with our policy so to do.

It is only when our rights are invaded or seriously menaced that we resent injuries or make preparation for our defense. With the movements in this hemisphere we are of necessity more immediately connected, and by causes which must be obvious to all enlightened and impartial observers.

The political system of the allied powers is essentially different in this respect from that of America. This difference proceeds from that which exists in their respective Governments; and to the defense of our own, which has been achieved by the loss of so much blood and treasure, and matured by the wisdom of their most enlightened citizens, and under which we have enjoyed unexampled felicity, this whole nation is devoted.

We owe it, therefore, to candor and to the amicable relations existing between the United States and those powers to declare that we should consider any attempt on their part to extend their system to any portion of this hemisphere as dangerous to our peace and safety. With the existing colonies or dependencies of any European power we have not interfered and shall not interfere, but with the Governments who have declared their independence and maintained it, and whose independence we have, on great consideration and on just principles, acknowledged, we could not view any interposition for the purpose of oppressing them, or controlling in any other manner their destiny, by any European power in any other light than as the manifestation of an unfriendly disposition toward the United States.

In the war between those new Governments and Spain we declared our neutrality at the time of their recognition, and to this we have adhered, and shall continue to adhere, provided no change shall occur which, in the judgment of the competent authorities of this Government, shall make a corresponding change on the part of the United States indispensable to their security.

The late events in Spain and Portugal shew that Europe is still unsettled. Of this important fact no stronger proof can be adduced than that the allied powers should have thought it proper, on any principle satisfactory to themselves, to have interposed by force in the internal concerns of Spain. To what extent such interposition may be carried, on the same principle, is a question in which all independent powers whose governments differ from theirs are interested, even those most remote, and surely none more so than the United States.

Our policy in regard to Europe, which was adopted at an early stage of the wars which have so long agitated that quarter of the globe, nevertheless remains the same, which is, not to interfere in the internal concerns of any of its powers; to consider the government de facto as the legitimate government for us; to cultivate friendly relations with it, and to preserve those relations by a frank, firm, and manly policy, meeting in all instances the just claims of every power, submitting to injuries from none.

But in regard to those continents circumstances are eminently and conspicuously different. It is impossible that the allied powers should extend their political system to any portion of either continent without endangering our peace and happiness; nor can anyone believe that our southern brethren, if left to themselves, would adopt it of their own accord. It is equally impossible, therefore, that we should behold such interposition in any form with indifference. If we look to the comparative strength and resources of Spain and those new Governments, and their distance from each other, it must be obvious that she can never subdue them. It is still the true policy of the United States to leave the parties to themselves, in the hope that other powers will pursue the same course.

If we compare the present condition of our Union with its actual state at the close of our Revolution, the history of the world furnishes no example of a progress in improvement in all the important circumstances which constitute the happiness of a nation which bears any resemblance to it. At the first epoch our population did not exceed 3,000,000. by the last census it amounted to about 10,000,000, and, what is more extraordinary, it is almost altogether native, for the immigration from other countries has been inconsiderable.

At the first epoch half the territory within our acknowledged limits was uninhabited and a wilderness. Since then new territory has been acquired of vast extent, comprising within it many rivers, particularly the Mississippi, the navigation of which to the ocean was of the highest importance to the original States. Over this territory our population has expanded in every direction, and new States have been established almost equal in number to those which formed the first bond of our Union. This expansion of our population and accession of new States to our Union have had the happiest effect on all its highest interests.

That it has eminently augmented our resources and added to our strength and respectability as a power is admitted by all, but it is not in these important circumstances only that this happy effect is felt. It is manifest that by enlarging the basis of our system and increasing the number of States the system itself has been greatly strengthened in both its branches. Consolidation and disunion have thereby been rendered equally impracticable.

Each Government, confiding in its own strength, has less to apprehend from the other, and in consequence each, enjoying a greater freedom of action, is rendered more efficient for all the purposes for which it was instituted.

It is unnecessary to treat here of the vast improvement made in the system itself by the adoption of this Constitution and of its happy effect in elevating the character and in protecting the rights of the nation as well as individuals. To what, then, do we owe these blessings? It is known to all that we derive them from the excellence of our institutions. Ought we not, then, to adopt every measure which may be necessary to perpetuate them?

e. Westward Expansion

With the official end of the era of British colonization of America, we find a new process which can be justly referred to as the 'internal colonization', i.e., American colonization of the continent through its continuous expansion towards the western frontier that so much determined the very essence of American uniqueness, democracy, and development (according to American scholars like Frederick Jackson Turner and others) that the end of the expansionist process due to the end of territory or land gave rise to 'frontier anxiety' among the Americans.

Decade by decade, the boundary of the map of the United States moved farther west than the last. Distinct advances of the frontier occurred, and by the census of 1820, the settled area included Ohio, Southern Indiana and Illinois, Southeastern Missouri, and about one-half of Louisiana.[21] The frontier region of the time lay along the Great Lakes, where Astor's American Fur Company operated in the Indian trade,[22] and beyond the Mississippi, where Indian traders extended their activity even to the Rocky Mountains; Florida also furnished frontier conditions. The Mississippi River region was the scene of typical frontier settlements. The rising steam navigation on western waters, the opening of the Erie Canal, and the westward extension of cotton cultivation added five frontier states to the Union in this period. The first great push of population to the far west occurred in the gold mines of California in 1848, Colorado and Nevada by 1858, Montana and Wyoming in the 1860s, and Dakota in 1870s.[23]

So far as the social history is concerned, the westward expansion began long back with the fur traders when these nomadic groups blazed the trails across the Piedmont and through the Appalachian Mountain barrier, pioneered on Kentucky, crossed the Mississippi, scaled the Sierras, and ran their trap lines through California's interior valleys.[24] The miners established communities in these regions and settled here permanently seeking opportunities and fortunes offered by the west. However, the real wealth proved to be in the grass and soil. Cattle-raising spread into the trans-Missouri region and ranching emerged as a booming occupation in the rich soil and pastures of Colorado, Wyoming, Dakota, Kansas, and Nebraska 'when enterprising men began to drive their Texas longhorns north across the open public domain.'[25] Between 1866 and 1888 around six million head of cattle were driven up from Texas on these high plains. The 'romantic' and 'wild' west gave place to the farmers and their families who settled here under the Homestead Act[26] soon ousting roaming ranchers within any entitlement to the land.

Ray A. Billington argues that the farmers made no compromise with nature, and unlike their predecessors, they did not adapt but conquered. They stripped millions of acres of virgin timber forests and viewed forests and grasslands as obstacles to overcome; they wanted to see the Indian tribes exterminated, '...their objective was to transform the western wilderness into replicas of eastern communities, with no trace of the natural environment remaining.'[27] The amount of exportable surplus mounted with the increased clearing of land, resulting in the division of labour (when the prospering farmers wanted to pay for services that they themselves performed formerly), and creating the basis for the towns and villages that climaxed the farmers' frontier.

The frontier process has to be understood in terms of man-nature contact and settlement pattern of two distinct groups – fur-traders, herdsmen, and others whose enterprise depended on preserving the wilderness and utilizing nature, and farmers, millers, merchants, speculators, and town-planters whose profits depended on an expanding economy subduing nature. The first group, however, preceded the later and the movement went on rapidly.[28]

Frederick Jackson Turner in *The Significance of the Frontier in American History*[29] saw the American westward expansion as a synonym to American development. The continually advancing frontier line for him represented the evolution of typical and unique American institutions, the progress to manufacturing civilization and societal development. He depicted a glorious saga of American expansion towards west which involved the capacities and potentialities of the Americans, 'in winning a wilderness, and in developing at each area of this progress out of the primitive economic and political conditions of the frontier into the complexity of city life.'[30] To Turner, the frontier represented the bifurcating line between 'savagery' and 'civilized'; that the we/they-, progressive/primitive-, savage/civilized-paradigm was deeply rooted in the Turner thesis is evident when he remarks, '…the frontier is the outer edge of the wave—the meeting point between savagery and civilization.'[31] And he found every justification of the evolution of American institutions and national development through the replacement or 'acculturation' (at times) of 'savageries' by the 'civilized'. Social evolution, '…begins with the Indian and the hunter; it goes on to tell of the disintegration of savagery by the entrance of the trader, the pathfinder of civilization; we read the annals of the pastoral stage in ranch life; the exploitation of the soil by the raising of unrotated crops of corn and wheat in sparsely settled farming communities; the intensive culture of the denser farm settlement; and finally the manufacturing organization with city and factory system.'[32] The westward expansion by replacing and making the former inhabitants adapt to the process of Americanization promoted the formation of a composite nationality for the American people.

The frontier thesis not only reflected the surging nationalism of the time, but Turner seemed to be intensely anxious to the waning away of the free lands across the frontier. In fact his thesis starts with this anxiety when he finds from the recent bulletin of the Superintendent of the Census for 1890 that, 'Up to and including 1880 the country had a frontier of settlement, but at present the unsettled area has been so broken into by isolated bodies of settlement that there can hardly be said to be a frontier line. In the discussion of its extent, its westward movement, etc., it cannot, therefore, any longer have a place in the census reports.'[33] Thus, he finally laments that, 'But never again will such gifts of free land offer themselves…the frontier has gone, and with its going has closed the first period of American history.'[34]

The Turner thesis has been criticized, countered, and questioned as it provided a one-sided portrayal of the glorious sojourn of newly liberated America without mere consideration of its impact on the inhabitants already existing in the areas, especially the Indian tribes, and the indentured servants who were brought by the colonizers. Hence what was 'liberty' for the newly settled advantageous American people was defeat and slavery for the disadvantaged 'savages'.

It is important to note here that the Indian tribes strongly resisted against the invasion of their land as a part of the 'internal colonization' that went on since the post-Revolutionary days, but they were defeated by stronger military organization of American troops. One must remember the Battle of Fallen Timbers (1794), a struggle between American Indian tribes affiliated with the Western Confederacy and the United States for control of the Northwest Territory (an area bounded on the south by the Ohio River, on the west by the Mississippi River, and on the northeast by the Great Lakes), and the rebellion of Tecumseh, the Shawnee leader in the Old North-west who was defeated by William Henry Harrison at the Battle of Tippecanoe in 1811, fought Battle of Thames in 1812, but finally killed by Americans at the Battle of Thames in Canada in 1813 leading to the disintegration of his confederacy. Other tribes such as the Miamis also fought a series of battles between 1795 and 1840 to resist forcible invasion of Ohio Valley; thousands of Cherokees, Chickasaws, Choctaws, Creeks, and Seminoles resisted against westward expansion, but were thoroughly defeated and exterminated during the regime of Andrew Jackson in the 1830s.[35] These were repeated in the fates of the Modocs, Mohaves, Paiutes, Shastas, Yumas, and others when California was ceded to become the thirty-first state of the Union.[36]

Coming back to the analysis of the Turner thesis, we find that its acceptability has been questioned by a number of scholars from different schools of thought. Marxist historian Charles A. Beard has pointed out that though Turner mentioned about the economic group conflicts as the outgrowths of the westward movement, but he omitted the contradiction between capitalists and organized labour.[37] Louis Hacker further elaborated Beard's argument and pointed out that Turner was ignorant about the growth of monopolistic capitalism and impending imperialism. The free lands actually ensured the agricultural base required for the international transfers for building a native industrial enterprise.[38] Writing in the late half of the 1960s, Richard Hofstadter brought the charge of a flawed American progressive in Turner; Turner could only see American achievements, but could easily miss the shameful aspects of expansion including riotous land speculation, vigilantism, and most importantly the tragic tale of the Indians, anti-Mexicans, and anti-Chinese nativism.[39] Donald Worster supplemented Hofstadter's view arguing that the Turner thesis obscured the fact that the west was the site of intense struggles over power and hierarchy between races, classes, genders, and other socio-ethnic entities.[40] The environmental historian Richard White mentions that Turner separated nature and culture as two isolated categories rather than reflecting on their intertwined inter-relationship.

Finally, Turner's model was stridently positivist and 'exceptionalist'; he belonged to the old western school of history which narrated a tale of 'progress' and 'improvement' restricted to the Middle West. It was nationalistic with roots of chauvinism that dominated the American scene for the subsequent decades in American history. William Appleman Williams saw in Turner thesis a prophecy of open door diplomacy and more active relations with foreign nations and markets.[41] This kind of history that provided the ideological justification for American 'exceptionalism' is no more accepted by the new western school, and western experience is now studied with a broad outlook emphasizing elements of cosmopolitanism (melting pot) and with the historical understanding that American development was not entirely exceptional and some roads of it led directly to failures and injuries.

Annotated Bibliography

- In *The Frontier in American History* (New York: H. Holt and Company, 1920), Frederick Jackson Turner's propagates his 'frontier thesis' that the westward expansion of America was pivotal behind American democracy and development. It is one of the first manifestations of the idea of American 'exceptionalism'.
- In *Westward Expansion: A History of the American Frontier* (New Mexico: University of New Mexico Press, 2001, 6th edition, abridged version), Ray

Allen Billington and Martin Ridge, along with an archetypal narrative of the new American nation's successful expansion, shed light on the social, environmental, and human cost of westward expansion.

- Everett S. Lee's 'The Turner Thesis Reexamined', (*American Quarterly*, Vol. 13, No. 1 [Spring 1961], pp. 77–83) and Jackson K. Putnam's 'The Turner Thesis and the Westward Movement: A Reappraisal', *The Western Historical Quarterly*, Vol. 7, No. 4 [Oct. 1976], pp. 377–404) provide historiographical interpretations of the Turner thesis by a number of scholars since the publication of the 'frontier thesis' till the present times.

f. John Marshall and the Evolution of the Judiciary

Ever since the constitution was passed at the Philadelphia Convention in 1787, there had been a tussle for power between the centre and the state and among states. The states nurtured a sense of resentment against the centre for being forced to part with many of their powers. A lot of unresolved problems had remained; when the constitution was on trial, George Washington lamented that America was still disunited. He bewailed the fact that the country was 'united by a rope of sand.' From such a situation the nation had to be built up. The Constitution, the cornerstone of the American Republic had to be safeguarded and correctly interpreted for the establishment of law and order and a stable government which would ultimately bring prosperity to the country. Therefore, the need for a very capable Chief Justice, who would be able to present just solutions to the constitutional problems, was strongly felt.

The choice fell on John Marshall, a contemporary of Thomas Jefferson. He seemed to be eminently suitable for the post of the Chief Justice of the Supreme Court. When the Constitution was being drawn up, Marshall joined the Federalist group led by Alexander Hamilton, even though he had been a Democrat earlier. The Federalists were in favour of a strong centre and protection of private property. The post of the Chief Justice was still innocuous, since his functions were not yet properly defined. The government was still in a very rudimentary stage. The capital was at Philadelphia and the government operated from the basement of a bank. No importance was yet attached to the Supreme Court. But due to his remarkable efficiency, Marshall, during his long tenure of office from 1801–35, was gradually able to establish the Court as one of the pillars of the American Constitution. As he dealt with the various judicial cases, more and more power accrued to the Supreme Court, and he could eventually turn it into a cornerstone of the American Republic.

The main task before Marshall was to firmly stabilize the federal government against the disorderly and disruptive tendencies of the individual states, to whom the federal government was the enemy. Marshall's task was to prove otherwise. Since the basic parameters of the powers of either the Supreme Court or the Chief Justice were not laid down, Chief Justice Marshall judiciously interpreted the Constitution in such a way that the Supreme Court would be gradually transformed into an awe-inspiring and powerful institution of the nation.

In order to strengthen the position of the Supreme Court, Marshall introduced the system of 'judicial review' which meant the right to review all the legislations and the decisions of the federal as well as the state governments. This right was not previously there in the Constitution, but Marshall introduced the practice, making it one of the basic principles of the American Constitution. Subsequently, it was copied in most of the constitutions of the world. Though initially there was a lot of opposition and a hot bed of controversy to the use of judicial review, but ultimately its wisdom came to be realized. In order to understand how far he was successful in establishing the principle of 'judicial review' it is necessary to study some of the individual cases.

In 1803 he handled his first case ***Marbury versus Madison***. Marbury, who was a Federalist and who had been appointed during the Federalist regime of John Adams, continued to remain in office when Jefferson, the Democratic Republican President came to power. Intent on removing all federalists from his office, Jefferson appointed Madison as the Secretary of State and directed him to force Marbury to relinquish his office. Accordingly, on some fake charge Madison dismissed Marbury who now went to the Supreme Court to present his case. Marshall was in a dilemma since there was no legal basis to remove Marbury from his office. At the same time he wanted to support the federal government under Jefferson. He used judicial review and made his judgment in favor of Madison. He argued that the President had a prerogative to remove all people from his office whom he thought were undesirable. This judgment undoubtedly smacked of high handedness, but Marshall was wise in pointing out that the Executive should not indulge in such practices very frequently.

In the ***Dartmouth College versus the Trustees*** in New York state case in 1810, Marshall displayed his strong stand against the state government. Dartmouth College was run by a private autonomous body, and the Trustees were the main body who ran the college. Somehow the state legislature intervened and tried to place their own candidates in the governing body of the college. The Trustees objected on grounds of interference into the management of the college. A conflict ensued and the case came up before the Supreme Court. Again by exercising judicial review, Marshall gave his verdict in favor of the college Trustees. His main argument was that the college was an autonomous body, its funds being raised through autonomous means, and therefore should be regarded as a private property. Neither the state nor the central government had the right of intervention in college administration. In this case, Marshall upheld the sanctity of private property. But his decision was also based on the good reputation and efficient running of the college, which he thought was really contributing to national progress. Had the Board of Trustees been corrupt or inefficient, his judgment would be definitely otherwise.

If in the earlier two cases he gave his verdict in favor of the federal government and the principle of private property, in the case between ***McCulloch versus Maryland*** in 1819, his judgment went in support of the state of Maryland. In this case, the federal government wanted to establish a branch of the Federal Bank, but the state government strongly protested against this move and interpreted this as a downright intervention in state affairs. Marshall did a thorough judicial review and commented that in the interest of the nation at large, the federal government had the right to establish a branch of the national bank in a state. But in case of a vehement opposition by the government and people of the state, the branch should be withdrawn. So his verdict went in favor of Maryland. It is interesting to note that Marshall was not dogmatic in his views. He always delivered a balanced judgment in a true democratic spirit.

In the ***Cohens versus Virginia*** case, which occurred over a dispute in lottery business, Marshall's verdict after a judicial review went in favor of the national agent, Cohens. In Virginia there was a state lottery run by state agents. Cohens wanted to float a national lottery business there, against which Virginia protested. Marshall reviewed the case minutely and came to the conclusion that since finance was a national issue, national funding process through lottery for developmental measures should not be restricted. In this way he asserted the right of the federal government over state issues in matters pertaining to finance; Cohens was allowed to operate a federal lottery and Virginia's objection was over-ruled.

A typical example of an inter-state conflict was the ***Gibbons versus Ogden*** case of 1824. This was about the boating rights of New York and New Jersey over River Hudson that runs between these two states. Both these states as well as some federal agents were keen on running a steamship service. Since it was the quickest mode of transport, it was felt that it should be a national priority. Marshall after reviewing the case pointed out that since the river transport service was meant to benefit the entire nation, it should be entrusted to the central government and should not remain a monopoly in the hands of New York and New Jersey. In this way, in the greater interest of the whole nation, Gibbons, the central government agent was given the federal charter to operate the steamship service on River Hudson.

Marshall dealt all these above-mentioned cases in a positively pragmatic, logical, and a forthright manner that enabled him to appear as an arbiter of American democracy. His goal was not personal aggrandizement; his principal aim was to strengthen the federal government and build a mighty democracy and a powerful Supreme Court to reckon with. The Constitution was clearly defined, and his judicial decisions had the force of law. His biographer Edward Baldwin is full of praise about John Marshall's achievements. Richard Hofstadter, in spite of his caustic comments in *American Political Traditions and the Men Who Made It,* also comments on Marshall's great strides towards creating a strong centre and a powerful Supreme Court. There is however an allegation against him that as a Federalist, Marshall's hidden agenda was to always support the propertied people and endow more power in the hands of those who were already powerful; he favoured the plutocrats against the poor people. He has also been dubbed as a power-monger. But such assessments seem to be unacceptable if his entire life-story is carefully studied. His only dream was to create a strong American nation and that is precisely what he achieved.

Annotated Bibliography

- Edward W. Corwin's *John Marshall and the Constitution: A Chronicle of the Supreme Court* (New Haven: Yale University Press, 1919; online edition at Project Gutenberg, available at: http://www.gutenberg.org/ebooks/3291)

date of access Nov 2012 is a chronicle of the establishment of the national judiciary.

- In *John Marshall: Definer of a Nation* (New York: Owl Books, 1998; reprint edition), biographer Jean Edward Smith has drawn an elegant portrait of John Marshall. Working on primary sources, Smith demonstrates the qualities of Marshall as lawyer, jurist, scholar, soldier, comrade, and friend.
- Herbert A. Johnson's *The Chief Justiceship of John Marshall, 1801–1835* (Columbia, South Carolina: University of South Carolina Press, 1997) is a political description of the judiciary functioning under the justiceship of John Marshall.
- Richard Hofstadter's *The American Political Tradition and the Men Who Made It* (New York: A. A. Knopf, 1948) is on the political history of the United States from the days of the founders to the presidency of Frederick Delano Roosevelt. The author argues that the dominant theme in American federal politics from Washington to FDR was a cautious and steadying process of ensuring the primacy of private property through compromises centred on the nation's unique incarnation of Lockean-tinged republican capitalism.

g. Evolution of Political Parties, 1840–60

The party system, an integral part of any democratic government, steadily developed in the United States mainly between 1840 and 1860. D.W. Brogan writes that it originated from the Hamilton-Jefferson controversy during the presidency of George Washington. Alexander Hamilton was the Secretary of State and Thomas Jefferson was the Secretary of Treasury in the first ever cabinet held by the first US President George Washington. As we have seen in ***section a*** of this chapter that these two most distinguished members of the cabinet belonged to two different schools of political thought. Whereas Hamilton believed in a strong centre, diminution of state rights, a strong federal structure, and a pro-British foreign policy, Jefferson believed in a soft centre, preservation of state rights and a pro-French foreign policy. Washington counted on the huge experiences of both these remarkable men of his cabinet. Their constant debates over every important issue connected with the nation-building process became famous as the Hamilton–Jefferson debates, and marked the origin of the party system in America.

The first basic point of difference between the two ministers veered round the question of state rights versus federal rights. In view of the fluid political situation in the country, Washington supported Hamilton on the question of a strong centre. A strong assertion of state rights could endanger the bond of unity in the new nation. However, he gave as much allowance as possible to Jefferson's view that state rights should also be preserved. A harmony was struck between federal rights and state rights. The second issue was concerned with the import and export of goods to and from America and on the issue of suitable excise duties. Jefferson stoutly resisted the idea of too much concentration of power in the Bank of United States or the Secretary of Treasury. He was also opposed to high tariffs and local duties of any kind. He felt that interference of the centre should be kept at minimum and the states should have some concurrent rights in the matter of taxation. There was a difference between the two stalwarts over foreign policy as well. Whereas Hamilton was a staunch Anglophil and wanted to emulate the British model of government, Jefferson was biased towards the French structure of democracy. Washington accommodated the divergent views of the two cabinet ministers by establishing a federal centre with provisions for state rights as well. Washington, by and large, adopted the tariff policies and excise duties suggested by Hamilton. America followed a pro-British foreign policy at least during the first cabinet and also more or less depended on a non-intervention policy.

After Washington, American political system underwent a marked change that led to the full-fledged emergence of the political parties. In the post-Washington era, the two opposing parties were the Democratic Republican Party headed by Thomas Jefferson and the Federalist Party led by Alexander Hamilton (and supported by John Borgian and James Madison). John Adams, who followed Washington in 1797, was a lawyer from Boston; he had been one of the framers of the Constitution, a rigid Anglophile and a strong Federalist. He wanted the financial institutions to be strengthened and state rights to be curtailed wherever possible, thereby enlarging the federal powers and strengthening the Federalist Party. It seemed that the Federalist Party would continue for a long time, but with the beginning of Thomas Jefferson's residency in 1803 there was a wind of change in both internal and foreign policies.

Under Jefferson, federal rights sought to be minimized, state rights were promoted in state conventions, and there was non-intervention in state matters. There was a reversal of foreign policy with Jefferson leaning more towards the French. A master-triumph of his pro-French policy was the purchase of Louisiana in 1803 for 45 million dollars from Napoleon. Louisiana's inclusion strengthened American democracy and Jefferson became immensely popular. All this resulted in a virtual eclipse of the Federalist Party and the spectacular rise of the Democratic-Republican Party.

The Democratic-Republican Party continued to flourish during the next presidency of James Madison from 1809. He was originally a Federalist and as a President he followed the lines laid down by Jefferson. In theory, he was still a Federalist, but in practice he became a democratic Republican. This resulted in the rapid decline of the Federalist Party and the rise of the Democratic-Republican Party to further greater heights.

Jefferson's triumph over the Democratic Party could however never turn it into a mass-based democratic party. Though he identified with the common people theoretically, his landed-aristocratic background prevented him from projecting himself as a people's man. It became a people's democracy only under Andrew Jackson who became the President in 1828 and served two terms from 1828–32 and 1832–36. Coming from a very humble origin, Jackson, 'a typical cowboy', whose friends were the ranchers and the land–speculators, he could easily identify himself with the ordinary folks. He came from the frontier region of Kentucky; he had good contact with the Middle West. The main thrust of his manifesto was the formation of a government for the common people that would include 'the planter, the farmer, the mechanic, and the labourer' and he really brought these four classes of people into play under his government. Merrill Jansen writes that for the first time new faces were coming up to create a new nation. These new men represented new states like Massachusetts and Virginia. There were the urban poor from New York and New Jersey also. Jackson's government was supported by both the landed people and the industrial folks. So he represented people from cross-sections of the country except the dye-hard aristocrats; and this has drawn a high-browed and an unfair remark from Richard Hofstadter that Jackson was a 'rural upstart'!

Against Jackson's Democratic Republican Party, there now emerged a new party of the blue-blooded aristocrats, the National Republican Party under the leadership of Nicholas Biddle, the President of the first Bank of United States. Biddle, backed by money-power, tried to put several road-blocks in the path of Jackson's success. He created an artificial financial crisis situation by withdrawing huge sums of money from the Bank of United States leading to a financial anarchy. Jackson reacted to the challenge by forming state banks, where federal money after being withdrawn was deposited. 'Wild cat banks', as they came to be called proved partially successful, and in the see-saw battle between National Republican Party and the Democratic Republican Party, Jackson ultimately won.

The following phase of the history of American political parties was completely taken over by the Democratic Republican Party. By the beginning of the 1840s, new factors had entered into American politics, thereby necessitating the emergence of new political parties. The period witnessed American expansion on two fronts: the westward expansion through the Midwest across the Mississippi, through Kansas, Nebraska, Tennessee (Mississippi itself as a state, trying to reach till Oregon towards the Rockies), and the south-west expansion at the cost of the Spanish government of Mexico. Texas and California by now was flooded by American immigrants. The migration intensified with the rumour that the area had gold mines, an episode immortalized by Charlie Chaplin's classic film made on the 'Gold Rush' of the late 1840s. There was a constant flow of migrants from the settled frontier of the east to the southwest or to the northwest. The lure of gold attracted more settlers in the southwest and made a clash of arms inevitable with the Mexican government. To annex Texas which had already applied for admission to the American Union, the latter entered into war with Mexico in 1846 during the Presidency of James Polk, an aggressive Democratic Republican. The Democratic Republican Party needed more and more land to broaden its base in order to gain more support from the rural population. Hence they strongly supported the expansionist policy. The Mexican War brought spectacular victory for America, thereby further strengthening the party base of the Democrat Republicans. The policy of 'splendid isolation' of the earlier years had obviously stood them in good stead for it had helped in conserving all their energy. Flushed with victory, the American government now demanded the entire territory called New Mexico, Arizona, Utah, and California. The Mexican government had no other alternative but to surrender, giving thousands of Americans the opportunity to migrate to California, the land of gold. An excellent portrayal of the gold migration is *The Age of Gold: The California Gold Rush and the New American Dream* by H.W. Brands.

The large-scale migration of people from the south as well as from the east raised the question whether they would be allowed to carry their slaves with them, as a part of their property in the new area of settlement since that was 'free-soil zone'. The issue on slavery and 'free-soil zone' came to be fiercely debated resulting in the emergence of two new parties: the Southern Democrats, arising out of the Democratic Republican Party of Jackson, and the Northern Democrats, changed as National Republicans during the time of Abraham Lincoln. In this way the monolithic unity of the original Democratic Republican Party split over the slavery issue which led to the outbreak of the Civil War in the subsequent decades (***chapter 4***).

Numerous anti-slavery societies, supporting the National Republican Party, and the pro-slavery societies, supporting the Southern Democrats cropped up that further widened the gulf between the two parties. There was also the 'free-soil' party which claimed that the slaves should remain free in the newly occupied areas, where they had not lived before.

The Minnesota Conference of 1850 could not solve the problem. Finally, a plebiscite was held for finding out a river-mouth to the problem. A vast exodus of people from the North to the South started in order to outnumber the supporters for the pro-slavery group. The pro-slavery group argued that slaves Constituted property which along with life and liberty was safeguarded by the constitution. So slavery could not be abolished and the slaves should be allowed to move into the newly occupied areas. Production of American cotton that was exported all over the world was dependent on slave labour. David Christy, a powerful pro-slavery leader wrote a pamphlet called *Cotton is King* which became very popular and strengthened the position of the Southern Democrats. On the other side, the anti-slavery group, who supported the National Republican Party argued that slavery was unconstitutional, unethical, and inhuman, and therefore should be abolished. The anti-slavery group was founded by the firebrand leader William Lloyd Garrison in Boston. However, the principal factor behind the anti-slavery movement was not so much on humanitarian or ethical ground as it was on the economic question. It was a conflict between slave-economy and free-economy. The economic mainstay in the North was based on industry which depended on free-labour. They could not compete with the slave-based economy of the South. If slave-based economy attacked the North then it would completely cripple industrial economy based on free labour.

In 1858, again a compromise was attempted. If one slave state had to enter the American Union then it had to be matched by a free state. In this way, equilibrium was established in the American Senate. Again, 1858 marks the advent of Abraham Lincoln's entry into politics as the leader of the National Republican Party. An excellent lawyer, a dynamic speaker, and truly a spokesman of the common people, he could readily impress the people with his power of words. During his election campaigns he stated that his programme included both the preservation of the American Union and the abolition of slavery. At this juncture a new issue cropped up. As many as six Southern states, fearing that Lincoln's victory in the election would lead to abolition of slavery, now applied for secession. After Lincoln's triumph in the election, he reiterated his earlier stand, and in order to preserve the American Union he sent federal troops to the south to bring back the rebel states one after another. By 1863 he also abolished slavery by a proclamation. With the Emancipation bill passed and the seceding states brought within the federal government, Lincoln was at the height of his victory.

So once again America reaffirmed its faith in 'life, liberty, and pursuit of happiness', and under Lincoln it had a new dimension. The abolition of slavery signified that abundance of free-labour from now on would be available in the North, where industries proliferated. It denoted that America was making the conscious choice of an industrial revolution as an alternative to the old agrarian democracy based on slaves.

Annotated Bibliography

- W.N. Chambers's *The American Party Systems: Stages of Political Development* (USA: Oxford University Press, 1975) is on the role of national parties in influencing democratic governmental processes since 1789.

- In *Economic Origins of Jeffersonian Democracy* (New York: the Macmillan Company, 1915), Charles Beard provides an economic background to early American law from the ratification period to the end of the Jefferson administration.
- Richard Hofstadter's *The Idea of a Party System: The Rise of Legitimate Opposition in the United States, 1780–1840* (Berkeley and Los Angeles: University of California Press, 1970) is a political account of the operation and functioning of party system in the United States between 1780 and 1840 and an exploration of the ideological undercurrent that played havoc in nation building.
- In 'Community and Consensus in Ante-Bellum America', (*The Historical Journal*, Vol. 19, No. 03 (September 1976), pp. 635–63), B.W. Collins makes a historio-graphical emphasis between national issues and the problems of community life experienced by Americans in the past.

Notes

1. Donald R. Hickey, *The War of 1812: A Forgotten Conflict* (USA: The University of Illinois, 2012), p. 3, Bicentennial Edition.
2. Reginald Horsman, *The Causes of the War of 1812* (Philadelphia: University of Pennsylvania Press, 1962), p. 264.
3. Harry L. Coles, *The War of 1812* (Chicago: The University of Chicago Press, 1965), pp. 2–3; Daniel Boorstein, ed, *The Chicago History of American Civilization* series.
4. Sir Robert Phillimore, *Commentaries upon International Law* (Philadelphia: T. and J.W. Johnson & Co. 1857), Vol. 3, p. 211.
5. Harry L. Coles, *The War of 1812*, p. 4.
6. Often deserters only carried 'protection' papers (instead of papers for naturalization), which could be purchased for as little as one dollar, Harry L. Coles, *The War of 1812*.
7. Paul A. Gilje, 'Free Trade and Sailors' Rights: The Rhetoric of the War of 1812', *Journal of the Early Republic*, Spring 2010, Vol. 30, No. 1, pp. 1–23.
8. The primary effect of the ordinance was the creation of the Northwest Territory as the first organized territory of the United States out of the region south of the Great Lakes, north and west of the Ohio River, and east of the Mississippi River.
9. Richard White, *The Middle Ground: Indians, Empires, and Republics in the Great Lakes Region*, 1650–1815 (New York: Cambridge University Press, 1991); reference cited in Donald R. Hickey, 'The War of 1812: Still a Forgotten Conflict?' *The Journal of Military History*, Vol. 65, No. 3 (July, 2001), pp. 741–69.

10. Paul Johnson, *The Birth of the Modern: World Society 1815–1830* (New York: Harper Collins, 1991), p. 10.
11. Albert K. Weinberg, *Manifest Destiny: A Study of Nationalist Expansion in American History* (New York: The Johns Hopkins University Press, 1958), p. 52ff.
12. *Annals of Congress*, 12th Congress, 1st Session (1812).
13. Alan Taylor, *The Civil War of 1812: American Citizens, British Subjects, Irish Rebels and Indian Allies* (New York: Alfred A. Knopf, 2010).
14. Jon Latimer, *1812: War with America* (Cambridge: Belknap Press, 2007), p. 101.
15. Noam Chomsky, *Hegemony Or Survival: America's Quest for Global Dominance* (New York: Henry Holt and Company, 2004), pp. 63–64.
16. George C. Herring *From Colony to Superpower: U.S. Foreign Relations Since 1776* (Oxford: Oxford University Press, 2008), pp. 153–55.
17. Paul S. Boyer, *The Oxford companion to United States history* (Oxford: Oxford University Press, 2006), p. 514.
18. John A. Crow, *The Epic of Latin America*, (New York: University of California Press, 1992), 4th edition, p. 676.
19. Ibid.
20. Gerhard Peters and John T. Woolley, *The American Presidency Project*, available at: http://www.presidency.ucsb.edu/ws/?pid=29465 (date of access: Nov. 2012).
21. *Scribner's Statistical Atlas*, xxxix, cited in Frederick Jackson Turner, *The Frontier in American History* (New York: H. Holt and Company, 1920), available at: http://xroads.virginia.edu/~hyper/turner/ (date of access: 25 May 2012).
22. Turner, *Character and Influence of the Indian Trade in Wisconsin* (Johns Hopkins University Studies, Series ix), p. 61ff, cited in ibid.
23. Keith W. Olson, Wood Gray, Richard Hofstadter, *An Outline of American History* (USA: United States Information Agency), p. 109.
24. Ray Allen Billington and Martin Ridge, *Westward Expansion: A History of the American Frontier* (New Mexico: University of New Mexico Press, 2001), 6th edition, abridged version, p. 4.
25. Keith W. Olson, *An Outline of American History*, p. 109.
26. A homestead act (the law passed in 1862) was one of the three United States federal laws that gave an applicant ownership at no cost of farmland called a 'homestead' consisting of 160 acres (65 hectares) of undeveloped federal land, west of the Mississippi River. It was an expression of the 'Free Soil' policy of Northerners who wanted individual farmers to own and operate their own farms, as opposed to slave-owners who would use the labour of the slaves.
27. Ray Allen Billington and Martin Ridge, *Westward Expansion*, p. 5.
28. Ibid., pp. 7–8.

29. Initially it was presented as a paper before the American Historical Association in Chicago on 12 July 1893; later incorporated into Frederick Jackson Turner, *The Frontier in American History*
30. Ibid.
31. Ibid.
32. Ibid.
33. Ibid.
34. Ibid.
35. Dee Brown, *Bury My Heart at Wounded Knee: An Indian History of the American West, The Illustrated Edition* (New York: Sterling Publishing Co., Inc., 2009), p. 9.
36. Ibid., p. 13.
37. Charles A. Beard, 'The Frontier in American History', *New Republic* (16 February 1921), pp. 349–50.
38. Louis M. Hacker, 'Sections – or Classes?', *Nation* 137 (July 26, 1933), pp. 108–110.
39. Richard Hofstadter, *The Progressive Historians: Turner, Beard, Parrington* (New York: Knopf, 1969), pp. 104–6.
40. Donald Worster, *Beyond the Agrarian Myth*, Patricia N. Limerick, Clyde A. Milner II, Charles E. Rankin, *Trails: Toward a New Western history* (Lawrence: University Press of Kansas, 1991).
41. William Appleman Williams, 'The Frontier Thesis: An American Foreign Policy', *Pacific Historical Review* 24 (November 1956), pp. 379–95.

4

'Two Americas': Regional Differences and Sectional Conflicts

The chapter includes the causes and course of the American Civil War which was fought between the industrial Northern and agrarian Southern states. It not only depicts the war as a political carnage but goes beyond to look into its socio-economic dimensions. That the war was decisive to the futuristic path of American History and made vast changes in the economic development of America is noted here. A critical interpretation revolves round the issue of slavery. The chapter ends with a biographical sketch of Abraham Lincoln, the chief architect of the victorious North in the war and the sixteenth President of the United States.

a. The Civil War

The American Civil War, fought between the Northern and Southern states with industrial and agrarian potentialities respectively, during the first half of the 1860s for over the secession of the Confederacy, should not only be looked as a political carnage but also from multi-variegated prisms – economic, societal, cultural, etc., as the outcome of the war was decisive to the futuristic path of American History. Charles A. and Mary R. Beard wrote in *The Rise of American Civilization* that the Civil War was a social war that made vast changes in the arrangement of classes, in the accumulation and distribution of wealth in the course of industrial development.

Causes of the War

Though recent historians disagree with the economic determinism prevalent in the writings of the economic historians of the US and argue that Northern and Southern economies were complementary, there were economic, political, regional, and cultural divides that promoted sectionalism among the Southern and Northern states when the interest of one was juxtaposed against that of the other.

The issue surrounding the abolition of slavery was one of the vital causes behind the outbreak of the Civil War. The origin of slavery can be traced back to pre-colonial times when African people were brought forcefully by the American shippers and fortune-hunters to the ports of Boston, New York, and Baltimore where they were sold as slaves to the planters for about 10 dollars per slave. There were three main kinds of plantations: cotton, tobacco, and sugarcane. All these plantations required hard, intensive physical labour for long hours. Ideally suited for this kind of labour, they slogged without a murmur of protest just like human beasts, thereby bringing great prosperity to the country. Cotton plantation was the most lucrative source of wealth. America produced long yarn which was the best and the most highly priced in the world. David Christie, author of the pamphlet *Cotton is King* justified the slavery-system on the ground of Southern cotton production solely dependent on slave-labour.

The anti-slavery movement in the United States had roots in the Declaration of Independence and slavery was banned in the Northwest Territory with the Northwest Ordinance of 1787. In 1807, the Congress banned the international slave trade. In this way though slavery faded in the border states and urban areas, but it expanded in highly profitable cotton states of the deep South. There was a systematic campaign in the North against slavery which gathered momentum with anti-slavery activists like William Lloyd Garrison, the founder of the Anti Slavery Society in 1820. Garrison and his supporters argued that slavery was against the ideals of Christianity, the norms of universal brotherhood, and economically unproductive too. The last argument was based on the fact that one could not hope to get the best out of the labour of a man if he was used as a beast and not allowed to think on his own. It was also downright unconstitutional since the American Constitution asserted the right of equality for all men. Slavery most of all was condemned on the moral and humanitarian ground. In his campaign against slavery he got the support of many of his contemporaries including the Evangelist leader Charles Wilberforce of England, the man behind the reformist policy of the British government in India during the same time.

The conflict reached a climactic point on the question of westward expansion. The great hunger for land and hence more opportunities led to armed clashes such as the War of 1812 and the war against Mexico in 1845. The Mexican War brought a number of territories to the south of America – New Mexico, Utah, Arizona, Texas, and finally California. These places were soon populated by fresh waves of people coming from the North-west. The balance maintained by the Minnesota Conference of 1850 drawing an artificial line of 36° 30′ between north and south could no longer be honoured due to the vast exodus of people from east to west. Matters became more complicated as people from the South wanted to carry their slaves to these lands which were actually free-soil areas. Disregarding the border line they moved on with their entire families and retinue of staff resulting in the notorious *Bleeding Kansas* and *Bloody Nebraska* incidents.

The slavery issue exploded in the 1850s. The newly available 'free soil' was a Northern demand and they wanted it to be available to the independent yeoman farmers and not to the rich slave owners who would buy up the best land and work it with slaves, forcing the white farmers onto marginal lands. With this mission the Free Soil Party was established in 1848. Charles C. Bolton reveals in *Poor Whites of the Antebellum South: Tenants and Laborers in Central North Carolina and Northeast Mississippi* that the demand of Free Soilers and Republicans enraged the Southerners who feared that it would attract west European immigrants and poor Southern whites. The new Republican Party angered slavery interests by demanding the end to its expansion and much of the political battle in the 1850s focussed on the expansion of slavery into these newly created territories. Eric Foner argues in *Free Soil, Free Labor, Free Men: The Ideology of the Republican Party before the Civil War* that both North and South assumed that if slavery could not expand, it would wither and die. With tobacco and cotton wearing out the soil so fast, the South needed to expand to new lands with hordes of slaves.

James G. Randall and David Donald mention in *Civil War and Reconstruction* that in 1860 the percentage of Southern families that owned slaves has been estimated to be 43 per cent in the lower South, 36 per cent in the upper South, and 22 per cent in the border states that fought mostly for the Union. Half the owners had one to four slaves. A total of 8,000 planters owned 50 or more slaves in 1850 and only 1,800 planters owned 100 or more; of the latter, 85 per cent lived in the lower South, as opposed to one percent in the border states. Ninety-five per cent of African-Americans lived in the South, comprising one-third of the population there as opposed to 1 per cent of the population of the North, chiefly in larger cities like New York and Philadelphia. Hence, fears of eventual emancipation were much greater in the South.

Gradually the slaves left the border states through sale, manumission, and escape; the border states had more free African-Americans and European immigrants than the lower South. This eventually increased Southern fears that prompted Southern efforts to make Kansas a slave state. By 1860, the number of white border state families owning slaves plunged to only 16 per cent of the total.

The states had certain rights. While the Southern position was that the citizens of every state had the right to take their property anywhere in the US which included slaves, Northerners rejected this 'right' as it violated the right of a free state to outlaw slavery within its borders. However, the Dred Scott Supreme Court decision of 1857, which overturned the ban on slavery in territory north of the 36°30′ parallel, bolstered the Southern case within territories and angered the North.

Finally, the South argued that each state had the right to secede, i.e., leave the Union at any point of time and the Constitution was an agreement among the states. The Northerners rejected such notion as opposed to the will of the Founding Fathers of the Constitution.

The slavery issue as the most severe bone of contention set the stage for other debates between North and South which irrevocably reflected the question of their divergent political economies. For example, the tariff laws in the 1830s, 1840s, and 1850s written by the Democrats kept reducing rates so much so that the 1857 rates were the lowest since 1816. This affected the Northern industrialists and factory workers, especially in Pennsylvania, who demanded protection for their growing iron industry.

The Whigs and Republicans were in favour of high tariffs to stimulate industrial growth. The Republicans called for an increase in tariffs in the 1860 election.

Consulting military camp newspapers and personal correspondence between soldiers and families during the Civil War, historian Chandra Manning shows that the war participants, i.e., both Union and Confederate soldiers believed slavery to be the cause of the Civil War. A majority of Confederate soldiers fought to protect slavery as it was an integral part of southern economy and culture. Historian Eric Foner argues that no two people held the same motivations. He argues that while some were motivated mainly by slavery, most were motivated by some mixture of politics, culture, nationalism, honour, or any other number of motivations.

The Course of the War

Abraham Lincoln's emergence as a national leader pushed the situation to a climactic point and in favour of industrial North. Beginning his career at county politics and thereafter being elected in the state legislature, Lincoln with his slogan for democracy, free labour, and free economy appeared as the great champion of the anti-slavery movement. The South began to fear that Lincoln's victory in the elections in 1860 would lead to the abolition of slavery and enforcement of free economy and democracy in the southern states.

Soon after Lincoln's victory in the election, the American Southern states – Georgia, Virginia, North Carolina, South Carolina, Florida, and Texas revolted and seceded from the American Union and formed a separate state. But Lincoln, after taking the oath of presidency, clearly pointed out that America was one country and one union which could not be broken into two independent states. He had no other option but to send troops against the recalcitrant states to bring them back into the American Union. In this way the Civil War began primarily on a deep-rooted conflict that had existed for a long time between the North and the South.

The Civil War ended with victory resting with the North signifying the triumph of democracy and free-economy. The emancipation of slaves was looked upon as the highest achievement of Abraham Lincoln, who said in the preamble to the proclamation of Emancipation of 1863, 'If my name ever goes down in history for any of my good works, it must be this one, that is the emancipation of slaves.[1] But the era of Reconstruction (1865–77) following the Civil War was an utter failure as emancipation without economic upliftment could not secure lives and livelihoods of the vast population of freed men. The regaining of power of the Southern Democrats in 1877 signified re-established of white supremacy and denial of civil and political rights of the blacks (see **chapter 10, section b**). Eric Foner rightly remarks, 'What remains certain is that Reconstruction failed, and that for blacks its failure was a disaster whose magnitude cannot be obscured by the genuine accomplishments that did endure.'[2]

On a closer analysis, the Civil War determined the future character of the American political economy. More than the humanitarian aspect of the abolition of slavery, it accelerated the process of industrialization in the United States with all the freed slaves now joining the vast force of free labour in the North and compete with the poor white labour for jobs. The northern white labourers also rushed to the southern states of Texas and Florida especially in search of better job opportunities. It signified the victory of industrial capitalism and solidified its ground in America. Ensuring a free democratic, capitalist, and industrialist economy to ultimately succeed in America the outcome of the war set on foot the rapid industrialization of America in the post-Civil War period.[3]

Annotated Bibliography

- In *Poor Whites of the Antebellum South: Tenants and Laborers in Central North Carolina and Northeast Mississippi* (North Carolina: Duke University Press, 1994), Charles C. Bolton sheds light on the lives of the often neglected landless white tenants and labourers and their relationship to yeoman farmers, black slaves, free blacks, and elite whites. He shows how poor whites represented a troubling presence in a society based on the principles of white independence and black slavery.
- In *Free Soil, Free Labor, Free Men: The Ideology of the Republican Party before the Civil War* (Oxford: Oxford University Press, 1970), Eric Foner brings out the causes of the American Civil War. Making a critical analysis of the causes and events of the war, Foner shows that even after the Civil War the assurance for 'free soil, free labor, free men' did not really apply for most Americans, especially the blacks.

- Chandra Manning's *What This Cruel War Was Over: Soldiers, Slavery, and the Civil War* (New York: Knopf, 2007) is an interpretation of the Confederate soldiers' perceptions of the war and the inter-relationship between slavery and individual and family interests in it.
- Eric Foner's *Reconstruction: America's Unfinished Revolution, 1863–1877* (New York: Harper & Row, 1988) is a fascinating account of the era of Reconstruction and how every American (black or white) responded to these unprecedented changes unleashed by the war and the end of slavery.
- In his article 'Did the Civil War Retard Industrialization', (*The Mississippi Valley Historical Review*, Vol. 48, No. 2 (September 1961), pp. 197–210), Thomas C. Cochran, on the basis of some quantitative studies, indicates that there was an immediate retarding effect of the Civil War on American economic growth due to the uncertainties of the times.

b. Abraham Lincoln

'As I would not be a slave, I would not be a master' and democracy signifies a form of government 'of the people, for the people and by the people' – the person whose remarks shook the Parliament and the then American society was Abraham Lincoln, the sixteenth President of the American nation. Though the various regimes of the Republican and Democratic government suited the political economy of the nation, yet it would be erroneous to underestimate the individual capacity and radicalism of Lincoln.

Born on 12 February 1809 to Thomas and Nancy Lincoln in a one-room log cabin in Hardin County, Kentucky, his childhood was not a bed of roses. Abraham's father Thomas Lincoln had to make his own way on the frontier when his grandfather was killed in an Indian raid in Kentucky. Thomas owned two 600-acres farmlands, several town lots, livestock, and horses, and was among the richest men in the county. But from propertied he became a pauper by 1816 when he lost all lands in court cases because of faulty property titles.[4] This made the family to move north across the Ohio River in Perry County, Indiana. Lincoln lost his last hope, his mother at the age of nine. His father was married to Sarah Bush Johnston. As a teen, Lincoln had to well equip himself with the hard frontier life and became an adept axe man in his work building rail fences. So far as education is concerned, he was mostly self-educated and was an avid reader. The Lincoln family moved west and settled on public land in Illinois, a free, non-slave state in 1830.

Abraham began his political career at the early age of 20 with his first campaign for the Illinois General Assembly. Kenneth J. Winkle remarks in *The Young Eagle: The Rise of Abraham Lincoln* that as one of his early political activities that drew popular support, he advocated navigational improvements on the Sangamon River.[5] In the New Salem precinct he received 277 of the 300 votes and won election to the state legislature.

His popularity spread across the country with his 'free soil' stance of opposing both slavery and abolitionism. In 1837 Lincoln remarked, 'Institution of slavery is founded on both injustice and bad policy, but the promulgation of abolition doctrines tends rather to increase than abate its evils.'[6] It is important to mention in this context that his training (self-training based on Blackstone's *Commentaries on the Laws of England*, etc.) and success as a lawyer helped to strengthen his argumentative skills.

Lincoln served to the US House of Representatives between 1846 and 1848. With abolitionist Congressman Joshua R. Giddings, he wrote a bill to abolish slavery in the Columbia District with compensation for the slave owners, enforcement to capture fugitive slaves, and also a popular vote on the matter, and abandoned it when it did not find much Whig supporters. General Zachary Taylor won the 1848 presidential election, and though Lincoln hoped to be appointed Commissioner of the General Land Office, his rival lawyer Justin Butterfield was appointed to the post. Lincoln was offered the post of Governor of the Oregon Territory but declined to the offer as it was a democratic stronghold and could have been fatal to his political career in Illinois.

Till the early half of 1850s, he was busy in the legal profession, and it was the pro-slavery Kansas–Nebraska Act of 1854 (which was the slavery-restricting Missouri Compromise of 1820) that ensured his return to politics again. Senator Stephen A. Douglas of Illinois argued that specified settlers had the right to determine locally whether to allow slavery in new US territory which Lincoln opposed vehemently. While the abolitionists and anti-slavery Radical Republicans of the Northeast saw slavery as a sin, the conservative Republicans thought it a curse as it hurt the interests of the white people and blocked progress. Eric Foner argues that Lincoln was a moderate in the middle; he opposed slavery primarily as it violated the republicanism principles of the Founding Fathers, especially the equality of all men as expressed in the Declaration of Independence.[7]

The Kansas–Nebraska Act created irreparable schism among the Whigs. Drawing on remnants of the old Whig party, the disenchanted Free Soil, Liberty, and Democratic party members, Lincoln was instrumental in providing shape to the new Republican Party. Lincoln sharply denounced the decision of the Chief Justice Roger B. Taney who opined that blacks were not citizens and derived no rights from the Constitution in *Dred Scott v. Sandford* (March 1857) case in the Supreme Court. Lincoln counter-argued that the Founding Fathers of the Declaration considered that 'all men are created equal, that they are endowed by their Creator with certain unalienable Rights, that among these are Life, Liberty and the pursuit of Happiness'.[8] After his nomination to the US Senate in 1858, Lincoln warned about the danger of disunion caused by the slavery debate and tried his best to rally Republicans across the North.

The stage was finally set for the fight between Lincoln and Douglas as the US senator for Illinois. James M. McPherson remarks in *Battle Cry of Freedom: the Civil War Era* that the seven Lincoln–Douglas debates of 1858 were the most famous political debates in American history.[9] The Democrats won more seats and Lincoln was defeated; but he gained national political reputation from the articulation of anti-slavery issue.

On 6 November 1860, Lincoln was elected the sixteenth President of the United States and the first President from the Republican Party, beating Democrat Stephen A. Douglas, John C. Breckinridge of the Southern Democrats, and John Bell of the new Constitutional Union Party. Lincoln's victory in the election made the secessionists to leave the Union; South Carolina took the lead by adopting an ordinance of secession on 20 December 1860 followed by Florida, Mississippi, Alabama, Georgia, Louisiana, and Texas by February 1861. While these states declared themselves to be a sovereign nation, the Confederate States of America with Jefferson Davis as its provisional President,[10] Lincoln refused to recognize the Confederacy and declared it illegal.

Lincoln made every effort to avoid war, but when the Confederate forces fired on Union troops at Fort Sumter on 12 April 1861, forcing them to surrender war was inevitable. Lincoln tried hard to put down the rebellion. He was compelled to use unprecedented powers. He expanded his war powers, imposed a blockade on all the Confederate shipping ports, disbursed funds before appropriation by the Congress, and after suspending *habeas corpus* arrested and imprisoned thousands of suspected Confederate sympathizers. Lincoln studied Henry Halleck's *Elements of Military Art and Science* from the Library of Congress to learn wartime and military specificities. Historian Richard Carwardine argues that Lincoln had to think wisely for preventing the war from becoming an international conflict.[11]

Due to the administration's failure to deliver a speedy end to the war along with other causes including rising inflation, new high taxes, and anxiety that freed slaves and undermined the labour market the Republicans encountered severe losses in the mid-term elections in 1862. On 19 June 1862 an act banning slavery on all federal territory was passed followed by the passage of the Second Confiscation Act which set up court procedures that could free the slaves of anyone convicted of aiding the rebellion. Freeing the slaves was necessary at the critical juncture for North to win the war. The Emancipation Proclamation of 1863 declared the slaves in 10 states (not then under Union control) with exemptions specified for areas already under Union control in two states. The Union armies advanced south and over three million slaves in Confederate territory were freed. Lincoln initiated a massive recruitment of Negro troops in the military service of the government. In 1864, Lincoln was re-elected in a landslide, receiving 78 per cent of the Union soldiers' vote. By April 1865, the war came to an end with the Northern victory. And with that, the profound objective of the Civil War, as perceived by Lincoln, a new birth of freedom in the nation was accomplished.

After the end of the Civil War, the most important tasks before him were reintegration of the conquered southern states and the free slaves' question. Senator Charles Sumner's Freedman's Bureau law had the provision of setting up a temporary federal agency designed to meet the immediate material needs of former slaves. The law also assigned land for a lease of three years along with the ability to purchase title for the freedmen.

The Lincoln era is also important for the passage of various other acts that carved the path towards industrial America. These include the Homestead Act of 1862 that made millions of acres of government-held land in the West available for purchase at very low cost, the Morrill Land-Grant Colleges Act of 1862 which provided government grants for agricultural colleges in each state. The Pacific Railway Acts of 1862 and 1864 granted federal support for the construction of the America's First Transcontinental Railroad, completed in 1869. McPherson points out that the passage of these acts was made possible by the absence of Southern congressmen and senators who had opposed the measures in the 1850s.[12]

Abraham Lincoln died a tragic death on 11 April 1865 when he was assassinated by John Wilkes Booth, the Confederate spy from Maryland. There is a debate among historians on the political image of Lincoln. Historians like Herman Belz, Norman Graebner, and Robert Smith argue that he was a hero to the political conservatives for his intense nationalism, support for business, insistence on the abolition of slavery, and his political and economic actions in terms of Lockean and Burkean principles on behalf of both liberty and tradition.[13] Gabor Boritt argues in *Lincoln and the Economics of the American Dream* that as a Whig activist, Lincoln was a spokesman for business interests, favouring high tariffs, banks, internal improvements, and railroads in opposition to the agrarian Democrats.[14] James G. Randall reveals in *Lincoln, the Liberal Statesman* that 'he was conservative in his complete avoidance of that type of so-called 'radicalism' which involved abuse of the South, hatred for the slaveholder, thirst for vengeance, partisan plotting, and ungenerous demands that Southern institutions be transformed overnight by outsiders.'[15] On the other hand Dirck and Cashin take a defensive stance and mention that he was not as bad as most politicians, and was a 'moral visionary' who deftly advanced the abolitionist cause, as fast as politically possible.[16] The emphasis has also shifted away from Lincoln-the-emancipator to an argument that blacks had freed themselves from slavery, or at least were responsible for pressuring the government on emancipation. However, in spite of these limitations, it is agreed by all, whether Republican or Democrat that Lincoln was a man of outstanding ability. Finally, it can be concluded with the opinion of David Herbert Donald in his 1996 biography that Lincoln was distinctly endowed with the personality trait of negative capability, defined by the poet John Keats and attributed to extraordinary leaders who were 'content in the midst of uncertainties and doubts, and not compelled toward fact or reason.'[17]

Annotated Bibliography

- Extensive biographies of Abraham Lincoln have been sketched by David Herbert Donald *Lincoln (*New York Simon and Schuster, 1996) and Richard Carwardine *Lincoln* (London: Pearson Education Ltd, 2003).
- James M. McPherson's *Battle Cry of Freedom: The Civil War Era* (New York: Oxford University Press, 1993) is a political account of the Civil War and the role of Abraham Lincoln in the victory of the Northern camp in it.
- In *Lincoln and the Economics of the American Dream* (Urbana: University of Illinois Press, 1994), Gabor Boritt mentions about Lincoln's ever deepening commitment to improvements of the nation and makes a connection between the rise of Lincoln and the economic realities of the time.
- Eric Foner's *The Fiery Trial: Abraham Lincoln and American Slavery* (New York: W.W. Norton & Company, 2010) traces the history of Lincoln from Whig to Republican and captures the entire sojourn of the end of slavery in America. In Foner's account, Lincoln appears to be neither the perfect saint of later myth nor the racist demon, but a complex, real man who had to meet the greatest challenge of his era.

Notes

1. *Proclamation of Emancipation of 1863* (available at: http://statelibrary.ncdcr.gov/ghl/themes/emancipation.html, date of access April 2012)
2. Eric Foner, *Reconstruction: America's Unfinished Revolution, 1863–1877* (New York: Harper & Row, 1988), p. 604.
3. Though Thomas C. Cochran ('Did the Civil War Retard Industrialization', *The Mississippi Valley Historical Review*, Vol. 48, No. 2 (September 1961), pp. 197–210) on the basis of referring to quantitative studies by other scholars indicated that there was an immediate retarding effect of the Civil War on American economic growth due to the uncertainties of the times, but overall it was conducive to American industrialization and set the permanent path towards an ideology justifying American industrialism as an established fact.
4. Carl Sandburg, *Abraham Lincoln: The Prairie Years* (New York: Harcourt, Brace & Company, 1926), p. 20.
5. Kenneth J. Winkle, *The Young Eagle: The Rise of Abraham Lincoln* (Dallas: Taylor Trade Publications, 2001), pp. 7–8.
6. David Herbert Donald, *Lincoln* (New York: Simon and Schuster, 1996), p. 134.
7. Eric Foner, *The Fiery Trial: Abraham Lincoln and American Slavery* (New York: W.W. Norton & Company, 2010), pp. 84–88.

8. *The Declaration of Independence* (July 4, 1776), available at: http://www.ushistory.org/declaration/document/index.htm, date of access: April 2013.
9. James M. McPherson, *Battle Cry of Freedom: the Civil War Era* (New York: Oxford University Press, 1993), p. 182.
10. The upper South and border states – Delaware, Maryland, Virginia, North Carolina, Tennessee, Kentucky, Missouri, and Arkansas initially rejected the secessionist appeal.
11. Richard Carwardine, *Lincoln* (London: Pearson Education Ltd, 2003), pp. 163–64.
12. James M. McPherson, ibid., pp. 450–52.
13. Herman Belz, 'Lincoln, Abraham', Bruce Frohnen, et al., eds, *American Conservatism: An Encyclopedia* (Wilmington, DE: ISI Books, 2006), pp. 514–18; Norman Graebner, 'Abraham Lincoln: Conservative Statesman', *The Enduring Lincoln: Lincoln Sesquicentennial Lectures at the University of Illinois* (Urbana: University of Illinois Press, 1959), pp. 67–94; Robert C. Smith, *Conservatism and Racism, and Why in America They Are the Same* (State University of New York Press, 2010), pp. 43–45.
14. Gabor Boritt, *Lincoln and the Economics of the American Dream* (Urbana: University of Illinois Press, 1994), pp. 196, 198, 228, 301.
15. James G. Randall, *Lincoln, the Liberal Statesman* (New York: Dodd, Mead, 1947), p. 175.
16. Brian Dirck, *Lincoln the Lawyer* (Urbana: University of Illinois Press, 2008), p. 31; Joan E. Cashin, ed, *The War Was You and Me: Civilians in The American Civil War* (Princeton: Princeton University Press, 2002), p. 61.
17. David Herbert Donald, *Lincoln*, p. 15.

5

Agrarian and Industrial Revolutions

This chapter provides an economic history of the two most important revolutions of America in the post-Civil War period: the agricultural and the industrial revolutions. Along with exploring the reasons behind these phenomena, the most important inventions are mentioned that changed the course of American History in the subsequent decades. The Industrial Revolution has been studied by a number of scholars across disciplines, the thrust varying from economics to social, technological, and environmental history. A brief discussion on the historiography of the industrial revolution covers all the important works from 1860s till the recent times.

a. Agricultural Revolution

The post-Civil War Agrarian Revolution resulted out of a combination of several factors. Huge availability of arable lands, equally large numbers of tillers of soil, startling inventions in agricultural implements, scientific researches in plant genetics, and techniques of crop production, all combined and brought about a spectacular breakthrough in the agrarian sector.

By the mid-nineteenth century, America came to possess a vast amount of arable lands which, between 1860 and 1900, increased from three million to 60 million and the number of farms from two million to six million. On an average the production went up by three times or 300 per cent. For example, in 1860 the production of wheat was 250 million bushels which jumped up to 655 million bushels by 1900. Similarly, the production of corn was a little less than one million bushels which leapt up to two and a half billion bushels in 1900. Production of cotton also took a giant leap from four million bales 1860 to 10 million bales in

1900. This colossal increase in crop-production not only made America self-sufficient in procurement of food but also created enough surpluses for export to European countries.

This spectacular phenomenon can be explained by two factors. In the first place, the opening of the West and the steady westward expansion from the East and the South created vast areas for farming. The plains and valleys of the West were primarily conducive to the growth of agriculture, and within a very short period the region began to produce a far greater volume of crops including wheat and corn, and even cotton, than other parts of the country. There was also a steady increase in agricultural labour with fresh waves of migration both from the east to the West as also from the Old World to different parts of the New World which provided a constant supply of fresh farmhands. It was mainly the underdogs of the industrial cities of the east and the north who found a gate of escape to the arable lands of the far West and settled down there happily. This was true of a considerable number of freed Black people of the South who joined the rank of the tillers in the West. Among the immigrants from the Old world, there were peasants from Ireland, Poland, and France, and the French peasants specially were extremely skilled.

The phenomenal increase in the areas of cultivable land and the strength of man-power, however, were not sufficient in bringing about the agricultural revolution. The farming techniques had to be mechanized and scientific. The second important factor therefore was the invention of a number of mechanical devices that expedited and increased the efficiency of farming. The first important invention was Eli Whitney's cotton gin in 1793 that revolutionized cotton production in the South. This was followed by the epoch-making invention of the chilled plow by John Deere in 1837. The invention of the mechanical reaper by the two farmers, Obed Hussey and Cyrus McCormick, greatly quickened the speed of reaping acres of land. In 1847, Hussey established his reaper factory in Baltimore; McCormick moved to Chicago to start his factory from where he started producing machines and selling them. In this way, the strenuous work of gathering up the grain and binding the stacks of crops with some kind of coil or wire could be easily carried out through a mechanical device. The machine also helped in loading the entire harvest into wagons, ready for transportation. In the 1880s, the reaper-thresher was invented which could reap, thresh, clean, and put the grain in sacks, all in a single operation.

Agriculture could now use mechanical devices. The crop reapers, corn planters, corn cutters, huskers, the manure spreader, and other useful inventions took away the manual strain of the tillers and greatly increased his efficiency.

Scientific researches in the agrarian sector started since the time of Washington and Jefferson, who were keen on introducing new plants, rotating crops, and improving their livestock. Jefferson is reported to have said, 'The greatest service which can be rendered to any country is to add a useful plant to its culture'. New experiments were carried out in plant physiology or plant genetics. Two new kinds of wheat, *Kubanka* and *Kharkov*, were introduced to Western America. Its seeds were brought from Mexico and Russia, and these could be easily grown on the American soil. Their chief merit was that these were rust-resistant crops. Many crops would degenerate and rot due to weather situations but now with such epoch-making inventions the crops could be saved.

Through the availability of fresh virgin soil, constant increase of manpower, and most importantly, the use of ingenious machines for production processes and new scientific inventions, an astounding agricultural revolution was effected in America. Peter D. McClelland, however, brings out an important point in his treatise *Sowing Modernity: America's First Agricultural Revolution*, often missed by us. He argues that though scholars have emphasized on the first widespread use of complex machinery, the systematic application of science and recourse to modern management techniques as revolutionary discontinuities in the farming sector, but the study of the beginning of the transformation process had been neglected and excluded. His study is a departure in the sense that it takes into account the importance of the early changes 'on the farm long before complex machines or modern chemistry or agribusiness was an integral part of American husbandry.'[1] To him, the later revolutionary modifications in the agrarian sector was preceded by a fundamental attitudinal shift among the agrarian producers in search for a better way that led to the generation and use of new techniques or devices. Once this attitudinal change was entrenched among the farming community, following the Darwinian principle, the fittest novelties survived 'with fitness defined primarily as a capacity to increase the profits of those who own the farm.'[2]

This phase can be defined as the 'first agricultural revolution', which once accomplished, reassured the subsequent agrarian innovations of the subsequent decades.

With the rapid mechanization of the rural sector, the old-world, pre-industrial pastoral life began to disappear. It seemed that the entire country had become a giant farm-house and the farmer's close bond with the soil was lost. He seemed to be replaced by a man-made machine that perfected the skill of planting, reaping, harvesting, and even packing the entire produce of crops. As he felt more and more separated from his ties with the land, he became increasingly alienated and lost in his sense of identity. The charm of pastoral life fast disappeared, a far cry that would be soon heard in the Granger and Populist Movements.

Annotated Bibliography

- In *Sowing Modernity: America's First Agricultural Revolution* (USA: University of Cornell Press, 1997), Peter D. McClelland surveys practices from crop rotation to livestock breeding, with a particular focus on the change in implements used to produce small grains and claims that transformation of American agriculture was an unmistakable revolution.
- Paul K. Conkin's *A Revolution down on the Farm: The Transformation of American Agriculture since 1929* (Kentucky: The University Press of Kentucky, 2008) captures the history of American agriculture, showing how New Deal innovations evolved into convoluted commodity programmes following World War II. Conkin argues that the greatest industrial revolution in history has occurred in agriculture since 1929 with an increased tenfold production on American farms.

b. Industrial Revolution

The Industrial Revolution in the United States was a spectacular phenomenon and 'As railroad networks, steam shipping routes, textile factories, telegraph and telephone lines, steel foundries, and mechanized harvesting machines blossomed across the land, they transfigured American life,' remarks Kevin and Laurie C. Hillstorm in *The Industrial Revolution in America: Automobiles, Mining and Petroleum, Textiles.*[3]

America stretched from the Atlantic in the east coast to the Pacific Sea and the Rockies in the west coast, and having vast stretches of land under its control, it had enough rural surplus which could be now generated for industrial growth. America was blessed with abundance of labour since the time of the early settlers. Migration of labour was a constant factor, encouraged by the pioneer farmers who had come in successive batches from the European continent and founded the United States. The East European countries, especially Russia, and Western European countries like Italy and France provided with cheap labour. After the emancipation of slaves in 1863, the freed men joined the rank of the labour force in the North.

America was rich in mineral resources. It had all the basic requisites for industrial growth that included coal, iron, oil, and eventually electricity. Abundance of coal was found in the entire plain of Illinois, Oklahoma, and Texas. Coal was discovered further North, just below the Great Lakes, in the newly emerged states of Dakota, Wyoming, and Idaho in the 1870s. Sale of coal naturally brought great monetary profit. Iron was found in plenty in the entire belt near the Great Lakes, north of Illinois. There were vast repositories of iron ore in the Mesabi iron mines, close to Chicago on the banks of Lake Michigan. Oil and first-grade petroleum was first discovered by Drexen in Pennsylvania 1845. Further excavations for oil were made in Texas, California, and Oklahoma. In general, the Middle states and the Southern states that were acquired after the Mexican War were oil-producing areas. Soon the annual production of oil increased enormously and the rush to the 'oil regions' rivalled the rush to the gold reserves to California a decade earlier. Copper reserves had been discovered in Michigan from very early times. From the 1880s, rich copper deposits were exploited in Montana and Arizona. In 1882, the Anaconda Mine was opened. Abundant availability of copper, the discovery of vast silver deposits in Colorado, Nevada, and Montana, and the 'gold rush' made into California rapidly transformed the economic status of a group of people in the society. By selling these raw-materials to the future industrial tycoons, they suddenly became very rich as 'copper-kings', 'gold-kings', or 'iron mongers'.

Thomas C. Cochran has made a brilliant analysis of both economic and socio-cultural factors which combined, leading to massive American industrialization in the nineteenth century. The study also applies a comparative framework with European, Latin American, and Asian countries to show that the availability of natural resources cannot be the only impetus if other non-economic factors would not have played a crucial role in utilizing these.[4] There were numerous factors unique to the American nation in the nineteenth century that boosted its industrialization. One such factor was immigration. The early American society was composed almost entirely of immigrants from the British Isles, France, Germany, and the Netherlands who brought with them some of the world's most advanced business and industry. For example, Holland led the seventeenth century world in most types of technology followed by England, and a large section of French immigrants (Huguenots) were highly skilled artisans. And added with this, the mere fact of immigration itself, the risking fact of the terrible ocean voyage, and of settlement in a country of savage climatic variations indicated a strong motivation for self-betterment and economic advance that went on without any obstacle from the indigenous soil as huge population of Indians were already exterminated.[5] As the United States was the major recipient of immigration throughout the nineteenth century, there was no dearth of workers and the continuing process of migration, either from abroad or within the nation stimulated economic growth. The migrant, detached from an extended family and friends, went ahead with his own ability to conform to even change his environment that stimulated innovation and transformed him into an 'economic man' rather than a social or communal one. [6]

The Americans applied a utilitarian calculus to the problems of competition and cooperation and took collective ventures merging their firms. This was a unique attitude quite different from the other nations emphasizing where mergers meant loss of identity. As Thorstein Veblen argues, this technological behaviour rather than ceremonial behaviour fostered American economic growth and advancement.[7]

Government support and initiative also had its positive outcomes. In America, government was not a rigid structure run for the traditional interests of a clerical or lay aristocracy, but rather a utility set up by enterprising citizens to provide order and aid cooperative endeavour. If a bank, canal, factory, or railroad could not secure adequate private financing but seemed economically desirable, government was called upon to make up the deficiency. There was no watertight division between the purposes of the professional politician and the private capitalist.[8]

The interaction of all these factors created a type of personality in the United States peculiarly suited to developing its resources. The American entrepreneur, with optimism towards success, was willing to take moderate risks for better returns. Cochran cogently remarks, 'This spirit of optimism, this continuing dream of high returns from further investment, put a premium on saving for the future rather than spending for present consumption. As a result, few Americans developed the gracious living of Europeans or wealthy Latin Americans, and leisure, even among those who could amply afford it, produced a feeling of guilt.'[9]

Startling innovations were made that changed the life of the American citizens. Robert Fulton's epoch-making steam-engine, much before the Civil War, Elias Howe's sewing machine, Charles Goodyer's vulcanized rubber, and Alexander Graham Bell's telephone were indeed testimonies to the inventive genius of the American scientists. Charles Brush invented dynamo in 1878 that could generate electricity in a small way. He patented an arc lamp that was used by some cities for street lighting. In 1882, Thomas Alva Edison built a generating and a distributing station in New York. Undoubtedly, the invention of electricity opened huge possibilities for industrial developments. In the 1890s, Edison startled the world by manufacturing a motion-picture machine that within a decade began the era of American movies. Another ingenious invention was the type-writer by Christopher Latham Sholes and Carlos S. Glidden, which was placed in the market in 1873. Within a short time this small gadget became indispensable in every business office. An interesting anecdote is related to the invention of the typewriter. Mark Twain, the famous American author was amused to no end to see how it piles up an awful stack of words on one page and commented, 'It don't muss things or scatter ink blots around'.[10]

Not only men, but American women were also great inventors. The telescope invented by Sarah Mather in 1845 made possible for sea vessels to explore ocean depths. Martha Coston is famous for the pyrotechnic flares (also known as night signals) by which ships could set up effective communications system. Fannie Farmer created cookbooks, and by establishing a standardized measuring system, introduced science into the kitchen. Women not only made great inventions in the domestic realm but their inventions reached beyond domesticity and contributed havoc in the industrial revolution in the US. Margaret Knight's safety device (by which a machine automatically stopped if a worker came too close to it) in textile mills drastically reduced the number of accidents and injuries in mills. Her inventions amassed 27 patents!

A testimony to all these remarkable inventions was the huge number of patents that the Federal patent office granted to the inventors. Between 1860 and 1900, about 676,000 patents were given to the inventors.

The saga of American industrial revolution would be incomplete without reference to the innovations in the transportation and automobile sectors that revolutionized the American economy. In 1794, a private company completed the Philadelphia-Lancaster Turnpike, a broad, paved highway similar to the good European highways at that time.[11] The completion of the Lancaster Turnpike resulted in a turnpike-building boom that lasted nearly 20 years. By 1821, nearly 4,000 miles of turnpikes had been completed mainly from state funds and mostly connecting the eastern cities. By 1852, the Cumberland Road (also called the 'National Road'), stretching 591 miles from Cumberland, in western Maryland, to Vandalia, in Illinois was completed using both federal and state aid.

As it was not much economical to ship bulky goods by land across the great distances in America, businessmen and inventors began concentrating on improving water transportation. Robert Fulton sent the first commercially successful steamboat, the Clermont, from New York City up the Hudson River to Albany in 1807. With this, steamboat spread rapidly and steamer transport was made available from New Orleans as far north as Ohio. By 1830, there were more than 200 steamers on the Mississippi. Steamboats opened the West and South to further settlement and stimulated the agricultural economy of the West by providing better access to markets at a lower cost.

While steamboats were conquering western rivers, canals improved connectivity in the Northeast. The Erie Canal was constructed as per the plan of New York Governor DeWitt Clinton, connecting the Hudson River with Lake Erie. Completed in 1825, the Canal ran 363 miles from Albany to Buffalo. It was a revolutionary achievement as it reduced travel time from New York to Buffalo from 20 days to six, reducing the cost of moving a ton of freight from $100 to $5; it also linked the Mississippi Valley and the Atlantic Ocean. Finally, the Canal provided a water route from New York to Chicago, via the Great Lakes, and marked the beginning of Chicago's rapid growth. The success of the Erie Canal sparked a canal-building mania that lasted for more than a decade and resulted in around 3,000 miles of waterways by 1840.

The most revolutionary and significant invention came through the construction of railroads. Much of the early railroad growth was developed by private investors. In 1828, development of the first railroad began in Baltimore, and in 1832, the Baltimore and Ohio Railroad reached 73 miles. By 1833, the Charleston and Hamburg Railroad extended 136 miles west of Charleston. By 1840, the United States had over 3,000 miles of tracks, nearly double the mileage in all of Europe. And by 1860, the US saw development of over 30,000 miles of railroad tracks, three-fourths of which were in the industrializing north.

Turnpike, canals, steamboats, and railways forged a truly continental economy. Finally, 'The emergence of the American automobile industry was a closing chapter in the nation's Industrial Revolution,' remarks Hillstorms.[12] The invention of the combustion engine in Europe played a major role in the development of the later automobile industry. In 1894, Elwood P. Haynes built a gasoline-powered automobile, followed by the launching of other motor carriages by Ransom E. Olds, Alexander Winton, and Henry Ford between 1894 and 1896. By 1895, over 500 patent applications relating to motor cars were filed with the US Patent Office. In 1900, more than 50,000 people gathered in Madison Square Garden in the New York City to attend the nation's first ever automobile show.[13] Numerous automotive companies flourished during this period. In 1902, the Cadillac Motor Company was founded by Henry M. Leland. In 1903, Henry Ford established the famous Ford Motor Company, and the same year David D. Buick founded the Buick Motor Car Company, which was sold the next year to William Durant and became the nucleus for the General Motors.[14]

What was revolutionary and unique of the American Industrial Revolution is not only the host of inventions, but the organizational strategies and capitalistic management or managerial skills to accelerate productivity that explains the rise and sustenance of 'big business' or giant corporations.

The rapid development in the size and power of the business organizations or trusts in America through large-scale mergers and consolidations startled economists worldwide. John Bates Clark and John Maurice Clark remarked in *The Control of Trusts*, 'The mere size of the

Table 5.1: Some Key Inventions

Person	Invention	Year
James Watt	First reliable Steam Engine	1775
Eli Whitney	Cotton Gin, Interchangeable parts for muskets	1793, 1798
Robert Fulton	Regular Steamboat service on the Hudson River	1807
Samuel F. B. Morse	Telegraph	1836
Elias Howe	Sewing Machine	1844
Sarah Mather	Telescope	1845
Isaac Singer	Improves and markets Howe's Sewing Machine	1851
Cyrus Field	Transatlantic Cable	1866
Alexander Graham Bell	Telephone	1876
Thomas Edison	Phonograph, Incandescent Light Bulb	1877, 1879
Charles Brush	Dynamo	1878
Nikola Tesla	Induction Electric Motor	1888
Rudolf Diesel	Diesel Engine	1892
Elwood Haynes	Gasoline-powered automobile	1894
Orville and Wilbur Wright	First Airplane	1903
Henry Ford	Model T Ford, Assembly Line	1908, 1913

Source: Information collected from Kevin and Laurie C. Hillstorm, *The Industrial Revolution in America: Automobiles, Mining and Petroleum, Textiles* (Santa Barbara, California: ABC-CLIO Inc., 2006), vol. 1; Corona Brezina', *The Industrial Revolution in America: A Primary Source History of America's Transformation into an Industrial Society* (New York: The Rosen Publishing Group, Inc., 2005).

consolidations which have recently appeared is enough to startle those who saw them in the making. If the carboniferous age had returned and the earth had re-peopled itself with dinosaurs, the change made in animal life would have scarcely seemed greater than that which has been made in the business world by these monster-like corporations.'[15]

The large funds needed for buildings and other large-scale industries went beyond the capacity of single individuals or partnerships and required the financial co-operation of many people which was made possible by the corporate firms. The consolidations contributed to other advantages to the big shots like: limited liability of stockholders, flexibility of management, and release of stockholders from managerial responsibilities. And finally, the businessman could command minority capital interests and retain control of the business.

In 1904, John Moody listed 46 combinations or trusts organized in 1901, and each with a capital of $1,000,000 or more, 63 in 1902, and 18 in 1903, making 127 in the three years.[16] The leading trusts were the US Steel Corporation formed by Andrew Carnegie, the Standard Oil Company formed by John D. Rockfeller, Hill, Harriman and Gould's Railway Trust, and Joshua and John Morgan's Trust of Banks. With the organization by Elbert H. Gary and J.P. Morgan of the giant United States Steel Corporation, the climax of the early consolidation movement was reached in 1901. Railroad and petroleum industries were among the very first to combine and consolidate.

Alfred Chandler rightly argues in *The Coming of Big Business* that American big business are not only unique by their size, but in the ways in which they are owned and managed. All the great firms were joint stock corporations and operated largely by professional managers.[17] Consolidation featuring technological progress and the availability of adequate capital gave birth to mass production. Frederick Taylor's scientific management and other corporate capitalistic strategies were imperative to ensure mass production for mass consumption, ensuring huge turnover to the giant capitalists. Henry Ford was one of the chief exponents of mass production, and to him it was, 'the focusing upon a manufacturing project of the principles of power, accuracy, economy, system, continuity and speed...And the normal result is a productive organization that delivers in quantities a useful commodity of standard material, workmanship and design at minimum cost.'[18] Mass production reached maturity with specialization of labour and standardization of work. Another important feature of the late nineteenth and the early twentieth century was the emergence of industrial laboratory (replacing individual workshop) financed by commercial concerns. Organized research was applied to organized production.

The growth of big business drew many responses and reaction mainly from the middle class, small entrepreneurs, businessmen, and the working class. Resisting voices sprouted in the form of anti-trust movement through protests, demonstrations, formation of labour, and other socialist organizations, and muckraking (*chapter 6*).

A Brief Historiography of the Industrial Revolution

The Industrial Revolution of the US has been studied by a number of scholars across disciplines and hence the thrust have been varied from economics to social, technological, and in recent days also environmental history.

Between 1860s and 1880s, the books and pamphlets dealing with the industrial revolution echoed nationalist perspectives where the revolution was seen with pride and glory. In this context, mention may be made of James P. Boyd's *Triumphs and Wonders of the 19th century*, Charles L. Flint's *One Hundred Years' Progress*, etc. From the 1880s, studies were pursued from critical perspectives revealing light on the contradiction between capital and labour. Caroll D. Wright in *The Industrial Evolution of the United States* provided one of the early accounts of the labour movement in the United States along with a depiction of the factory system.

The Progressive historians' writing in the post-WWI period provided economic interpretations of American History in general. These new economic historians included Louis C. Hunter, Caroline F. Ware, and George R. Taylor, who were all Harvard scholars under the guidance of Edwin F. Gay and Arthur H. Cole. They revealed light on technological processes in the US industrialization, the themes cutting across textiles, transport, etc. The path shown by the new economic historians paved the way towards the growth of a new kind of scholarship in the 1960s with emphasis on the questions concerned on economic growth and analytical methodology in place of empirical and narrative approaches. H.J. Habakkuk's *American and British Technology in the Nineteenth Century* followed a comparative methodology and addressed complex economic themes and issues like rates of investment, trade cycles, demand factors, etc. Though his work had certain limitations, other seminal works followed to critique and refine the themes that he advanced.

The 1960s also saw the advent of the 'new social history' prompted by the civil rights movement, feminist movement, Vietnam War, etc. This school was influenced by the Annales School and Marxist historiography and hence were critical to the glorious portrayal of nationalistic (often chauvinistic) history of the past generations. Elites were replayed by ordinary men as the key actors in history; the tensions experienced by the common people in the US transition from agrarian to industrial period found reflection in their research. The new social historians did not find the entire truth in Alfred Chandler's 'managerial revolution', and deeply felt that it excluded the workers. Following E.P. Thompson and Sidney Pollard, these scholars focussed on family networks, work cultures, occupational mobility, etc., to capture the bigger picture of life under the factory system.

In the 1980s and 1990s, regional history was written and there were case-studies combining political, technological, and cultural histories. Judith McGaw's *Most Wonderful Machine,* dealing with a paper industry in western Massachusetts and Carlyn Cooper's 1991 article published in the journal of *Technology and Culture,* revealing light on the patent system and the politics of patent management are path-breaking.[19]

The environmental impact of industrialization has been dealt by Theodore Steinberg in *Nature Incorporated* which narrates the history of how large textile corporations owned by the Boston associates bought up much of the Merrimack River's watershed, built dams, and controlled the flow of water to the mill towns from Manchester, New Hampshire to Lawrence, Massachusetts affecting human health and also the health of the river.[20]

Despite these case-study approaches, we also find the big picture of the US industrialization being drawn by some historians. These include David Nye's *American Technological Sublime* and Robert B. Gordon and Patrick M. Malone's *The Texture of the Industry,* a path-breaking work using artefacts and other objects of material culture to supplement the analytical framework.[21]

Donald MacKenzie and Judy Wajcman in *The Social Shaping of Technology* have applied social constructivist approach, i.e., analyzed technology as a social product.[22] Charles Seller's *The Market Revolution* has provided a composite principle that interlinked diverse social, cultural, and political developments with the greater framework of the capitalistic transformation of the nineteenth century.[23] This approach had a far-flung impact on historiography of the 1990s and 'More implicitly than explicitly, the new view moved away from longstanding economic and technological forces of production toward a consumer-driven model of change that emphasized the centrality of politics and social turmoil while black-boxing complex processes of technological change,' remarks Merritt Roe Smith and Robert Martello in their recent 2010 publication from the Massachusetts Institute of Technology.[24]

Another school of historians called the 'new institutionalists' emerged during the late 1990s whose analysis once again revolved round the state and political economy. Richard John is one of them who argue that federal policies and state initiatives were critical for US industrialization. Another interesting study has been conducted by Carter Goodrich.[25] He has provided the 'state in, state out' approach where he argues that the public and the private operated in a co-operative rather than a competitive manner. The state and federal governments 'got in' in matters of internal improvements, subsidizing and supporting risky business ventures; and once the venture became profitable, the government 'got out' and the enterprise continued under private ownership.[26]

Annotated Bibliography

- Thomas C. Cochran's essay 'Industrialization' in C.V. Woodward, ed, *The Comparative Approach to American History* (New York, Oxford: Oxford University Press, 1997, pp. 175–86, new edition) applies a comparative framework to study American industrialization and industrialization of European, Latin American, and Asian countries covering a wide array of economic and non-economic factors.
- Corona Brezina's *The Industrial Revolution in America: A Primary Source History of America's Transformation into an Industrial Society* (New York: The Rosen Publishing Group, Inc., 2005) traces the transformation of the United States into the world's foremost industrial power using primary evidences like newspaper articles, letters, and pamphlets, patents, etc.
- Jennifer L. Goloboy ed., *Industrial Revolution: People and Perspectives* (Santa Barbara, California: ABC-CLIO, Inc., 2008) is a collection of nine essays shedding light on the impact of American industrialization on the multi-layered, heterogeneous society including white male artisans, free women workers, slaves, manufacturers, middle class, immigrants, etc., finally leading to deepening class divisions and expanding consumerism.

- Jeff Horn, Leonard N. Rosenband, and Merritt Roe Smith ed., *Reconceptualizing the Industrial Revolution* (Massachusetts: Massachusetts Institute of Technology, 2010) is a collection of essays offering new perspectives on the Industrial Revolution as a global phenomenon. A lengthy chapter is dedicated to the American Industrial Revolution including historiography.
- In *The US Industrial Revolution* (USA, North Mankato, Minnesota: ABDO Publishing Company, 2011), Robert Grayson charts the context of the industrial revolution in America, mentions the inventions, and analyses its socio-economic impact.

Notes

1. Peter D. McClelland, *Sowing Modernity: America's First Agricultural Revolution* (USA: University of Cornell Press, 1997), p. 7.
2. Ibid., p. 8.
3. Kevin and Laurie C. Hillstorm, *The Industrial Revolution in America: Automobiles, Mining and Petroleum, Textiles* (Santa Barbara, California: ABC-CLIO Inc., 2006), vol. 1, p. vii.
4. Thomas C. Cochran, 'Industrialization', C.V. Woodward, ed, *The Comparative Approach to American History* (New York, Oxford: Oxford University Press, 1997), pp. 175–86; new edition.
5. Ibid., p. 176.
6. Ibid., p. 178.
7. Ibid., p. 179.
8. Ibid., pp. 179–80.
9. Ibid., p. 181.
10. A. Nevins and H.S. Commager, *A Short History of the United States* (New York: Random House, 1945).
11. It was called a 'turnpike' because as drivers approached the tollgate they were confronted with a barrier of sharp spikes that was turned aside when they paid their toll.
12. Kevin and Laurie C. Hillstorm, *The Industrial Revolution in America,* p. 1.
13. Ibid., p. 5.
14. Ibid., p. 9.
15. John Bates Clark and John Maurice Clark, *The Control of Trusts,* (New York: The Macmillan Company, 1912), pp. 14–15.
16. John Moody, *The Truth about the Trusts* (New York: The Moody Publishing Company, 1904), pp. 453–69.

17. Alfred Chandler, 'The Coming of Big Business' C.V. Woodward, ed, *The Comparative Approach to American History* (New York: Basic Books, 1968), pp. 220–37.
18. *Encyclopaedia Britannica* (New York: Encyclopaedia Britannica), 13th ed., vol. II, p. 821.
19. Judith McGaw, *Most Wonderful Machine: Mechanization and Social Change in Berkshire Paper Making, 1801–1885* (Princeton, New Jersey: Princeton University Press, 1987); Carlyn Cooper, 'Making Inventions Patent', *Technology and Culture*, Vol. 32, No. 4, Special Issue: 'Patents and Invention' (October 1991), pp. 837–45.
20. Theodore Steinberg, *Nature Incorporated: Industrialization and the Waters of New England* (New York: Cambridge University Press, 1991).
21. David Nye, *American Technological Sublime* (Cambridge, Massachusetts: The MIT Press, 1994); Robert B. Gordon and Patrick M. Malone, *The Texture of Industry: An Archaeological View of the Industrialization of North America* (New York: Oxford University Press, 1994).
22. Donald MacKenzie and Wajcman, eds, *The Social Shaping of Technology* (Philadelphia: Open University Press, 1985).
23. Charles Seller, *The Market Revolution: Jacksonian America, 1815–1846* (New York: Oxford University Press, 1991).
24. Merritt Roe Smith and Robert Martello, 'Taking Stock of the Industrial Revolution in America', Jeff Horn, Leonard N. Rosenband and Merritt Roe Smith, eds, *Reconceptualizing the Industrial Revolution* (Massachusetts: Massachusetts Institute of Technology, 2010), p. 184.
25. Carter Goodrich, *Government Promotion of American Canals and Railroads, 1800–1890* (New York: Columbia University Press, 1960); *The Government and the Economy, 1783–1861* (Indianapolis: Bobbs-Merrill, 1967).
26. Merritt Roe Smith and Robert Martello, 'Taking Stock of the Industrial Revolution', p. 186.

6

Resisting Voices

It is a saga of social activism and political reform against the excesses of corporate capitalism. Various strands of resistances have been explored from populist trends in the agrarian context to middle-class progressivism to moderate labour organizations like American Federation of Labour to politically motivated radical Marxist labour organizations like Industrial Workers of the World. The chapter explores the heterogeneity in socialist challenges as the nation moved on to its mature stage of industrial (including monopoly and finance) capitalism.

a. Agrarian Anxiety and Populism

The wrenching changes in American economy and society in the post-Civil War period and the rise of big business created two polarized worlds within the nation creating an affluent class and a distressed community who were untouched with the benefits of industrial and national growth. Populism emerged as a political ideology of struggle that pitted 'a virtuous and homogeneous people against a set of elites and dangerous 'others' who were together depicted as depriving (or attempting to deprive) the sovereign people of their rights, values, prosperity, identity, and voice.'[1] The Granger Movement mainly in the Mid-West can be considered as a prelude to the 'Farmers Alliance' and the formation of the Populist Party in America.

The Granger Movement, 1867–70s

The causes of the movement, as Solon Justus Buck argues, can be primarily sought in economic conditions, and to a less extent in political, social, and intellectual conditions that affected the American farmer.[2] The characteristics of the movement varied regionally as per differences in agricultural situations. The great prairie of states of the Upper Mississippi Valley, stretching from Ohio to Kansas and Nebraska was the centre of agricultural discontent where 'the protective movement among the farmers manifested most vigorously.'[3] The farmers in these areas which produced wheat and corn as the main crops, were feeling the depression in the wheat industry as early as the 1850s, most severely in Wisconsin and Illinois. They faced severe competition from the virgin wheat fields of the farther West that forced them to switch over to more diversified agriculture. The farmers of Wisconsin and Illinois, and also parts of Minnesota and Iowa were soon burdened with debt and looked after the bankers, railways, legislatures, tariff system, and monopolies as the causes of their misfortunes.

With the spread of railroads across the nation, the prosperity of the farmers depended on their ability to send crops to consumers cheaply and get back their required articles for consumption which again required a cheapening of transportation and a reduction of the cost of handling commodities by the middlemen who stood between producers and consumers, the two important agendas of the Granger Movement.[4]

When President Andrew Johnson commissioned Oliver Kelley to go to the Southern States and to collect data to improve Southern agricultural conditions, he toured the war-torn countryside in the South and was appalled by the outdated farming practices. He saw the need for an organization that would bring people from the North and South together in a spirit of mutual cooperation; and after many letters and consultations with the other founders like William Saunders, Francis M. McDowell, John Trimble, Caroline Hall, and others, the National Grange of the Order of Patrons of Husbandry was born in 1867 to promote the economic and political well-being of the community and agriculture. Membership in the Grange increased dramatically from 1873 (200,000) to 1875 (858,050) as many of the state and local granges adopted non-partisan political resolutions, especially regarding the regulation of railroad transportation costs. It is interesting to note that women were encouraged to participate and four of the elected positions could only be held by women.

Rapid growth infused the national organization with money from dues, and many local granges established consumer cooperatives, initially supplied by the wholesaler Aaron Montgomery Ward. Poor fiscal management, combined with organizational difficulties resulting from rapid growth, led to a massive decline in membership, but by the turn of the twentieth century, the Grange rebounded and membership stabilized.

Although established originally for social and educational purposes, the local granges became political forums and increased in number as channels of farmer protest against economic abuses through cooperative enterprise. The Granger Movement succeeded in regulating the railroads and grain warehouses. The birth of the Cooperative Extension Service, Rural Free Delivery, and the Farm Credit System were largely due to Grange lobbying. The grangers captured several state legislatures in the Middlewest and secured the passage in Illinois, Wisconsin, Minnesota, and Iowa of the so-called Granger laws, setting or authorizing maximum railroad rates and establishing state railroad commissions for administering the new legislation. The peak of their political power was marked by their success in *Munn v. Illinois* (1876), which held that the grain warehouses were a 'private utility in the public interest', and therefore could be regulated by public law. However, this achievement was overturned later by the Supreme Court in *Wabash v. Illinois* (1886) that severely limited the rights of states to control interstate commerce and led to the creation of the Interstate Commerce Commission.

Since the later part of the 1870s, the Greenback Party, the Farmers' Alliance, and, finally, the Populist Party expressed much of the agrarian protest, and the granges reverted to their original role, as purely social organizations and continued to exist in the East, especially in New England, where they had been least active politically.[5] The significance and legacy of the Granger Movement is well reflected in the words of Solon Justus Buck,

> If the Granger Movement had been a mere episode in American history, it would still have been worthy of investigation because it exhibits the conditions, opinions, and desires, which prevailed among large numbers of American farmers during the seventies, and because it actually played a considerable part in the history of the decade. Many, however, of these conditions, opinions, and desires, which were first brought into prominence by the Granger Movement, have remained active forces in American history to the present day.[6]

Populist Trends: Greenback Party, Farmers' Alliance, and the Populist Party

The rise of the Greenback Party has to be contextualized within the Panic of 1873 which began with a crisis in the overextended railroad industry, when the brokerage house Jay Cooke & Company found itself unable to sell enough Northern Pacific Railroad bonds to meet its financial obligations, leading to a default on loans and setting off a financial chain reaction. The depression continued till 1878. The Congress was expected to alleviate the business crisis through re-inflation of the currency, pitting railroad promoters and the iron industry against Eastern bankers and the merchant elite, who favoured a stable, gold-based currency. Within this temporal context, as historian Paul Kleppner argues, the Greenback Party originated in the state of Indiana, where early in 1873, a group of reform-minded farmers and political activists declared themselves free of the established parties and declared themselves as the Independent Party.[7] The group nominated a slate for state-wide office, running on a platform which called for expansion of the national currency.

The name of the Greenback Party is referred to the non-gold-backed paper money, commonly known as 'greenbacks' which was issued by the North during the American Civil War and shortly afterward. The party opposed the deflationary lowering of prices paid to producers entailed by a return to a bullion-based monetary system, the policy favoured by the dominant Republican Party. They believed that the continued use of unbacked currency would better foster business and assist farmers by raising prices and making debts easier to pay. Several regional conventions took place in 1875, merging the activities of local political parties towards a single end; the attendees mainly comprised of farmers or lawyers, with few urban wage workers or trade union officials as historian Philip S. Foner has pointed out, the union movement shattered and atomized following the Panic of 1873.[8] The first national convention was held in Indianapolis, Indiana in May 1876.

The Greenbackers condemned the harmonization of the silver dollar and regarded that the Coinage Act of 1873 was in fact utterly ruthless. They also opposed the National Banking System, created by the National Banking Act of 1863 and the Resumption Act of 1875, which mandated that the US Treasury hard currency in exchange for greenback currency upon its presentation for redemption beginning on 1 January 1879, thus returning the nation to the gold standard. The Greenbacks contended that these measures created an inflexible currency controlled by banks rather than the federal government and favoured creditors and industry to the detriment of farmers and labourers.[9]

In 1880, the Greenback Party broadened its platform to include support for an income tax, an eight-hour day, and women's right to vote. However, the Greenback party gradually declined since the 1880s, failed to win seats in the election of 1884 and 1886, and few delegates attended in the fourth National Convention held in Cincinnati, Ohio, in May (first session) and September (second session) 1888. With no nominations and the failure of the convention, the Party ceased to exist.

Though the organization faded into oblivion, its basic programme was reborn under the aegis of the Populist Party and both the parties were finally successful in moving the Democratic Party to espouse looser monetary policy and an ultimate abandonment of the gold standard.

The Farmers' Alliances emerged as political organizations with elaborate economic programmes to unite the farmers of America for their protection against class-legislation and the encroachments of concentrated capital. Their programme, known as the *Ocala Demands* also called for the regulation of the railroads; currency inflation to provide debt relief; the lowering of the tariff; and the establishment of government-owned storehouses and low-interest lending facilities.[10]

Working with sympathetic Democrats in the South and small third parties in the West, the Farmer's Alliance made a push for political power during the late 1880s when a series of droughts devastated the West; Western Kansas lost half its population during a four-year span, and by 1890, there was widespread agrarian distress. During their move towards consolidation in 1889, the leaders of the Southern Farmers' Alliance and the Agricultural Wheel organizations contacted Terence V. Powderly, leader of the Knights of Labor, and Matthew Gild has rightly pointed out,

> This contact between leaders of the farmers' movement and Powderly helped pave the way for a series of reform conferences held between December 1889 and July 1892 that resulted in the formation of the national People's (or Populist) Party.[11]

Its first convention was held in Omaha, Nebraska, in 1892 when delegates from farm, labour and reform organizations determined to make their mark on a political system that was hopelessly corrupted by the moneyed interests of the industrial and commercial trusts. The platform called for the abolition of national banks, a graduated income tax, direct election of Senators, civil service reform, a working day of eight hours, and Government control of all railroads, telegraphs, and telephones. The Populists showed impressive strength in the West and South in the 1892 elections, and their candidate for President James B. Weaver received 1,027,329 votes.

While the pragmatic portion of the Populist platform focussed on issues of land, railroads, and money, including the unlimited coinage of silver, conservative groups and the financial classes, on the other hand, insisted that railroad bonds should be payable in gold because if fares and freight rates were set in half-price silver dollars, railroads would go bankrupt in weeks, throwing hundreds of thousands of men out of work and destroying the industrial economy. This debate intensified with the financial Panic of 1893 which was marked by the collapse of railroad overbuilding and shaky railroad financing, resulting in a series of bank failures. The impact of the crisis – bank failures, rise in crop prices, and unemployment in the South and Midwest provided tough blow to the Democratic Party.

With the defeat of the Democrats-nominated William Jennings Bryan to Republican William McKinley by a margin of 600,000 votes in the election of 1896, the Populist Party doomed to failure, its fusion with the Democratic Party leading to a disastrous impact in the South. The Populist/Republican alliance which had governed North Carolina fell apart, and by 1898, the Democrats used a violently racist campaign to defeat the North Carolina Populists, and in 1900, the Democrats ushered in disfranchisement.

Populism never recovered from this and Populist Party was demoralized by a diminishing membership and puzzled and split by the dilemma of whether to fight the state-level enemy (the Democrats) or the national foe (the Republicans and Wall Street); it was a mere shadow of what it once was. The Party disbanded; populist activists either retired from politics or joined a major party or followed the new Socialist Party. Though the party was re-organized in 1904, Thomas E. Watson being the nominee for President in 1904 and 1908, the party disbanded again in 1908.

Nature of Populism

Since the emergence of the populist trends itself, there is a debate among historians regarding the nature of populism. While some historians see the populists as forward-looking liberal reformers, others view them as reactionaries trying to recapture an idyllic and utopian past, for some they are radicals out to restructure American life, and to some they are economically hard-pressed agrarians seeking government relief.

Frederick Jackson Turner depicted the Populist as responding to the closure of the frontier,

> The Farmers' Alliance and the Populist demand for government ownership of the railroad is a phase of the same effort of the pioneer farmer, on his latest frontier. The proposals have taken increasing proportions in each region of Western Advance. Taken as a whole, Populism is a manifestation of the old pioneer ideals of the native American, with the added element of increasing readiness to utilize the national government to effect its ends.[12]

Following the line of Turner, John D. Hicks emphasized economic pragmatism over ideals, presenting Populism as interest group politics, with have-nots demanding their fair share of America's wealth which was being leeched off by non-productive speculators. Though Hicks asserted that drought had ruined huge numbers of Kansas farmers, but he also pointed to financial manipulations, deflation in prices caused by the gold standard, high interest rates, mortgage foreclosures, and high railroad rates, and moreover corruption that accounted for populist outrages. All these led Populists to argue and struggle for the popular control of government. Hicks's research was read with much importance by later students of republicanism.[13]

In the 1930s, C. Vann Woodward stressed the Southern base, seeing the possibility of a black-and-white coalition of poor against the overbearing rich; Georgia politician Tom Watson serving as his hero.[14] In the 1950s, however, scholars like Richard Hofstadter portrayed the Populist Movement as an irrational response of backward-looking farmers to the challenges of modernity and discounted third-party links to Progressivism, arguing that Populists were provincial, conspiracy minded, and had a tendency toward scapegoatism that manifested itself as nativism, anti-Semitism, anti-intellectualism, and Anglophobia. The antithesis of anti-modern Populism was modernizing Progressivism according to Hofstadter's model, with leading progressives as Theodore Roosevelt, Robert LaFollette, and George Norris and Woodrow Wilson being vehement enemies of Populism, though William Jennings Bryan did cooperate and accepted the Populist nomination in 1896.[15]

Much recent scholarship including the works of Robert Miller and Gene Clanton emphasize Populism's debt to early American republicanism.[16] Clanton stresses that Populism was 'the last significant expression of an old radical tradition that derived from Enlightenment sources that had been filtered through a political tradition that bore the distinct imprint of Jeffersonian, Jacksonian, and Lincolnian democracy,' the tradition that emphasized human rights over the cash nexus of the Gilded Age's dominant ideology.[17] The latest work by Charles Postel offers thorough criticism to Hofstadter's argument that the Populists were traditionalistic and anti-modern, and argues that the Populists aggressively sought self-consciously progressive goals. They sought diffusion of scientific and technical knowledge, formed highly centralized organizations, launched large-scale incorporated businesses, and pressed for an array of state-centred reforms. Hundreds of thousands of women committed to Populism sought a more modern life, education, and employment in schools and offices. And even a large section of the labour movement looked to Populism for answers, forging a political coalition with farmers that gave impetus to the regulatory state.[18]

Annotated Bibliography

- In *The Granger Movement: A Study of Agricultural Organization and Its Political, Economic and Social Manifestations, 1870–1880* (Harvard: Harvard University Press, 1913), Solon Justus Buck offers a comprehensive treatment of the movement, analyzing the deeply rooted economic factors leading to its origin, the course of events, and its significance and legacy. Public documents and other archival materials have been provided at the end of the book which may be useful to readers interested in accessing primary sources. C.W. Pierson's essay 'Rise of the Granger Movement'

(*Popular Science Monthly*, xxxii (December 1887), pp. 199–208) provides an ensuing account of the origins of the Patrons of Husbandry.

- Paul Kleppner's 'The Greenback and Prohibition Parties' in Arthur M. Schlesinger, ed, *History of U.S. Political Parties: Volume II, 1860–1910, The Gilded Age of Politics* (New York: Chelsea House, 1973) provides both facts and interpretation relating to the origin of the Greenback Party and its course of actions in the next few years
- There have been a number of studies with regional approach. While C.V. Woodward in his article 'Tom Watson and the Negro in Agrarian Politics' (*The Journal of Southern History*, Vol. 4, No. 1 (February 1938), pp. 14–33) has concentrated on populism in Georgia, the Oklahoma experience is very well narrated in Robert Miller's, *Oklahoma Populism: A History of the People's Party in the Oklahoma Territory* (Norman and London: University of Oklahoma Press, 1987).
- Matthew Gild's *Greenbackers, Knights of Labor, and Populists, Farmer-Labor Insurgency in the Late-Nineteenth Century South* (Athens & London: The University of Georgia Press, 2007) is a thorough and detailed study of populist trends in the United States with greatest emphasis on the agendas and strategies of the parties.

Annexure: The Ocala Demands

Source: *US History Resources*
(available at: http://1.scds.org/resources/US-History/1890_The%20Ocala%20 Demands.pdf, date of access: 12.11.2012)

1. a. We demand the abolition of national banks.

b. We demand that the government shall establish sub-treasuries or depositories in the several states, which shall loan money direct to the people at a low rate of interest, not to exceed two per cent per annum, on non-perishable farm products, and also upon real estate, with proper limitations upon the quantity of land and amount of money.

c. We demand that the amount of the circulating medium be speedily increased to not less than $50 per capita.

2. We demand that Congress shall pass such laws as will effectually prevent the dealing in futures of all agricultural and mechanical productions; providing a stringent system of procedure in trials that will secure the prompt conviction, and imposing such penalties as shall secure the most perfect compliance with the law.

3. We condemn the silver bill recently passed by Congress, and demand in lieu thereof the free and unlimited coinage of silver.

4. We demand the passage of laws prohibiting alien ownership of land, and that Congress take prompt action to devise some plan to obtain all lands now owned by aliens and foreign syndicates; and that all lands now held by railroads and other corporations in excess of such as is actually used and needed by them be reclaimed by the government and held for actual settlers only.

5. Believing in the doctrine of equal rights to all and special privileges to none, we demand —

a. That our national legislation shall be so framed in the future as not to build up one industry at the expense of another.

b. We further demand a removal of the existing heavy tariff tax from the necessities of life, that the poor of our land must.

c. We further demand a just and equitable system of graduated tax on incomes.

d. We believe that the money of the county should be kept as much as possible in the hands of the people, and hence we demand that all national and state revenues shall be limited to the necessary expenses of the government economically and honestly administered.

6. We demand the most rigid, honest and just state and national government control and supervision of the means of public communication and transportation, and if this control and supervision does not remove the abuse now existing, we demand the government ownership of such means of communication and transportation.

7. We demand that the Congress of the United States submit an amendment to the Constitution providing for the election of United States Senators.

b. The Progressive Movement

The Age of Progressivism in America with the turn of the twentieth century was characterized by social activism and political reform in almost every sectors of American life which sprouted as resisting voices against the excesses of corporate capitalism. Regarding periodization of the progressive era, John D. Buenker, John C. Burnham, and Robert M. Crunden point out that it flourished from the 1890s to the 1920s.[19] The phenomenal growth in big business led to the rise of big trusts and monopolies crushing the power and status of smaller entrepreneurial houses. Trusts became all pervasive in American life and the formation of monopolies led to the introduction of monopolistic prices. Trusts and the monopolies created an undemocratic, anti-people, and a supremely selfish ambience sometimes leading to the Progressive Movement against industrial America. The undue advantage of liberalism and liberty given to the big entrepreneurs resulted in the curtailment of people's democratic rights. The big industries soon swallowed the smaller industries; Cooper put it pithily, it was 'industrial despotism' that came to be established in the place of democracy.

Origin of the Movement

B.K. Srivastava argue in his article 'The Progressive Movement: Through the Historian's Prism' that the movement was called 'Progressive' 'because it believed in the limitless possibilities of human progress...'[20] It emerged out of the social ferment which came into existence as a result of the earlier years of sustained economic growth and massive capitalist accumulation among the giant corporate. The insecurity of the smaller industries, excess of liberty in the hands of a few, and concentration of wealth among a coterie of rich businessmen created a complete polarization between the plutocrats and the people and drove many sections of people to look for protection from the Federal government. The plutocrats backed by the Republican Party were forced to reconsider the modes of function of their existing trusts and monopolies. So there was a pressure on them, both from the central government as well as from below. There was also the problem of over-production, i.e., when production levels surpassed the buying capacity of consumers. This brought about a recession and finally depression in the market. So to keep the industries running and also to democratize the system it became imperative to introduce certain governmental measures that would rectify the economic anomalies.

The countless associations and leagues like Women's Club, National Consumers League, National Consumers League, and National Municipal Reform League in the cities and a number of farm organizations in the country-side provided enduring substance to the Progressive Movement. These associations had diverse objectives lacking common interest. The leagues mostly operated at the local level and expressed a widening social consciousness among the middle class with few Americans working at the national level. Hence, at the initial phase, the Progressive Movement operated, as Robert H. Wiebe point out in *The Search for Order: 1877–1920*, at a split level often without much co-ordination or linkages.[21]

Gradually, from a series of diffused local movements, the Progressive Movement was transformed into a sharply focussed nationally oriented movement as small- and middle-class businessmen started winning their battles and making their resisting voices heard. Wiebe remarks, 'Businessmen who had sought an amenable efficient government, experts who had fought for an opportunity to administer, doctors and lawyers who had suddenly discovered a world ignorant of their wisdom, even humanitarians who had criticized the neglected schools and street corner parks, all had won measures of victory, as much in certain cases as they had ever anticipated.'[22]

Theodore Roosevelt and the Square Deal

It fell upon Theodore Roosevelt, the first messiah of progressivism and President of America from 1901 to provide with a chain of measures which he christened as the 'Square Deal' that sought to bring in a wave of progressivism in the society. One can surmise that 'Square Deal' was actually the precursor of New Deal of Roosevelt and New Freedom of Woodrow Wilson.

Born in an affluent family in New Jersey, he graduated from Harvard University, after which he joined the Navy. As a naval captain he fought against Spanish authorities to acquire South Pacific islands like Samoa and Haiti. He won the presidential election by a huge margin, after the assassination of the Republican President McKinley in 1901.

Theodore's chief concern as the President was to remove the abuses of capitalism and reach out to the common people. He was an aristocrat turned into a democrat and a realist. But above all he was regarded a Progressive, a new term in American political lexicography that continued to remain in fashion during the presidency of Franklin Roosevelt too. In contrast to his predecessor William McKinley, Roosevelt was a Republican who believed in government action to mitigate social evils. He denounced the representatives of predatory wealth as guilty of all forms of iniquity from the oppression of wage workers to defrauding the public. Richard Hofstadter describes Theodore as a conservative Republican who tried to be a liberal Progressive Democrat.

The origins of 'Square Deal' dates back to the presidencies of Hughes, Garfield, and Grover Cleveland who also attempted to pass special anti-trust acts and thought of inter-state commerce commissions to regulate trade and commerce across the border of states. They also thought of enacting industrial policies and autonomy of states and municipal corporations. The 'Square Deal' therefore grew out of a legacy of the past. As the name suggests, it was expected to bring a fair deal or justice to the society at large. Mark Klopfenstein argues in *The Progressive Era (1900-1920)* that The 'Square Deal' was formed upon three basic ideas: conservation of natural resources, control of corporations, and consumer protection.

A number of Acts were passed to become Federal laws:

- The **Reclamation Act of 1902** was passed to initiate large-scale irrigation projects at the expense and supervision of the Federal government.
- The **Elkin's Act of 1903** was an anti-trust act which was basically a revival of the same Act that was passed during Grover Cleveland's Presidency. It laid down that formation of new trusts would no longer be allowed and the existing monopolistic trusts should be dislocated. Conglomeration of companies was also banned and wherever possible trusts were broken into individual companies.
- The **Working men's Compensation Act** was passed between **1903 and 1906** which granted two crucial demands of improvement in wages and reduction in hours of work. The Act conceded that the profit-margin of the entrepreneurs had grown so much that a share of their increased wealth should be given to the workers. The Act also provided for a number of fringe benefits, improved work-place conditions, wage non-discrimination between male and female labour, and abolition of child labour etc.
- The **Hepburn Act of 1906** was a repetition of the inter-state commerce Act, the main purpose of which was to regulate inter-state commerce in the name of democratic federalism. Wherever

there were malpractices, the government sought to remove them. Theodore insisted that democracy within industrialism must be restored.

- The **Antiquities Act of 1906** gave the president authority to restrict use of particular public land.
- The **Pure Food and Drug Act of 1906** provided the federal inspection of meat products and forbade the manufacture, sale, or transportation of poisonous patent medicines.
- A nature-lover, conservationist, and known as the 'Father of Green Movement', Roosevelt took advantage of the **Forest Reservation Act of 1891** and set aside 180 million acres of forest areas for preservation.

In his last annual message to the Congress in 1908, Roosevelt recommended a host of progressive measures – regulation of the stock market, personal income and inheritance taxes, limitation of injunctions, compulsory investigation of labour disputes, and extension of eight-hour law for federal employees.[23]

The Taft Administration

The path set by Theodore Roosevelt was followed by his successor William Howard Taft whose presidency began from 1908. His style of functioning was a combination of maintaining a low profile but wielding the 'big stick' whenever necessary.

During the four years of Taft administration between 1908 and 1912, the Progressives in the Congress got better organized as they followed a common interest and strategy against two issues that caused apple of discord between the Progressives and the conservative elements within the Republican Party. The first controversy was over the issue of the downward revision of tariff. The downward revision was immediately required to meet consumer interest as high duties ensured a protected and secured market and could artificially maintain a higher price for the goods in the consumer market. The second cause that united the Progressives was the Pinchot-Ballinger controversy over conservation. T.R. Ballinger was appointed the Secretary of Interior by President Taft. Gifford R. Pinchot, Chief Forester, appointed by Roosevelt charged Ballinger with permitting the Morgan-Guggenhelm interests to acquire reserve coal lands in Alaska. When Taft dismissed Pinchot over the charge of gross indiscipline, it was looked into as a betrayal of Roosevelt's policy on conservation. These united and transformed the Progressives into a cohesive group on one hand, and on the other, the relationship between these two wings of the Republican Party was further strained.

Woodrow Wilson and the Progressive Era

The Republican Party was split and the Progressive Party was born in 1912 with Theodore Roosevelt as its leader. While Roosevelt campaigned for 'New Nationalism', Wilson's 'New Freedom' promised the restoration of competition and hence freedom among the small groups of entrepreneurs. Wilson and his Democratic Party won the contest.

The advent of Woodrow Wilson as the President in 1913 generated new hopes. It was widely believed that the new President was imbued with noble idealism and strongly wanted the good of the people of the world at large. His programme of 'New Freedom' included the re-assurance of the basic liberties of the American people at large, equal improvement of both agriculture and industry, and de-centralization of American economy as far as possible. Wilson successfully carried out some anti-trust reforms, tariff revision, and reforms in the banking and currency sector. The first modern presidential press conference was held at his behest on 15 March 1913, where news reporters were given a platform to ask him questions. Wilson initiated a new policy to encourage competition among the businessmen through the Federal Trade Commission that tried to stop unfair trade practices. Besides, with the Clayton Anti-Trust Act that was passed at his initiative, some business practices such as price discrimination, agreements prohibiting retailers from handling other companies' products, and directorates and agreements to control other companies were made illegal. This was a powerful piece of legislation by which private individual officers of corporations could be held responsible if their companies violated the laws. More importantly, the new laws set out clear guidelines that corporations could follow which was a dramatic improvement over the previous uncertainties. In 1916, an impending threat of a national rail-road strike was thwarted by the introduction of a new law that increased the existing wages and reduced the working hours of railroad employees.

There is a debate among historians regarding Wilson's actual position so far as progressivism was concerned. John M. Blum remarks in *The National Experience*, 'Indeed he (Wilson) had a right to boast that the Democrats had opened their hearts to 'the demands of social justice' and came very near to carrying out the Progressive Party as well as their own.'[24] To Arthur S. Link, Wilson 'either obstructed or refused to encourage the fulfilment of a large part of the Progressive platform.'[25] However, under Wilson's regime, the Congress successfully took the task of downward revision of tariff, established a sound banking system, and enacted several progressive or humanitarian measures with the active support and co-operation of the Progressives.

The waning away of the movement

The movement withered away with the disappearance of the objective conditions that contributed to its rise and spread. In the post-World War I period, suppression of civil liberties and the rise of racism and nativism represented the new social realities of the time.[26] However to some historians and scholars, the movement did not really came to an end in the 1920s; rather it survived to re-emerge in the 1930s. Russel B. Nye reflects in *Mid Western Progressive Politics* that the World War I merely suspended progressivism and the future of freedom was being settled on a large scale.[27] Link further argues that even during the war, the Progressive coalition not only survived but had several victories and proved it adept in restraining corporate business.[28]

The Progressive Movement remained weak in the 1920s and gradually declined. In the post-War period, 'American capitalism had passed through a managerial revolution absorbing the energies of the urban middle classes which had previously flowed into reform movement.

The middle class professionals and intellectuals discovered that it was much more profitable to be a junior executive in a corporation than a reformer.'[29]

Historiography

Historians' view on the nature of Progressive Movement has varied according to the intellectual currents of their respective times. Interpretations have changed from viewing the movement as a just, people-oriented movement to a reactionary, groundless, utopian wave of thought, imperative to protect capitalism.

To the first generation of writers like Harold U. Faulkner and Charles Beard, in the 1920s the movement was a successful culmination of a right kind of just struggle against the excesses of big business and giant capitalism.[30] John D. Hicks in his *The Populist Revolt: A History of the Farmers' Alliance and the People's Party* saw the progressives as the direct descendants of the populists.[31] Charles and Mary Beard compared the Progressive Movement with the French Revolution and saw the era as a direct outgrowth of the earlier Populist and Granger Movements.[32] According to these scholars, progressivism declined on the verge of the Great War when the government had no other option but to rely on big business. This interpretation had a lasting influence at least till the 1940s.

The 'consensus school' of historians provided a critical view and played down the importance of conflict in America's past. In *The American Political Tradition* (1948) and *The Age of Reform* (1955), Richard Hofstadter criticized the progressive heroes, and sharply dissenting with the view of the early generation writers, argued that the progressives were a completely different group from the populists.[33] To him, it was a reactionary movement led by the old aristocratic families undergoing a 'status revolution' due to their loss of status with the rise of the rich industrialists. He remarked that it was 'the complaint of the unorganized against the consequences of organization'[34] and could not bring significant revolutionary changes in America in terms of social legislation, organization of unskilled workers, etc. In *Anti-Intellectualism in American Life,* Hofstadter blatantly criticized the progressive intellectuals including John Dewey and his progressive educational reforms.[35] George

Mowry supplemented Hofstadter's argument and carried on a socio-psychological analysis in *The California Progressives* and *The Era of Theodore Roosevelt and the Birth of Modern America.*[36] Mowry pointed out that the progressives were young, middle-class, economically secure, romantically nationalistic people who believed in the goodness of man but in the inferiority of blacks and immigrants and felt threatened by big business on one side and organized labour on the other. Arthur S. Link's *Woodrow Wilson and the Progressive Era* supplements this earlier critical view.[37] According to Link, Wilson's progressivism was 'superficial' and 'There is little evidence that Wilson had any deep comprehension of the far-reaching social and economic tensions of the time.'[38] Louis Hartz discovered in *The Liberal Tradition in America* that as America lacked the feudal tradition, hence it also lacked ideological conflict.[39] Daniel Boorstin followed the Hartzian paradigm and emphasized on the absence of political theory in American History in *The Genius of American Politics.*[40]

The early 1950s saw the introduction of regional study to progressivism. These include the works of C. Vann Woodward (*Origins of the New South, 1877–1913*), Russell B. Nye (*Midwestern Progressive Politics*), Arthur Mann (*Yankee Reformers in the Urban Age*), etc.[41] The 1950s also visualized a number of works on the intellectual origins of progressivism, almost all of which countered Hartz and Boorstin's line of analysis. Eric Goldman in *Rendezvous with Destiny* termed the dominant intellectual ideas of the Gilded Age as 'Conservative Darwinism' and compared it with 'Reform Darwinism', a new set of ideas that came from Henry George, Thorstein Veblen, Louis D. Brandeis, and Walter Rauschenbusch. While 'Conservative Darwinism' preached that man is free, there are absolute truths, and progress comes only through changes in heredity, in 'Reform Darwinism' one finds that man is not free, truth is relative, and progress comes through changes in the environment.[42] Daniel Aaron in *Men of Good Hope* criticized the Progressives for not being true liberals, and to David Noble in *The Paradox of Progressive* groundless, optimism and utopianism were the central problems of the progressive thought.[43]

In the late-1950s and 1960s, the tradition of consensus interpretation began which was different from the early consensus arguments provided by Hofstadter, Mowry, and Goldman. Samuel P. Hays in *The Response to Industrialism* viewed the progressive period as part of a larger era between 1885 and 1914 when the dominant motif in America was not reform but industrialism. This affected all and Hays tried to analyze the responses of the various groups to it.[44] Robert H. Wiebe in *The Search for Order, 1877–1920* pointed out that the progressives were the new middle-class true innovators who developed values suitable for an industrial society unlike the Grangers who tried to apply old values to the new problems of trusts, slums, etc., and populists who sought radical utopian reforms but failed at last.[45]

The 'New Left' historians have interpreted the movement as a requi site towards protection of capitalism. William Appleman Williams in *The Contours of American History* described the movement as a part of the age of corporate capitalism where the federal government became a syndicalist state and adopted a policy of aiding business and the public.[46] Williams recognized three types of reformers: the old feudal gentry; Theodore Roosevelt-type patricians who saw themselves as stewards of the public welfare; the industrial gentry, far-sighted businessmen and intellectuals like Hanna and Croly who understood that laissez faire individualism was obsolete and saw the need to recognize labour and, with government guidance, to cooperate in achieving greater efficiency; and middle-class reformers, small businessmen and farmers who wanted to open up the system at the bottom to allow for more competition and advancement.[47] To Gabriel Kolko, the era did not signify government control of business, but business control of the government. The various legislations like the Hepburn Act, meatpacking legislation, the Federal Trade Commission, etc., were all drawn up by businessmen to protect their own interests. The progressives created a state to protect capitalism.[48]

In spite of such New Left critiques, there are some works that revived the old liberal interpretation. Allen Davis' *Spearheads for Reform: The Social Settlements and the Progressive Movement, 1890–1914* deals with the social justice aspect of the Progressive Movement.[49] She argues that the war destroyed the progressive spirit when social work became a profession rather than an emotional commitment.[50] Gilbert Osofsky in *Harlem: The Making of a Ghetto* showed that in Harlem white progressives like Mary White Ovington were dedicated to helping the blacks.[51]

These are the major trends in the historiography of the Progressive Movement. Any new work seem to get fitted within any of these broader schools of thought unless there is the rise of any new school using innovative methodologies and analytical framework.

Annotated Bibliography

- In *The Quest for Social Justice, 1898–1914* (New York: Macmillan, 1931), Harold U. Faulkner captures the entire sojourn of the Progressive Movement and looks into the Progressive Movement as a just struggle against the excesses of big business and giant capitalism.
- In *The Age of Reform: From Bryan to F.D.R.* (New York: Vintage Books, 1955) and *Anti-Intellectualism in American Life* (New York: Vintage Books, 1963) Richard Hofstadter sketches Progressive Movement as a reactionary movement led by the old aristocratic families undergoing a 'status revolution' due to their loss of status with the rise of the rich industrialists.
- In *The Liberal Tradition in America: An Interpretation of American Political Thought since the Revolution* (New York: Harcourt Brace & Company, 1955) Louis Hartz proposes for a 'liberal tradition' in America which is followed by Daniel J. Boorstin in *The Genius of American Politics* (Chicago: University of Chicago Press, 1953).
- Eric F. Goldman's *Rendezvous with Destiny: A History of Modern American Reform* (New York: Alfred A. Knopf, 1952) is a story of the lives of the dissenters, Populists, and Progressives in the days of reform.
- With a broader framework of looking into the Progressive Movement as a superficial and reactionary struggle, in *Woodrow Wilson and the Progressive Era* (New York: Harper & Brothers, 1954), Arthur S. Link argues that President Wilson was not dedicated to the deeper socio-economic tensions of his times.
- Samuel P. Hays's *The Response to Industrialism, 1885–1914* (Chicago: University of Chicago Press, 1957) is a narrative and analysis of the response and reaction of multiple communities in American society to the Progressive Movement.
- William Appleman Williams's *The Contours of American History* (Cleveland World Publishing Company, 1961) and Gabriel Kolko's *Railroads and Regulation, 1877–1916* (Princeton: Princeton University Press, 1965) and *The Triumph of Conservatism: A Reinterpretation of American History, 1900–1916* (New York: Free Press, 1963) are powerful Marxist narratives which argue that Progressive Movement was an eye wash to protect capitalism in reality.
- Robert H. Wiebe's *The Search for Order: 1877–1920* (New York: Hill and Wang, 1967) is a description of the transformation of the Progressive Movement from a series of diffused local movements into a sharply focussed national-oriented movement.
- In 'Progressivism: An Historiographical Essay' (*The History Teacher*, Vol. 6, No. 3 (May 1973), pp. 427–52), William G. Anderson provides a historiography of the movement with a rich and wide coverage of the various schools of thought.

c. Labour Unrest and Trade Unionism

It is a fact of history that industrialization and capitalism always bring in their wake impoverishment and socio-economic deprivation for the factory workers, the labouring masses whose labour is exploited by the capitalists causing the greatest contradiction between capital and labour as Marx propounded long ago. The response to this severe oppression takes place in the form of labour unrest and trade union movements. American was not an exception to this. That America did not observe the tumultuous tide of socialism as capitalism promised plenty to the masses and managed to curb the socialist culture through an evil entente between the state and civil society is no more an accepted fact.

Parallel to the growth of enormous wealth, there was increasing poverty, a situation of deprivation, and an acute feeling of discontent among the labour class leading to a state of irreconcilable class conflict in the American society, and the sources of this conflict lay hidden in the capitalistic structure of society itself. Howard Zinn in *The Socialist Challenge* has carried out a deep analysis of the causes and patterns of this class-conflict in America following its economic success in the era of big business and rapid industrialization.[52]

Working Conditions and Cost Cutting Mechanisms

The dismal working conditions in the factories equally matched their living conditions in the slums and the ghettos which were uncomfortable and appalling. John Spargo's *Bitter Cry of the Children* published at the turn of the twentieth century is a moving account of the inhuman sufferings of the child labourers in the coal-mines of Pennsylvania and West Virginia. The author made a detailed study of the number of child workers, the excruciatingly long hours which they put in, and the poor wages they received, which were not even enough to buy two square meals. A woman labourer recalls the conditions of work in one of the garment factories of 500 garment factories in New York:

> ...dangerously broken stairways...windows few and so dirty...the wooden floors that were swept once a year...Hardly any other light but the gas jets

> burning by day and night…the filthy, malodorous lavatory in the dark hall. No fresh drinking water…mice and roaches…
>
> During the winter months…how we suffered from the cold. In the summer we suffered from the heat…
>
> In these disease-breeding holes we, the youngsters together with the men and women toiled from seventy and eighty hours a week! Saturdays and Sundays included!...A sign would go up on Saturday afternoon: "If you do not come in on Sunday, you need not come in on Monday."…Children's dreams of a day off shattered. We wept, for after all, we were only children.[53]

In the first flush of their success, the American capitalists who were also 'trust' builders tried to maximize their profits and minimize their labour costs. They extorted the maximum hours of work from the workers, i.e., 10 to 12 hours a day in lieu of minimum wages. Women and children were also employed as labourers, and with the same working hours, they got only-half and one-fourth of the wages respectively in comparison to their adult male counterparts. Black workers made one-third of the earnings of the white workers. In the following extract the renowned poet Edwin Markham has sharply denounced against child labour and the overall working conditions in the garment and sweatshops in New York where the working class mostly constituted of the new immigrants in the city.

> In unaired rooms, mothers and fathers sew by day and by night. Those in the home sweatshop must work cheaper than those in the factory sweatshops…And the children are called in from play to drive and drudge beside their elders…
>
> All the year in New York and in other cities you may watch children radiating to and from such pitiful homes. Nearly any hour on the East Side of New York City you can see them – pallid boy or spindling girl – their faces dulled, their backs bent under a heavy load of garments piled on head and shoulders, the muscles of the whole frame in a long strain…
>
> Is it not a cruel civilization that allows little hearts and little shoulders to strain under these grown-up responsibilities, while in the same city, a pet cur is jeweled and pampered and aired on a fine lady's velvet lap on beautiful boulevards?[54]

There were also the incidents of disasters like fires and accidents at workplaces injuring and killing workers. In one year 50,000 accidents occurred in New York factories alone! A number of other diseases were affecting workers. According to a report of the Commission on Industrial Relations, in 1914, 35,000 workers were killed in industrial accidents. Quarrymen were inhaling deadly chemicals, lithographic printers were getting arsenic poisoning, and hat and cap makers were getting respiratory problems.[55]

While the workers were already suffering from such poor working conditions, on the other hand, they had to face further less remuneration and insecurity at jobs. Big capitalists were facing a number of challenges since the dawn of the twentieth century. There was financial collapse accompanied with panic; the profits were not high as per their expectation and there was an acute requirement of the formulation and designing of strategies for cost cutting. It is important to look into Frederick W. Taylor's 'scientific management' in this context. It was a system of finely detailed division of labour, increased mechanization, and piecework wage systems to increase production and profits. Taylor had a condescending view of less intelligent workers and often compared them to draft animals.[56] Harry Braverman has pointed out in *Labour and Monopoly Capital: The Degradation of Work in the Twentieth Century* that the purpose of 'scientific management' (also known as Taylorism) was to make workers interchangeable for doing simple tasks that was necessary for the new division of labour – like standard parts divested of individuality and humanity, bought and sold as commodities.[57] Ellen Rosen remarks in *Improving Public Sector Productivity: Concepts and Practice*, 'The worker was taken for granted as a cog in the machinery.'

In order to reduce high employee turnover, Henry Ford applied the 'assembly line' concept to increase production in factories. In this manufacturing process parts, usually interchangeable parts were added to a product in a sequential manner using optimally planned logistics to create a finished product much faster than with handcrafting-type methods. In spite of the apparent improved aspects of industry such as reduced labour hours and increased production of numbers and parts, the resulting larger demand actually allowed further economies of scale to be exploited.

Taylorism and Fordism not only invented ways to economize production by making jobs less remunerative and less secure, but by disconnecting a worker to the entire process of production, jobs became unpleasant to the former who became a 'stupefied automaton' at work.

Labour Organizations and Trade Unionism

The discontent and the sufferings of the labourers could not find expression in the early phase when they were largely unorganized as a class. Gradually they realized the need of coming together and solidify as a group to voice their common set of grievances. The earliest labour organization was the **Noble order of the Knights of Labor** founded in 1869 by Terence Powderly. Its main purpose was to break down the isolation of the labour class and build up a sense of social solidarity by offering them better amenities and spreading education among them. It was open to all working men, both skilled and unskilled including farmers, miners, artisans, and mill workers, and aimed at realizing through non-violent means a good government that would enable the labourers to have a proper share of the wealth that they help to create. It established branches in many industrial cities.

At this early stage of struggle, there was no consolidated programme of class-struggle. America's situation was different from the European countries as the wage indices were much higher than the rest of the world. Again, because of the constant wave of immigration, common group interest could not easily percolate among the divergent social and ethnic composition.

The history of organized unionism actually starts with the emergence of the **American Federation of Labour (AFL)** founded in Columbus, Ohio in December 1886 by Solomon Gompers, a Dutch Jew. After closing his cigar-making shop in London, Solomon arrived in America in 1863 and soon started working towards building a trade union movement. Solomon gained enough knowledge of labour history and economics through his experience of running the cigar shop. With his in-depth understanding of the then situation of trade unionism in America, he devised his first task to diligently knit together the different workers' units. In 1881, he founded the **Federation of Organized Trade and Labor Unions of the United States and Canada,** and finally in 1886, the AFL was born consisting of craft unions disaffected from the Knights of Labor.

AFL was composed of a number of self-governing trade-unions with clear-cut pragmatic goals. Concentrating on the removal of socio-economic grievances, politics was left out from the agenda. AFL believed that industries should survive and there should be a fair share of the profit for the workers. Wages for both men and women should be such as to improve the workers' quality of life and that should bring in fringe benefits; there should be good housing, good health insurance, good education and free supply of fuel like coal to the working families. Besides, they demanded reduced hours of labour, i.e., from 12 hours to eight hours and more humane treatment for the women labourers. Advocating the abolition of child-labour, AFL questioned the efficacy of child labour on grounds of social justice. By 1892, the AFL had the 250,000-member mark.[58]

The AFL, however, was not really a radical organization and had certain limitations. The Federation favoured pursuit of workers' immediate demands rather than challenging the property rights of owners. It took pragmatic view of politics that favoured tactical support for particular politicians over formation of a party devoted to workers' interests. Melvyn Dubofsky has pointed out in *We Shall Be All* that AFL at best can be regarded as 'the conservative alternative to working class radicalism.'[59] Again, 'The AFL was an exclusive union – almost all male, almost all white, almost all skilled workers,' as Howard Zinn rightly remarks.[60] AFL based itself on 'business unionism' and its skilled workers were called business agents, 'trying to match the monopoly of production by the employer with a monopoly of workers by the union.'[61] Hence it bargained and won better conditions for some workers and left most workers out.

In this atmosphere of exclusivity in unionization and the excluded wanting for more radical reforms, there emerged the first politically motivated Marxist labour organization, the **Industrial Workers of the World (IWW)** affiliated to the same organization in England and Germany. It was founded in Chicago in June 1905 at a convention of 200 socialists, anarchists, and radical trade unionists from all over the United States who opposed to the policies of the AFL. Among the first groups of organizers were William D. ('Big Bill') Haywood, Daniel De Leon, Eugene V. Debs, Thomas J. Hagerty, Lucy Parsons, 'Mother' Mary Harris Jones, Frank Bohn, William Trautmann, Vincent Saint John, Ralph Chaplin, and others. Its agenda was the establishment of communism and dictatorship of the proletariat which could be attained only through violent revolution. It was very much influenced by two European leaders, Molly Maguires and Johann Most who had migrated to the United States for some time and attempted to give the American labour movement a revolutionary slant.

IWW broke with the AFL idea of craft unions and the reason is well enumerated in one of its pamphlets:

> The directory of unions of Chicago shows in 1903 a total of 56 different unions in the packing houses, divided up still more in 14 different national trades unions of the American Federation of Labour.
>
> What a horrible example of any army divided against itself in the face of strong combination of employers...[62]

The IWW was radical, militant, courageous, and most importantly inclusive. It organized mass meetings and parades. It was the only American union (besides the Knights of Labor) to include all workers including women, immigrants, African-Americans, and Asians into the same organization. Many of its early members were immigrants, and some, like Carlo Tresca, Joe Hill, and Mary Jones, rose to prominence in the leadership. In 1923, the organization claimed 100,000 members and could marshal the support of approximately 300,000 workers. But despite a few successes in the mining camps in the west and in the textile centres of the east, IWW lacked a large mass base and numerical strength. The organization therefore had a short life and it closed down being unable to face the brutal force of the industrialists. In 1915, the vigilantes in Montana seized IWW organizer Frank Little, tortured him, and hanged him, leaving his body dangling from a railroad trestle. Its membership declined dramatically after severe government repression as part of the first Red Scare and a 1924 split brought on by internal conflict.

From the last quarter of the nineteenth century till the beginning of the twentieth century, there were innumerable labour strikes, some of which were short-lived and local, and some others affected the whole nation. Out of these, the **Pullman strike of 1894** was the most widespread and successful in achieving its ends. Named after Francis Pullman, an industrialist who owned factories for construction of railway coaches, the town of Pullman in Illinois offered much higher wages and better living conditions to its labourers than anywhere else. But with the onset of the economic depression of the 1890s, their wages were drastically reduced. When their appeal to Francis Pullman to treat the wage issue in a more humanitarian manner went unheeded, the workers were forced to strike work. Under the leadership of **Eugene V. Debs**, the head of the **American**

Railway Union, the strike gathered great momentum practically paralyzing most of the railroads in the North and the West. Unable to meet the challenge, an employer organization called the **General Managers' Association** sought for Federal government's intervention to restore normal railway service. The government responded by a strict order for withdrawal of the strike. As complete anarchy broke out against this stricture, Federal troops were sent to the state to crush the labour movement. Debs was imprisoned for contempt of court. However, with the sympathetic attitude of Governor Altgeld of Illinois, eventually many of the strikers' grievances were removed. The government relented ultimately and passed Federal laws to mete out social justice.

So far as strikes were concerned, the differences between AFL and IWW can be noticed. While AFL organized a number of mainly nonviolent strikes, IWW found that, 'Strikes are mere incidents in the class war; they are tests of strength, periodical drills in the course of which the workers train themselves for concerted action. This training is most necessary to prepare the masses for the final "catastrophe," the general strike which will complete the expropriation of the employers.'[63] IWW profoundly believed in workers strength and solidarity and direct violent action which is evident from IWW-led strike or direct action of 6,000 workers in 1909 against an affiliate of the US Steel Company and a series of other such actions.

Historians' Views

Divergent views have been professed by historians on labour conflict and trade union movement in the United States. The British historian Henry Pelling categorically rejects the existence of a Marxist model of an industrial society and class-struggle in the American society. To him, there was a healthy labour movement and trade unionism that fetched a better standard of living, collective bargaining, improvement in wages and hours of work, and finally abolition of child labour. Treading the same non-Marxist path, Sidney Hook in his classic work *From Hegel to Marx* puts it succinctly when he says '...capitalism tackled socialism and Marxism by holding the horns of the bull'. Hook argues that there was no scope for class-struggle and dictatorship of the proletariat in the United States since the American capitalists on their own would grant various reforms and benefits to the workers.

The Marxist school of historians including Eric Foner, Eric Hobsbawm, and Jaden Forster offer their own theories. Foner says that in spite of genuine labour grievances, American conditions were not ripe for a political revolution. The capitalists tried to keep the workers happy with concessions. During the Progressive Era, all the presidents from Theodore Roosevelt to Franklin D. Roosevelt through the New Deal measures improved the lot of the labour class; so much so that the proletariat class began to adopt many bourgeois habits. Hobsbawm also thinks that the class-situation was not rigid and bi-polar in America, which is why no class-struggle could take place. Forster the author of *History of American Trade Union Movement* thinks that there was enough opportunity for class-mobility and ample concessions were granted to the labourers by the capitalists. Compared to the rest of the world, the American labour class was better off; there was absence of a polarized situation – capital versus labour in America. But nevertheless, there was a deep sense of deprivation among the proletariat as they found themselves impoverished compared to the other classes in their country. According to Forster, it was this relative impoverishment that was at the root of this profound sense of deprivation, but actual class-struggle could not begin as the American capitalists from time to time gave them large doses of economic benefits.

Not only the distribution of economic benefits and reforms, the American capitalist society actually knew the strategies of protest management and control. The **National Civic Federation (NCF)** emerged to get better relations between capital and labour and Samuel Gompers was its vice-president for a long time. The Progressive reforms to a great extent succeeded to stabilize the capitalist system 'by repairing its worst defects, blunt the edge of the Socialist movement, restore some measure of class peace in a time of increasingly bitter clashes between capital and labour.' So, it would be misleading to accept that the contradiction did not grow, spread, or took radical steps. The workers continued to agitate and the first few decades of the twentieth century visualized one of the greatest socialist challenges through labour unrest and trade unionism, though there were various levels of protests, severe suppressions, and compromises at times.[64]

Annotated Bibliography

- Frederick W. Taylor's *The Principles of Scientific Management* (New York: Harper & Brothers, 1911) is an influential essay contacting the tenets of modern organization and decision theory. Here, Taylor puts forward mechanisms and strategies (of finely detailed division of labour, increased mechanization, and piecework wage systems) to increase production and hence profits.
- Howard Zinn's *A People's History of the United States* (New York: Perennial Classics, 2003) is a portrayal of the American history from the perception of the common people. It contains a radical analysis of the socialist challenge (labour movement) in the US.
- William C. Roberts ed,. *American Federation of Labor: History, Encyclopedia, Reference Book* (Washington, DC: American Federation of Labor, 1919) contains a detailed history and descriptive analysis of the American trade union movement.
- Marc Karson's *American Labor Unions and Politics, 1900–1918* (Carbondale: Southern Illinois University Press, 1958) is a political account of the US labour movement with an interpretation of the politics of labour unions.

Notes

1. Daniele Albertazzi and Duncan McDonnell, *Twenty-First Century Populism: The Spectre of Western European Democracy* (New York and London: Palgrave Macmillan), p. 3.
2. Solon Justus Buck, *The Granger Movement: A Study of Agricultural Organization and Its Political, Economic and Social Manifestations, 1870–1880* (Harvard: Harvard University Press, 1913), p. 3.
3. Ibid., p. 7.
4. Ibid., p. 9.
5. *The Columbia Electronic Encyclopedia* (2011) sixth edition; available at: http://www.infoplease.com/encyclopedia/history/granger-movement.html, date of access: 12.11.2012.
6. Solon Justus Buck, *The Granger Movement*, 302.
7. Paul Kleppner, 'The Greenback and Prohibition Parties', Arthur M. Schlesinger, ed, *History of U.S. Political Parties: Volume II, 1860–1910, The Gilded Age of Politics* (New York: Chelsea House, 1973), p. 1557.
8. Philip S. Foner, *History of the Labor Movement in the United States: Volume 1, From Colonial Times to the Founding of the American Federation of Labor* (New York: International Publishers, 1947), pp. 476–77.

9. Matthew Gild, *Greenbackers, Knights of Labor, and Populists, Farmer-Labor Insurgency in the Late-Nineteenth-Century South* (Athens & London: The University of Georgia Press, 2007), pp. 20–21.
10. In 1890, the Southern Alliance, the Farmers' Mutual Benefit Association, and the Colored Farmers' Alliance met jointly in Ocala, Florida. They formed a Supreme Council of the National Farmers' Alliance and drew up the following list of demands in December, just after the Alliance movement had had a sharp impact on the fall elections in the South and the states of the Great Plains region. *U.S. History Resources* (available at: http://1.scds.org/resources/US-History/1890_The%20Ocala%20Demands.pdf, date of access: 12.11.2012).
11. Matthew Gild, *Greenbackers, Knights of Labor, and Populists*, p. 123.
12. Frederick Jackson Turner, *The Frontier in American History* (New York: H. Holt and Company, 1920), also available at: http://xroads.virginia.edu/~hyper/turner/ (date of access: 25.05.2012), p. 148.
13. John D. Hicks, *The Populist Revolt: A History of the Farmers' Alliance and the People's Party* (Minneapolis: University of Minnesota Press, 1931); Martin Ridge, 'Populism Revolt: John D. Hicks and The Populist Revolt', *Reviews in American History*, Vol. 13 (March 1985), pp. 142–54.
14. C.V. Woodward, 'Tom Watson and the Negro in Agrarian Politics', *The Journal of Southern History*, Vol. 4, No. 1 (February 1938), pp. 14–33.
15. Richard Hofstadter, *The Age of Reform: From Bryan to F.D.R.* (New York: Vintage Books, 1955).
16. Robert Miller, *Oklahoma Populism: A History of the People's Party in the Oklahoma Territory* (Norman and London: University of Oklahoma Press, 1987); Gene Clanton, *Populism: The Humane Preference in America, 1890-1900* (Boston: Twayne Publishers, 1991).
17. Gene Clanton, *Populism*, p. xv.
18. Charles Postel, *The Populist Vision* (New York: Oxford University Press, 2007).
19. John D. Buenker, John C. Burnham, and Robert M. Crunden, *Progressivism* (Cambridge: Schenkman Publication Company, 1986).
20. B.K. Srivastava, 'The Progressive Movement: Through the Historian's Prism', Dwijendra Trivedi and S.C. Tiwari, eds, *Themes and Perspectives in American History: Essays in Historiography*, (American Studies Research Centre, 1978), p. 116.
21. Robert H. Wiebe, *The Search for Order: 1877–1920* (New York: Hill and Wang, 1967), p. 185.
22. Ibid., p. 211.
23. B.K. Srivastava, 'The Progressive Movement', p. 119.
24. John M. Blum et al., *The National Experience* (New York: Harcourt, Brace & Company, 1963), p. 553.

25. Arthur S. Link, *Woodrow Wilson and the Progressive Era* (New York: Harper & Brothers, 1954), p. 59.
26. B.K. Srivastava, 'The Progressive Movement', p. 140.
27. Russel B. Nye, *Mid Western Progressive Politics* (East Lansing: Michigan State University Press, 1959), p. 126.
28. Arthur S. Link, 'What happened to the Progressive Movement in the 1920's?', *American Historical Review*, Vol. 64, No. 4 (July 1959), pp. 833–51.
29. B.K. Srivastava, 'The Progressive Movement', p. 143.
30. Harold U. Faulkner, *The Quest for Social Justice, 1898–1914* (New York: Macmillan, 1931); Charles and Mary Beard, *The Rise of American Civilization* (New York: Macmillan, 1927), 2 volumes.
31. John D. Hicks, *The Populist Revolt.*
32. Charles and Mary Beard, *The Rise of American Civilization*, vol. 2, p. 543.
33. Richard Hofstadter, *The American Political Tradition and the Men Who Made It* (New York: Alfred A. Knopf, 1948); *The Age of Reform: From Bryan to F.D.R.*, ibid.
34. Richard Hofstadter, *The Age of Reform: From Bryan to F.D.R.*, p. 216.
35. Richard Hofstadter, *Anti-Intellectualism in American Life* (New York: Vintage Books, 1963).
36. George Mowry, *The California Progressives* (Berkeley: University of California Press, 1951); *The Era of Theodore Roosevelt and the Birth of Modern America, 1900–1912* (New York: Harper and Row, 1958).
37. Arthur S. Link, *Woodrow Wilson and the Progressive Era, 1910–1917.*
38. Ibid., p. 80.
39. Louis Hartz, *The Liberal Tradition in America: An Interpretation of American Political Thought Since the Revolution* (New York: Harcourt Brace & Company, 1955).
40. Daniel J. Boorstin, *The Genius of American Politics* (Chicago: University of Chicago Press, 1953).
41. C. Vann Woodward, *Origins of the New South, 1877–1913* (Baton Rouge: Louisiana State University Press, 1951); Russell B. Nye, *Midwestern Progressive Politics: A History of Its Origins and Development, 1870–1958*, ibid.; Arthur Mann, *Yankee Reformers in the Urban Age: Social Reform in Boston, 1880–1900* (Cambridge, Massachusetts: The Riverside Press, 1954).
42. Eric F. Goldman, *Rendezvous with Destiny: A History of Modern American Reform* (New York: Alfred A. Knopf, 1952).
43. Daniel Aaron, *Men of Good Hope, A Story of American Progressives* (New York: Oxford University Press, 1951); David W. Noble, *The Paradox of Progressive Thought* (Minneapolis: University of Minnesota Press, 1958).
44. Samuel P. Hays, *The Response to Industrialism, 1885–1914* (Chicago: University of Chicago Press, 1957).

45. Robert H. Wiebe, *The Search for Order, 1877–1920*.
46. William Appleman Williams, *The Contours of American History* (Cleveland World Publishing Company, 1961).
47. William G. Anderson, 'Progressivism: An Historiographical Essay', *The History Teacher*, Vol. 6, No. 3 (May 1973), pp. 427–52.
48. Gabriel Kolko, *Railroads and Regulation, 1877–1916* (Princeton: Princeton University Press, 1965); *The Triumph of Conservatism: A Reinterpretation of American History, 1900–1916* (New York: Free Press, 1963).
49. Allen Davis, *Spearheads for Reform: The Social Settlements and the Progressive Movement, 1890–1914* (New York: Oxford University Press, 1967).
50. William Appleman Williams, *The Contour of American History*.
51. Gilbert Osofsky, *Harlem: The Making of a Ghetto* (New York: Harper and Row, 1963).
52. Howard Zinn, 'The Socialist Challenge', *The Twentieth Century, A People's History of the United States* (New York: Perennial Classics, 2003), pp. 31–76.
53. Cited in ibid., p. 36.
54. Edwin Markham, *Cosmopolitan* magazine (January 1907), cited in Zinn, p. 35.
55. Howard Zinn, 'The Socialist Challenge', pp. 38–39.
56. Frederick W. Taylor, *The Principles of Scientific Management* (New York: Harper & Brothers, 1911), p. 59. He argued, 'Now one of the first requirements for a man who is fit to handle pig iron is that he shall be so stupid and so phlegmatic that he more nearly resembles in his mental makeup the ox than any other type.'
57. Ibid., p. 35.
58. William C. Roberts, ed, *American Federation of Labor: History, Encyclopedia, Reference Book* (Washington, DC: American Federation of Labor, 1919), p. 63.
59. Melvyn Dubofsky, *We Shall Be All* (Urbana: University of Illinois Press, 2000), pp. 5–6.
60. Howard Zinn, The Socialist Challenge', p. 39.
61. Ibid., p. 41.
62. Ibid., p. 43.
63. Ibid., pp. 43–44.
64. Ibid., p. 72.

7

American Foreign Policy: Post-Monroe Doctrine to World War I

It sheds light on how the American foreign policy gradually shifted from 'Splendid Isolation' to 'Manifest Destiny' to suit the politico-economic realities of the time. With the success of the Monroe Doctrine in the domestic front, it began to look outward with imperialist aspirations. Gradually, the Monroe Doctrine re-evolved to define a recognized sphere of American control in several countries including Cuba, Venezuela, Mexico, Nicaragua, Panama, etc. Along with the political history of annexation and conquest, the chapter explores US strategies and tactics to legitimize political control. The second part is on the US involvement in the WWI and how and why the policy of 'armed neutrality' was replaced by opposition against Triple Alliance.

a. From 'Splendid Isolation' to 'Manifest Destiny'

The Monroe Doctrine which had essentially been a doctrine for isolation underwent a gradual transformation, its principle and ideology being re-interpreted and applied to pave the way towards 'Manifest Destiny' especially since the fag end of the nineteenth century, though the process already initiated few decades before that. It is worth mentioning here that American Foreign Policy was the indispensable midwife to the birth of the American Republic.[1] 'It is a tale of the halting, even muddled, progression of the United States from a struggling state trying to establish its authority over the still-raw North American Atlantic seaboard to a sophisticated "hyperpower"...'[2] In the formative years, the American nation under

President George Washington and his successors, being conscious of the capacity of the newly independent nation, wanted itself to avoid entanglements to foreign alliances and partiality to any other power. The next stage was followed by the project of continental expansion or internal colonization where Americans entered into an arena of international intrigues with British, Spanish, French, and Mexican contenders and rivalries with the Native Indians succeeding at their aim of encroaching and settling into the last corner of the western frontier. With its consolidation in the home front and the success of the Monroe Doctrine in obstructing intervention from other European powers to uphold the democratic spirit, it began to look outward with its ever-swelling aspirations which proved to be imperialist in turn.

On 2 December 1845, the US President James Polk announced to the Congress that the principle of the Monroe Doctrine should be strictly enforced and that the United States should aggressively expand into the West, often termed as 'Manifest Destiny'. On the issue of American settlement in Texas, a war with the Mexican government became imminent. The war began in 1846, and it soon threatened to assume an international character since Mexico was under Spanish rule. America by now had also begun settlements in Utah, Arizona, New Mexico, and California. In 1842, the US President John Tyler applied the Monroe Doctrine to Hawaii; while Britain was not allowed to interfere there, the process of American annexation was successfully accomplished.

In 1862, French forces under Napoleon III invaded and conquered Mexico, giving it to Austrian-born Emperor Maximilian. Americans sharply resisted this French attempt and proclaimed it as a violation of the doctrine. But they could not intervene immediately as the nation was torn apart by the tumultuous tide called the American Civil War. With the end of the Civil War, the US brought troops down to the Rio Grande in hopes of pressuring the French government to end its occupation. Mexican nationalists eventually captured the Emperor and executed him, reasserting Mexico's independence. In the 1870s, President Ulysses S. Grant and his Secretary of State Hamilton Fish expanded the Monroe Doctrine to replace European influence in Latin America with that of the United States. It was reasserted, 'hereafter no territory on this continent (Central and South America) shall be regarded as subject to transfer to a European power.'[3]

In 1880s, James G. Blaine formulated the 'Big Brother' policy which was an extension of the Monroe Doctrine that aimed to rally Latin American nations behind the US leadership and to open their markets to the American traders. As a part of the policy, Blaine arranged and led the First International Conference of American States in 1889.

The American President Grover Cleveland, through his Secretary of State, Richard Olney, cited the Doctrine in 1895 in context of the Venezuelan crisis which was, 'one of the most momentous episodes in the history of Anglo-American relations in general and of Anglo-American rivalries in Latin America in particular.'[4] Venezuela sought to involve the US in a territorial dispute with Britain over Guayana Esequiba. America stated that British behaviour over the issue was unacceptable and a gross violation of the Monroe doctrine. It also threatened strong action against the United Kingdom if the British failed to arbitrate their dispute with Venezuela. In a 20 July 1895 note to Britain, Olney stated, 'The United States is practically sovereign on this continent, and its fiat is law upon the subjects to which it confines its interposition.'[5] The United States objected to British Prime Minister Lord Salisbury's proposal for a joint meeting to clarify the scope of the Monroe Doctrine.

Gradually, the Monroe Doctrine came to define a recognized sphere of American control that few dared to challenge. The Spanish-American War of 1898 over the issue of Cuba reflected strong economic imperialist motivation and design of America in the Latin American countries. The Spanish rule in the Latin American countries had all the vices of a feudal administration which was carried out through governors virtually independent of their authorities at home and often misusing their power and exercising tyranny over the people. The Cuban people had been suffering under the oppressive rule of the Spanish governor for a long time. Industry and trade were put under great strain due to intolerable levies. Agriculture and mining greatly suffered due to heavy excise taxes. Moreover, the Spanish manufacturers and traders enjoyed monopoly rights of charging excessively high prices. Life was insecure, the courts were completely in the hands of the Spanish rulers, freedom of press was practically denied, and the Church was corrupt and dominated by the Spanish nobles. Seething in discontent and suppressed anger, underground guerilla war had started since the 1870s. It intensified after the depression of 1895 with the Cuban patriot Jose Marti giving the clarion call of a revolt against the Spanish rule.

Initially there was an earnest attempt by the American government to maintain a neutral stand. But as the war continued, its economic effects on America were staggering since huge amount of American capital was invested in Cuba. The Spanish government poured in all its resources to crush the rebellion and also tried to prevail upon the European powers to stop United States from intervention. On the other hand, the rebels led by Jose Marti appealed to the US government for help. Popular sympathy for the rebel cause had also a role to play. By 1898, the US government also realized the efficacy of intervention in Cuban affairs and fished into the troubled water. There was great economic stake for the American capitalists in Cuba, particularly in sugarcane and tobacco plantations, where the estimated investment was one billion US dollar per year. So promptly the slogan 'Cuba libre' or 'liberation for Cuba' was raised by the American government to perpetuate its own economic interest to a great extent.

Theodore Roosevelt had proclaimed the rationale of the Monroe Doctrine in supporting intervention in the Spanish colony of Cuba in 1898. Roosevelt, the future President of America, played a crucial role in the war. An ex-Naval officer and the current Republican Governor of New York, Roosevelt was elevated to the rank of a colonel. He found the first US Volunteer Cavalry Regiment called the 'Rough Riders'. It was a short, quick war, won with ease and with laurels resting with America and Roosevelt. The people of Cuba undoubtedly had been liberated from the tyrannical Spanish rule, but America now emerged as the new controlling power. In 1898, following the Spanish-American War, Spain ceded to the United States for the sum of $20 million, Puerto Rico, the Philippines, Guam, and Cuba.

The victory in Cuba accelerated the spirit of jingoism and set America on the path of further expansion in other regions with Roosevelt's presidency from 1901. After he became President, and following the Venezuela Crisis of 1902–3, Roosevelt added the Roosevelt Corollary to the Monroe Doctrine in 1904.[6] Roosevelt's December 1904 annual message to the Congress declared,

> All that this country desires is to see the neighboring countries stable, orderly, and prosperous. Any country whose people conduct themselves well can count upon our hearty friendship. If a nation shows that it knows how to act with reasonable efficiency and decency in social and political

> matters, if it keeps order and pays its obligations, it need fear no interference from the United States. Chronic wrongdoing, or an impotence which results in a general loosening of the ties of civilized society, may in America, as elsewhere, ultimately require intervention by some civilized nation, and in the Western Hemisphere the adherence of the United States to the Monroe Doctrine may force the United States, however reluctantly, in flagrant cases of such wrongdoing or impotence, to the exercise of an international police power.[7]

It was the most significant amendment to the original doctrine and asserted US domination essentially making her a 'hemispheric policeman.'

The short experiment in imperialism ended as the US turned its attention to the Panama Canal and the stabilization of regions to its south, including Mexico. Roosevelt wanted to construct a canal through the narrow Central American isthmus and link the Pacific and Atlantic oceans. With the solidified interests of America in Panama which was the northernmost province of Colombia, both Colombia and the French company that was to provide the construction materials raised their prices. At this critical juncture, the US refused to pay the higher-than-expected fees and engineered a revolution in Colombia.[8] Roosevelt struck a deal with rebels who were dissatisfied with Colombian rule, offering them independence and American protection in exchange for land to build the canal. In 1903, the revolt broke out and the US Navy prevented Colombian troops from marching into Panama. Roosevelt immediately recognized Panama's independence and sent Secretary of State John Hay to sign the Hay–Bunau–Varilla Treaty, which relinquished ownership of the canal lands to the United States. The construction on the Panama Canal began the following year and was completed in 1914. Panama became a new republic, receiving $10 million from the US alone and also gained an annual payment of $250,000 and guarantees of independence.

The United States could also gain its foothold in the Far East. It intervened in China which was under the Manchu dynasty and where the European imperialists were already involved in a scramble for power. Roosevelt issued the Hay Doctrine in 1901, which laid down that if China was to be divided into spheres of influence among England, France, and Germany who had already made an entry as early as the 1870s, then US must also have its share.

Relations between the United States and Japan soured during the Roosevelt years. In 1905, Roosevelt mediated a dispute between the Russians and the Japanese to end the Russo–Japanese War. In December 1907, to demonstrate American prowess, Roosevelt sent 16 US battleships on a tour of the world. When the Great White Fleet stopped in Tokyo in 1908, Japanese and American officials signed the Root–Takahira Agreement, in which both countries agreed to respect the Open Door policy in China and each other's territorial integrity in the Pacific.

Between 1908 and 1913, the US government tried to legitimize its gains and consolidate the acquired territories. The Wilsonian regime (which noticed the outbreak of WWI) heralded a new age so far as American Foreign Policy was concerned when the nation had a quest for a new world in the immediate aftermath of the WWI, yet it followed a policy that Herring calls, 'involvement without commitment'.[9]

Though Wilson apparently seemed to avoid the aggressive stance Theodore Roosevelt had taken toward Latin America, he did not shrink from intervention on behalf of American values. He remarked in 1913, 'I am going to teach the South American republics to elect good men.'[10] Between 1914 and 1918, the United States intervened in Latin America, particularly in Mexico, Haiti, Cuba, and Panama and maintained troops in Nicaragua. Wilson ordered the military occupation of the Dominican Republic shortly after the resignation of its President Juan Isidro Jimenes Pereyra in 1916. Isabel Brown records how the US military worked in concert with wealthy Dominican landowners to suppress the *gavilleros* (guerrilla force fighting the occupation), and in the occupation that lasted until 1924, the soldiers were notorious for its brutality against those in the resistance.[11]

Annotated Bibliography

- In *From Colony to Superpower: U.S. Foreign Relations since 1776* (New York: Oxford University Press, 2008), George C. Herring traces the story of America's rise from 13 colonies to the world's greatest superpower. It not only provides a unilinear account of America's stunning successes but also tragic failures while capturing the interaction of the nation with other nations of the world. It is till date the bestseller on United States' foreign relations and diplomacy.

- Ernest May's *The World War and the American Isolation, 1914–17* (Cambridge: Harvard University Press, 1959) is a historical account of the neutrality period with rich coverage on the interplay of American, British, and German policies.
- Richard William Leopold's *The Growth of American Foreign Policy: A History* (New York: Alfred A. Knopf, 1962) is a narration of the key events of American foreign policy along with a critical interpretation of the ideological elements in it.
- In 'Catalyst for the Roosevelt Corollary: Arbitrating the 1902–1903 Venezuela Crisis and Its Impact on the Development of the Roosevelt Corollary to the Monroe Doctrine' (*Diplomacy and Statecraft*, Vol. 20, No. 3, 2009, pp. 383–402), Matthias Maass explores the context (the 1902/03 Venezuela Crisis) that led to President Theodore Roosevelt's decision to amend the Monroe Doctrine and propagate what came to be known as the 'Roosevelt Corollary', a landmark in United States foreign policy.

b. America and the WWI

When World War I began in 1914, Woodrow Wilson formally proclaimed that America would take a neutral stand, and in his address to the Congress in 1914, mentioned that it would be fatal for the American citizens to take sides in the War.[12] Such a policy had to be given up soon. With the intensification of German submarine warfare, greatly jeopardizing American security on the high seas, a wave of shock overtook the nation. Woodrow Wilson delivered his *War Message* to the Congress on the evening of 2 April 1917 and announced that his previous position of 'armed neutrality' was no longer tenable now that the Imperial German Government had announced that it would use its submarines to sink any vessel approaching the ports of Great Britain, Ireland, or any of the Western Coasts of Europe. On Good Friday, 6 April 1917, the United States joined the War ostensibly, 'to make the world safe for democracy'.

Without the support of men, money, and material from America, it would not have been possible for the Allies to defeat Germany in the end. Wilson insisted from the beginning that the war was not with the people of Germany but only against the autocratic government of the country. He was therefore against meting out a severe punishment and crippling the power of Germany after its defeat as he believed that peace terms should not be stringent and must not include annexation of unwilling people. Subsequently in January 1918, in a message to the Congress, he submitted his famous *Fourteen Points* as the basis for a just peace emphasizing mutual guarantees of political independence and territorial integrity (annexure).

Lloyd George of Britain and Clemenceau of France, present at the Versailles Peace Conference, were sceptical about Wilsonian idealism and dismissed the major part of the 'Fourteen Points' as unrealistic, unworkable, and impractical. Most of it was rejected as the Treaty of Versailles in an atmosphere of hatred, greed, and fear concluded a dictated peace, putting the entire war-guilt on Germany. But in accordance with the Wilsonian principle of self-determination, new states including Czechoslovakia, Yugoslavia, Poland, and Finland were recognized by fresh treaties. Another significant principle of the 'Fourteen Points', the formation of a 'general association of nations' found expression in the creation of the League of Nation, which was probably Wilson's greatest achievement.

It was believed that America had returned empty-handed from Versailles. The Old World nations seemed to have a tacit agreement among themselves; believing that European matters should be settled by Europeans themselves. American participation in the Continental game of politics was not to be tolerated even though a huge supply of human and material resources had been sent by America.

The question that arises is why US joined the World War I. George Kennan explains this in *American Diplomacy* that America had no other option but to join the War. It was not out of any altruistic motive that America had supplied war materials, merchandise, cereals, and most importantly, huge capital in form of money. It was this financial contribution which Wilson wanted back from the participants of the Allied bloc.[13] Richard Hofstadter in *American Political Traditions* writes that Wilson decided to join the War not out of any noble idealism; rather he was a pragmatist who was motivated by financial gains.[14] Thomas H. Buckley and Edwin B. Strong remarks in *American Foreign and National Security Policies, 1914–1945* that, 'More important than the propaganda factor was the question of economic ties with the belligerents.'[15] From August 1914 to April 1917, the US sold approximately $6 billion worth of goods to the Allies which was an increase in trade to them from $825 million to $3.25 billion a year.[16] That American economic stake in an Allied victory was great as recognized by Wilson.

America's economic mission was successful in the scramble for diplomatic leadership in international politics; the adolescent American nation needed few more years to dominate and establish hegemony over the entire global scene.

Annotated Bibliography

- Thomas H. Buckley and Edwin B. Strong, *American Foreign and National Security Policies, 1914–1945* (Knoxville: University of Tennessee Press, 1987) is a political account of US' national security laws and policies since the beginning of the WWI till the end of WWII.
- Ronald Schaffer's *America in the Great War: The Rise of the War Welfare State* is a fascinating tale of how the WWI wrought a dramatic revolution in America, wrenching a diverse, unregulated, nineteenth-century society into the modern age. The author shows how the Wilson Administration used persuasion, manipulation, direct control, and the cooperation of private industries and organizations to mobilize a freewheeling, individualist country.
- Glenn P. Hastedt's *Encyclopedia of American Foreign Policy* (New York: Facts on File, 2004) is a collection of 500 entries on key people, organizations, countries, influential offices, international organizations, theories of foreign policy formation, and court cases.

Annexure: Wilson's fourteen Points

1. Open covenants of peace, openly arrived at, after which there shall be no private international understandings of any kind but diplomacy shall proceed always frankly and in the public view.
2. Absolute freedom of navigation upon the seas, outside territorial waters, alike in peace and in war, except as the seas may be closed in whole or in part by international action for the enforcement of international covenants.
3. The removal, so far as possible, of all economic barriers and the establishment of equality of trade conditions among all the nations consenting to the peace and associating themselves for its maintenance.

4. Adequate guarantees given and taken that national armaments will be reduced to the lowest point consistent with domestic safety.
5. A free, open-minded, and absolutely impartial adjustment of all colonial claims, based upon a strict observance of the principle that in determining all such questions of sovereignty the interests of the populations concerned must have equal weight with the equitable claims of the government whose title is to be determined.
6. The evacuation of all Russian territory and such a settlement of all questions affecting Russia as will secure the best and freest cooperation of the other nations of the world in obtaining for her an unhampered and unembarrassed opportunity for the independent determination of her own political development and national policy and assure her of a sincere welcome into the society of free nations under institutions of her own choosing; and, more than a welcome, assistance also of every kind that she may need and may herself desire. The treatment accorded Russia by her sister nations in the months to come will be the acid test of their good will, of their comprehension of her needs as distinguished from their own interests, and of their intelligent and unselfish sympathy.
7. Belgium, the whole world will agree, must be evacuated and restored, without any attempt to limit the sovereignty which she enjoys in common with all other free nations. No other single act will serve as this will serve to restore confidence among the nations in the laws which they have themselves set and determined for the government of their relations with one another. Without this healing act the whole structure and validity of international law is forever impaired.
8. All French territory should be freed and the invaded portions restored, and the wrong done to France by Prussia in 1871 in the matter of Alsace-Lorraine, which has unsettled the peace of the world for nearly 50 years, should be righted, in order that peace may once more be made secure in the interest of all.
9. A readjustment of the frontiers of Italy should be effected along clearly recognizable lines of nationality.
10. The peoples of Austria-Hungary, whose place among the nations we wish to see safeguarded and assured, should be accorded the freest opportunity to autonomous development.
11. Romania, Serbia, and Montenegro should be evacuated; occupied territories restored; Serbia accorded free and secure access to the sea; and the relations of the several Balkan states to one another determined by friendly counsel along historically established lines of allegiance and nationality; and

international guarantees of the political and economic independence and territorial integrity of the several Balkan states should be entered into.

12. The Turkish portion of the present Ottoman Empire should be assured a secure sovereignty, but the other nationalities which are now under Turkish rule should be assured an undoubted security of life and an absolutely unmolested opportunity of autonomous development, and the Dardanelles should be permanently opened as a free passage to the ships and commerce of all nations under international guarantees.
13. An independent Polish state should be erected which should include the territories inhabited by indisputably Polish populations, which should be assured a free and secure access to the sea, and whose political and economic independence and territorial integrity should be guaranteed by international covenant.
14. A general association of nations must be formed under specific covenants for the purpose of affording mutual guarantees of political independence and territorial integrity to great and small states alike.

Notes

1. George C. Herring, *From Colony to Superpower: U.S. Foreign Relations Since 1776* (New York: Oxford University Press, 2008), editor's introduction, p. xiv.
2. Ibid.
3. Ibid., p. 259.
4. R.A. Humphreys, 'Anglo-American Rivalries and the Venezuela Crisis of 1895', Presidential Address to the Royal Historical Society, *Transactions of the Royal Historical Society*, Vol. 17, Dec. 10, 1966, pp. 131–64.
5. George C. Herring, *From Colony to Superpower*, p. 307.
6. Matthias Maass, 'Catalyst for the Roosevelt Corollary: Arbitrating the 1902–1903 Venezuela Crisis and Its Impact on the Development of the Roosevelt Corollary to the Monroe Doctrine', *Diplomacy and Statecraft*, Vol. 20, No. 3, (2009), pp. 383–402.
7. House Records HR 58A-K2, Records of the U.S. House of Representatives, Record Group 233, Center for Legislative Archives, National Archives, cited in http://www.ourdocuments.gov, date of access: 8.11.2012.
8. Bishop, Joseph Bucklin, *Uncle Sam's Panama Canal and World History, Accompanying the Panama Canal Flat-globe: Its Achievement an Honor to the United States and a Blessing to the World*, (New York: J. Wanamaker expressly for the World Syndicate Company, 1913).
9. George C. Herring, *From Colony to Superpower.*

10. Paul Horgan, *Great River: The Rio Grande in North American History* (Middletown, CT: Wesleyan University Press, 1984), p. 913.
11. Isabel Zakrzewski Brown, *Culture and Customs of the Dominican Republic* (USA: Greenwood Press, 1999).
12. 'Such divisions amongst us would be fatal to our peace of mind and might seriously stand in the way of the proper performance of our duty as the one great nation at peace, the one people holding itself ready to play a part of impartial mediation and speak the counsels of peace and accommodation, not as a partisan, but as a friend.' Primary Documents: U.S. Declaration of Neutrality, 19 August 1914, available at: http://www.firstworldwar.com/source/usneutrality.htm, date of access: 07.05.2012.
13. George Kennan, *American Diplomacy, 1900–1950* (Chicago: University of Chicago Press, 1951).
14. Richard Hofstadter, *American Political Traditions and the Men Who Made It* (New York: Vintage Books, 1948).
15. Thomas H. Buckley, Edwin B. Strong, *American Foreign and National Security Policies, 1914–1945* (Knoxville: University of Tennessee Press, 1987), p. 28.
16. Ibid., p. 29.

8

The Great Crisis and Its Recovery

This chapter is on the Great Depression of 1929 that marked the dawn of a new era of plenitude and prosperity. The impact of the American economic depression was severe at the home front and the European world and its colonies. By throwing light on various economic theories and arguments like that of the classical theories, Keynesian economics, debt-deflation analyses, etc., it tries to answer the most intriguing question concerning generation of scholars: Did the crash occur suddenly? While the first section generates pessimism, the next one is of hope when US followed the path of economic recovery under New Deal of Franklin D. Roosevelt. The chapter ends with the outbreak of the WWII.

a. The Great Depression of 1929

The hopeful era ushered in by Harding and Coolidge in the post-WWI period, proved to be short lived. Coming a long way from Wilsonian idealism, America in the 1920s, gave itself over to crass materialism and to ruthless making and spending of money. When Herbert Clark Hoover became the President in 1929, the nation thrived in affluence, which inspired the new president to comment, 'we in America are nearer to the final triumph over poverty than ever before in the history of any land.' There was boom in big business and technological goods and factory productions could not keep up with the increasing greed for newer and newer gadgets; stocks and shares skyrocketed. It was the dawn of a new era of plenitude and prosperity. But this euphoria did not last long. In October 1929, all on a sudden the crash came, and America was all steeped in an economic depression. Business houses were forced to lock doors, innumerable investors lost their savings, and factories shut down, banks crashed and unemployment increased by leaps and bounds. When America sneezed, the whole world caught cold – the depression had a chain impact on several countries of the world, especially the European world and its colonies.

Table 8.1: Economic Indicators, 1929–32

	Unites States	Great Britain	France	Germany
Industrial production	–46%	–23%	–24%	–41%
Wholesale prices	–32%	–33%	–34%	–29%
Foreign trade	–70%	–60%	–54%	–61%
Unemployment	+607%	+129%	+214%	+232%

Source: Jerome Blum, Rondo Cameron, and Thomas G. Barnes, *The European World: A History* (Boston: Little Brown & Co. 2nd edition 1970), p. 885.

The Great Depression was triggered by a sudden, total collapse in the stock market which is famous in history as the Wall Street Crash. Four phases—Black Thursday, Black Friday, then Black Monday, and Black Tuesday are commonly used to describe this collapse of stock values. All four are appropriate, for the crash was not a one-day affair. The initial crash occurred on Thursday (24 October 1929) but the catastrophic downturn of Monday (28 October) and Tuesday (29 October) precipitated widespread alarm and the onset of an unprecedented and long-lasting economic depression for the United States and the world. Did the crash occur suddenly? Different theories and schools of thought have different opinions on the issue.

The Classical School

The school of classical economics was influenced by the macroeconomic thought of nineteenth-century British economist David Ricardo and his book entitled *Principles of Political Economy and Taxation*. Ricardo admitted that there could be temporary periods when employment would fall below the natural level. His emphasis was on the long run and he argued that in the long run, things could be set right by the smooth functioning of the price system.

Influenced by Ricardian principles, economists of the classical school saw the massive slump in the late 1920s and early 1930s as a short-run aberration and the economy would right itself in the long run by returning to its potential output and to the natural level of employment.

Keynesian Economics

John Maynard Keynes contradicted with the argument of the classical school. While Ricardo pointed out about the 'temporary effects', for Keynes 'In the long run we are all dead'. Keynes's 1936 book, *The General Theory of Employment, Interest and Money* shifted the thrust of macroeconomic thought from the concept of aggregate supply to the concept of aggregate demand. Ricardo focussed on the economy's tendency to operate at a level of output given by the long-run aggregate supply curve. Keynes on the other hand, argued that recessionary or inflationary gaps could be created by shifts in aggregate demand. Keynesian Economics asserted that changes in aggregate demand can create gaps between the actual and potential levels of output; such gaps can be prolonged. Proper use of fiscal and monetary policy can close such gaps.

The Great Depression was caused when there was a reduction in aggregate demand that took the economy from above its potential output to below its potential output, and the resulting recessionary gap lasted for more than a decade. The plunge in aggregate demand began with a collapse in investment. The investment boom of the 1920s had left firms with an expanded stock of capital. As the capital stock approached its desired level, firms did not need as much new capital, and started cutting back investment. The stock market crash of 1929 shook business confidence, further reducing investment. Real gross private domestic investment plunged nearly 80 per cent between 1929 and 1932. The stock market crash also reduced the wealth of a small fraction of the population (just 5 per cent of Americans owned stock at that time), but it certainly reduced the consumption of the general population. It also reduced consumer confidence throughout the economy. The reduction in wealth and confidence reduced consumption spending and shifted the aggregate demand curve to the left.

Fiscal policy also acted to reduce aggregate demand. As consumption and income fell, governments at all levels found their tax revenues falling.

They responded by raising tax rates in an effort to balance their budgets. The federal government, for example, doubled income tax rates in 1932. Total government tax revenues as a percentage of GDP shot up from 10.8 per cent in 1929 to 16.6 per cent in 1933. Higher tax rates tended to reduce consumption and aggregate demand.

Other countries were suffering declining incomes as well. Their demand for US goods and services fell, reducing the real level of exports by 46 per cent between 1929 and 1933. The Smoot-Hawley Tariff Act of 1930 dramatically raised tariffs on products imported into the United States and led to retaliatory trade-restricting legislation around the world. This act, which more than 1,000 economists opposed in a formal petition, contributed to the collapse of world trade and to the recession.

Moreover, the federal government conducted a sharply contractionary monetary policy in the early years of the Depression. It took no action to prevent a wave of bank failures that swept the country at the outset of the Depression. Between 1929 and 1933, one-third of all banks in the United States failed. As a result, the money supply plunged 31 per cent during the period. The federal government could have prevented many of the failures by engaging in open-market operations to inject new reserves into the system and by lending reserves to troubled banks through the discount window. But it generally refused to do so; the federal government officials sometimes even applauded bank failures as a desirable way to weed out bad management.

The plunge in aggregate demand produced a recessionary gap. Such a gap produced falling wages, shifting the short-run aggregate supply curve to the right. Nominal wages plunged roughly 20 per cent between 1929 and 1933. But the shift in short-run aggregate supply was insufficient to bring the economy back to its potential output. The failure of shifts in short-run aggregate supply to bring the economy back to its potential output in the early 1930s was partly the result of the magnitude of the reductions in aggregate demand, which plunged the economy into the deepest recessionary gap ever recorded in the United States. The short-run aggregate supply curve began shifting to the right in 1930 as nominal wages fell, but these shifts, which would ordinarily increase real GDP, were overwhelmed by continued reductions in aggregate demand.

A further factor blocking the economy's return to its potential output was the federal policy. President Franklin. D. Roosevelt thought that falling wages and prices were in large part to be blamed for the Depression. Programmes initiated by the Roosevelt administration in 1933 sought to block further reductions in wages and prices. That stopped further reductions in nominal wages in 1933, thus stopping further shifts in aggregate supply. With recovery blocked from the supply side and with no policy in place to boost aggregate demand, the economy remained locked in a recessionary gap so long.

The Debt-deflation Theory

Irving Fisher argued in his article entitled *The Debt-Deflation Theory of Great Depressions* that the predominant factor leading to the Great Depression was over-indebtedness and deflation. He outlined nine factors interacting with one another under conditions of debt and deflation to create the mechanics of boom to bust. [1]

1. Debt liquidation and distress selling;
2. Contraction of the money supply as bank loans are paid off;
3. A fall in the level of asset prices;
4. A still greater fall in the net worths of business, precipitating bankruptcies;
5. A fall in profits;
6. A reduction in output, in trade, and in employment;
7. Pessimism and loss of confidence;
8. Hoarding of money; and
9. A fall in nominal interest rates and a rise in deflation adjusted interest rates.

Ben Bernanke in his article *Non-Monetary Effects of the Financial Crisis in the Propagation of the Great Depression* has revived the debt-deflation theory of the Great Depression originated by Fisher. [2]

Monetarist Theory

In their 1963 book, *A Monetary History of the United States, 1867–1960*, Milton Friedman and Anna Schwartz concluded that the Great

Depression was not the necessary and direct result of the stock-market crash of October 1929. It was caused by a speculative investment bubble. The popping of the 'bubble' may have been instigated by the Federal Reserve's raising of the discount rate – the interest rates the Fed charges on loans to commercial banks – in August 1929. The stock-market crash of October 1929 made it more difficult for many businesses to repay their loans to the banks, and many banks found their balance sheets impaired as a result. But the most important cause of the bank runs that began in October 1930 was bad times in the farm belt, where the banks were especially weak and poorly diversified. The number of bank runs increased exponentially in December 1930 – in that single month 352 banks failed. Most of the failing banks were in the Midwest, their failures caused by farmers who defaulted on their loans because they were hit hard by the economic downturn. No sooner did the first wave of bank runs subside than another got underway in the spring of 1931, creating what Friedman and Schwartz described as a 'contagion of fear' among bank depositors. Bank crises continued to come in waves until the spring of 1933.

Hence, according to the monetarists, the Great Depression was mainly caused by monetary contraction, the consequence of poor policy-making by the American Federal Reserve System, and continued crisis in the banking system. In this view, the Federal Reserve, by not acting, allowed the money supply to shrink by one-third from 1929–33, thereby transforming a normal recession into the Great Depression. Friedman argued that the downward turn in the economy, starting with the stock market crash, would have been just another recession.

The Austrian School

This includes Austrian economist Friedrich Hayek and American economist Murray Rothbard. They agree with monetarists' view that the Federal Reserve was much responsible for the crisis; but in contradiction with the monetarists, the Austrian school argues that the key cause of the Depression was the expansion of the money supply in the 1920s that led to an unsustainable credit-driven boom. The inflation of the money supply in turn led to an unsustainable boom in both asset prices (stocks and bonds) and capital goods. By the time the Fed tightened its grip in

1928, it was far too late leading to a significant economic contraction. Hence, the artificial interference in the economy was a disaster prior to the Depression, and government efforts to prop up the economy after the crash of 1929 only worsened the situation.

The Marxist School

Marx saw recession and depression as unavoidable under free-market capitalism as there are no restrictions on accumulations of capital other than the market itself. The Marxist school emphasizes on the tendency of capitalism to create unbalanced accumulations of wealth, leading to over accumulations of capital and a repeating cycle of devaluations through economic crises.

Marxist scholars argued that the boom of 1920s was more rhetoric than reality. Wages rose by a total of 6.1 per cent between 1922 and 1929 (with no increase after 1925); the manufacturing workforce remained stagnant, and industrial production only expanded by about a third. The classical Marxist scholar Lewis Corey pointed out in *The Decline of American Capitalism* that during the 1920s, the growth of luxury consumption, unproductive expenses, and credit put stress on the economy. Incomes from dividends and managerial salaries rose much faster than real wages. The decade was marked with upsurges of non-productive speculative investment in real estate and the stock market. Recent Marxist interpretation has been provided in the accounts of Antonio Carlo (*The Crisis of the State in the Thirties*), Martin J. Sklar (*The United States as a Developing Country: Studies in US History in the Progressive Era and the 1920s*), and Chris Harman (*Zombie Capitalism: Global Crisis and the Relevance of Marx*).[3]

Whatever the causes may be, the impact was severe. The Depression became a worldwide business downturn of the 1930s that affected almost all countries. International commerce declined quickly. There was a sharp reduction in tax revenues, profits, and personal incomes. It affected both countries that exported raw materials and industrialized countries. It led to a sharp decrease in world trade as each country tried to protect their own industries and products by raising tariffs on imports. Governments reduced their spending, which led to decreased consumer demand. Construction came to a standstill in many nations. Some nations changed their heads and their type of government. World Trade collapsed with trade in 1939 still below the 1929 level. In Germany, weak economic conditions led to the rise to power of Adolf Hitler. Germany suffered greatly because of the huge debt the country was burdened by following World War I. The Japanese invaded China and developed mines and industries in Manchuria. Japan thought this economic growth would relieve the Depression. The Depression had profound political effects. In countries such as Germany and Japan, reaction to the Depression brought about the rise to power of militarist governments who adopted the aggressive foreign policies that led to the World War II. In countries such as the United States and Britain, the government intervened which ultimately resulted in the creation of welfare systems. Thousands of investors lost large sums of money and several were wiped out, losing everything. Banks, stores, and factories were closed and left millions of people jobless, penniless, and homeless. Many people came to depend on the government or charities to provide them with food.

The impact of the Great Depression on India, the then British colony was severe. The price decline from late 1929 to October 1931 was 36 per cent, compared to 27 per cent in Britain and 26 per cent in the US. The impact of the crisis on agrarian, trade, industrial, and transport sectors have been extensively covered by the path-breaking works of K.A. Manikumar (*A Colonial Economy in the Great Depression, Madras (1929–1937)*) and G. Balachandran (*John Bullion's Empire: Britain's Gold Problem and India Between the Wars*).[4]

Annotated Bibliography

- John Maynard Keynes's *The General Theory of Employment, Interest and Money* (Cambridge: Cambridge University Press, 1936) is a path-breaking work emphasizing on the concept of aggregate demand to understand crisis. Keynes's work is central to the debate on the causes of the Great Depression of 1929.
- Milton Friedman and Anna Schwartz's *A Monetary History of the United States, 1867–1960* (Princeton: Princeton University Press, 1963) is an analysis of historical data of around a century to show that monetary policy of the nation mattered the most in managing American economy and navigating serious economic fluctuations.

- In *America's Great Depression* (USA: the Ludwig Von Mises Institute, 2000, 5th edition), the Austrian economist Murray Rothbard uses the business cycle theory to show how expansive monetary policies could be responsible for generating imbalances between investment and consumption.
- In 'The Debt-Deflation Theory of Great Depressions' (*Econometrica*, October 1933, Vol. 1, No. 4, pp. 337–57), Irving Fisher develops the 'debt-deflation' theory attributing crises to the bursting of a credit bubble and outlines nine factors interacting with one another under conditions of debt and deflation to create the mechanics of boom to bust.
- In 'Non-Monetary Effects of the Financial Crisis in the Propagation of the Great Depression' (*American Economic Review*, June 1983, Vol. 73, No. 3, pp. 257–76), Ben Bernanke explains the reasons behind the unusual length and depth of the Depression and proposes that malfunctioning of financial institutions during the 1930s was an important cause.

b. Roosevelt, the New Deal and the Outbreak of the World War II

The 1930s marked a watershed and came as a dividing line in the American past. Roosevelt's New Deal can be regarded as the bordering line between the two phases of governance in America. H. Hoover, elected in 1928 and functioning as the Secretary of Governance found the root of the Depression in panic and the solution lay in the restoration of self-belief and confidence. But this view was limited and Hoover could not assume the globality of the crisis. He requested easier money, self-liquidating public works, low personal and corporate income taxes, and commodity stabilization corporations. These initiatives were however inadequate. Commodity stabilization corporations lacked the funds and agricultural prices kept plummeting. However, Hoover was reluctant to launch drastic, immediate government action and could not realize that his own government surfaced business interests where power was privileged by a relatively few leaders in each functional bloc formed and operating as an oligarchy. He was a republican conservative, believer in voluntarism, and not a Darwinist by principle; he continued to lock himself in the delusion and self-created bubble, waiting for the recovery to come by itself, while the problems associated with the Great Depression kept on clouding the American firmament.

1932 came as a landmark year with the election of Roosevelt who was by then a popular figure as the Governor of New York. To him, the only thing to fear was fear itself – nameless, unrecognizing, unjustified terror; he realized that the American people were not stricken by plague of locusts, plenty was at the doorstep, but the problem remained in the generous use of languishes in the very sight of the supply. Since the President was able to identify the problems, the common people had great hopes in the new government. Historians like Arthur Link, Frank Friedel, William Current, and Richard McGreaver regard Franklin Roosevelt as one of the finest statesmen in the history of America.

There is controversy among scholars regarding the economic framework of New Deal. Though some scholars argue that Roosevelt was highly influenced by Keynesian theory of 'deficit spending', D. Fusfield argues in *The Economic Philosophy of Franklin. D. Roosevelt and the Origins of the New Deal* that FDR disagreed with Keynesian theories from tie-and-again and he had his own economic thought (he was a graduate in economics from Harvard). There was also controversy in the cabinet among economists like Tugwell, believers of the institutional school of Veblen and John Commons, staunch supporter of structural reforms. The New Deal actually represented a sustained effort and effective experiment in the Keynesian middle way. Its pragmatism and resourcefulness could forge faith as a man who moved through safe channels and shrank from the dogmatism of bankrupt right and fanatic left.

The New Deal rested on three pillars – *relief* (immediate action to halt the economy's deterioration), *recovery* (temporary programmes to restart the flow of consumer demand), and *reform* (programmes to avoid another depression and ensure citizens against national disasters).

Developing a legislative framework to launch policies in the most severely affected industrial and agricultural sector, part of his recovery programme also launched public sector projects. Relief or immediate action was taken in the banking sector as soon as his hundred days of administration began.

Banking Sector

On 3 March 1933, all banks were closed until any new legislation passed. On 9 March, the Emergency Banking Relief Act was passed which led to

Table 8.2: Families on Relief, 1936–41

Relief Cases 1936–1941 (monthly average in 1,000)

	1936	1937	1938	1939	1940	1941
Workers employed						
WPA	1,995	2,227	1,932	2,911	1,971	1,638
CCC and NYA	712	801	643	793	877	919
Other federal work projects	554	663	452	488	468	681
Public assistance cases						
Social security programs	602	1,306	1,852	2,132	2,308	2,517
General relief	2,946	1,484	1,611	1,647	1,570	1,206
Total families helped	5,886	5,660	5,474	6,751	5,860	5,167
Unemployed workers (Bur Lab Stat)	9,030	7,700	10,390	9,480	8,120	5,560
Coverage (cases/ unemployed)	65%	74%	53%	71%	72%	93%

Source: Gene Smiley, 'Recent Unemployment Rate Estimates for the 1920s and 1930s', *Journal of Economic History*, vol. 43 (June 1983), pp. 487–93.

the opening of several banks under the supervision of the treasury department and federal loans were also available if required. Billions of dollars in hoarded currency and gold flowed back to the people within a month. By June, there was a steady, sharp, and upward recovery. But according to Milton Friedman and Anna Schwartz, the curve came close being worse than disease when during 1933, 4,004 small banks merged into larger banks. To deal with deflation, the nation went off the gold standard. In March and April, in a series of laws and executive orders, the government suspended the gold standard for United States currency. Anyone holding significant amounts of gold coinage was mandated to exchange it for the existing fixed price of US dollars, after which the US would no longer pay gold on demand for the dollar, and gold would no longer be considered valid legal tender for debts in private and public contracts. The dollar was allowed to float freely on foreign exchange markets with no guaranteed price in gold, only to be fixed again at a significantly lower level a year later with the passage of the Gold Reserve Act in 1934. Markets immediately responded well to the suspension, in the hope that the decline in prices would finally end.

Agricultural Sector

Agricultural prices fell from 147 per cent in 1929 to 65 per cent in 1932. In this scenario, while the rich classes with substantive capital wanted government assurance of limited production to sketch a balance between demand and supply, the marginal farmers looked for direct financial assistance. The Agricultural Adjustment Act was launched in May 1933 with the advice of R. Tugwell, George Peek, and Henry Wallace. It functioned with its sister organization Credit Commodity Corporation. Its aim was to raise prices for commodities through artificial scarcity. The total output of corn, cotton, dairy products, hogs, rice, tobacco, and wheat was set by using a system of domestic allotments. The farmers themselves had a voice in the process of using government to benefit their incomes. The agricultural adjustment administration paid land owners subsidies for leaving some of their lands idle with funds provided by a new tax on food processing aiming to force up farm prices to the point of parity, an index based on 1910–4 prices. To meet 1933 goals, 10 million acres (40,000 km^2) of growing cotton was ploughed up, bountiful crops were left to rot, and six million baby pigs were killed and discarded. The idea was the less produced, the higher the wholesale price and the higher income to the farmer. Farm incomes increased significantly in the first three years of the New Deal, as prices for commodities rose.

Industrial Sector

From 1929 to 1933, the industrial economy had been suffering from a vicious cycle of deflation. In June 1933, the National Industrial Recovery Act (NIRA) was passed. It established the National Resources Planning Board (NRPB) to assist in planning the economy by providing recommendations and information. Fredric A. Delano was appointed head of the NRPB. The NIRA guaranteed to workers the right of collective bargaining and allowed union organizing activity. To prime the pump and cut unemployment, the NIRA created the Public Works Administration (PWA). From 1933 to 1935 PWA spent $3.3 billion with private companies to build 34,599 projects including building bridges, airports, dams, post offices, courthouses, and thousands of kilometres of road. Huge numbers of unemployed persons were put to work in this government-financed public works projects. Through reforestation and flood control, millions of hectares of soil were reclaimed and protected from erosion and devastation.

The NIRA also established the National Recovery Administration (NRA), which attempted to stabilize prices and wages through cooperative code authorities involving government, business, and labour. The NRA allowed business to create a multitude of regulations imposing the pricing and production standards for all sorts of goods and services. Most economists were dubious because it was based on fixing prices to reduce competition. The NRA was ended by the Supreme Court in 1935. The judges interpreted their measures as a megalomaniac attempt on the part of the President to augment his own power and influence in the name of justice. The conservative members in the Supreme Court, who were in favour of trusts, monopolies, and private capitalists, felt that too much of federal intervention would destroy individual rights of life, liberty, and property in the United States. There was lack of proper auditing for public expenditure. So opposition grew strong and general unrest spread in the country.

By the time NRA ended in May 1935, industrial production was 55 per cent higher than in May 1933. In the spring of 1935, responding to the setbacks in the Court, the Administration endorsed several significant new initiatives which historians refer to as the 'Second New Deal' and note that it was more radical, more pro-labour, and anti-business than the 'First New Deal' of 1933–4. The National Labor Relations Act (NLRA) (also known as the Wagner Act), passed in June 1935, revived and strengthened the protections of collective bargaining contained in the original NIRA. This resulted in a tremendous growth of membership in the labour unions composing the American Federation of Labor. Labour thus became a major component of the New Deal political coalition. Roosevelt nationalized unemployment relief through the Works Progress

Administration (WPA), headed by Harry Hopkins. It created hundreds of thousands of low-skilled blue collar jobs for unemployed men (and some for unemployed women and white collar workers). The National Youth Administration, later used as a model for some of the Great Society programs in the 1960s, fell under the semi-autonomous WPA program..

The most important programme of 1935 was the Social Security Act, which established a system of universal retirement pensions, unemployment insurance, and welfare benefits for poor families and the handicapped. It established the framework for the US welfare system. Roosevelt insisted that it should be funded by payroll taxes rather than from the general fund.

In spite of mounting resistance against his administration, FDR was re-elected for the second term in 1936 and emerged as being more pragmatic and resolute than in the earlier term of presidency. Determined to root out all opposition in the Supreme Court, he cleverly manoeuvred in replacing some of the earlier judges by his own men of choice. Next, deciding to directly communicate with the trade unions, he invited some labour organizations like, American Federation of Labour, Knights of Labour, etc., and discussed his new programme with them. He promised to raise their wages and reduce their working hours. This ultimately led the trade unions to withdraw their opposition.

Roosevelt's response to the recession of 1937 was even more radical. He moved left and unleashed a rhetorical campaign against monopoly power, which was cast as the cause of the new crisis. Automaker Henry Ford, steelmaker Tom Girdler, and the superrich *Sixty Families* who supposedly comprised the living centre of the modern US industrial oligarchy came under attack. To create an economic upturn, he launched a $5-billion spending programme in the spring of 1938 to increase mass purchasing power.

The Waning Away of the New Deal Programme

Roosevelt's domestic programme was interrupted by changes in the international scene, leading to the outbreak of the World War II. He returned to power once again and his third term of presidency began in 1940.

The roots of the WWII lay in the rise of three totalitarian states – Nazi Germany, Fascist Italy, and Japan, which were following an aggressive policy in the Far East. Germany, angered by the restrictions, imposed on it by the Versailles Treaty was bent on taking revenge on the major world powers. Under Adolf Hitler, who had successfully organized his National Socialist Party and had come to power in 1933, Germany played the first move by attacking Poland. The three powers soon joined hands to form the Axis bloc against France and England. US continued to stand aloof, feeling smug and safe in its policy of 'splendid isolation'. But as the crisis deepened, with Hitler's runaway victories in Europe, Japan spreading its claws over the Pacific region and threatening to capture Philippines, Haiti, and Guam, and the Pearl Harbour incident, America took alarm, and at last decided to join the war. There were other motives also behind America's participation. American big business had produced enormous industrial ware including a great amount of military hardware that needed to be sold in the continental market. Ideologically too, America felt the moral pressure of taking up arms against Nazism and Fascism and ally with France and England to protect democracy.

The outcome of American participation in the WWII was the final victory of the Allies over the Axis powers. The newly invented Atom bomb, hurled on Hiroshima and Nagasaki in Japan, causing irreparable losses in terms of human lives forced Japan to make an unconditional surrender. One by one the Axis Powers accepted defeat in the hands of the Allied powers, thanks to Franklin Roosevelt. The world was at last made safe for democracy, and democracy triumphed against totalitarianism. The upshot of it all was that America now emerged as a dominant leader of the world; its economy was restored and it took over the great task of re-building the war-ravaged world.

Critical analysis and Review of the New Deal

When democracy was under attack, the New Deal played a significant role. Heirs of Enlightenment, the New Dealers launched a broad humanistic movement to make man's life in earth more tolerable and some day even to achieve co-operative commonwealth. It has been interpreted in different ways – state capitalism (Louis Hacker), break with the past (R. Hofstadter), levelling aims of communism (E. Robinson), and beneficent liberalism (Eric Goldman).

Though the New Deal could not achieve recovery, but at least relieved the nation from sufferings. Its failures had to be understood within the broader framework of the shortcomings of American liberal democracy. When America entered the World War I, federal assistance to corporate capitalism and acceptance of private property created a wide gap between the promise of equality and reality. Conservatives like John Davis and Al Smith pointed out that with New Deal, American life was meshed up with bureaucratic interventionism which clashed with the American notion of liberty. Leftists like Huey Long argued that FDR did not propound for the federal ownership of industry or business. It was a radical rhetoric, a garb beneath which its pro-capitalist face was concealed. According to New leftists Paul Conkin and Howard Zinn, it was generous to select business groups but insufficient for the marginal people belonging to the communities of share-croppers, tenant-farmers, farm-labourers, unskilled workers, etc. Actually, one has to take notice of the political constraints that the New Deal encountered. Conservative scepticism about government remained strong both in the Congress and among certain segments of the population. Thus, some scholars have stressed that the New Deal was not just a product of its liberal backers, but also a product of the pressures of its conservative opponents. Economists like Harold Cole and Lee Ohanian believe that the New Deal prolonged and further worsened the Depression and the New Deal cartelization policies were a key factor behind the weak recovery. The abandonment of these policies coincided with the strong economic recovery of the 1940s.

There were some limitations in his programmes, but FDR had naïve intentions to bring smooth recovery of the US economy. One can evaluate a government administration or policy according to its good intentions; others can by measuring its actual consequences. These two set of evaluations will provide two contradictory balance sheets. The same holds true so far as Roosevelt's administration and his New Deal is concerned.

Annotated Bibliography

- A detailed description of the reforms and policies under the rubric of Roosevelt's New Deal is evident in William. E. Luchtenburg's *Franklin. D. Roosevelt and the New Deal* (New York: Harper and Row, 1963) and B.J. Bernstein's *Towards a New Past: Dissenting Essays in American History* (New York: Pantheon Books, 1968).
- Howard Zinn, ed,. *New Deal Thought* (New York: American Heritage Series, 1966), Paul Conkin's *The New Deal* (New York: Crowell, 1967), and Harold Cole and Lee Ohanian's 'New Deal Policies and the Persistence of the Great Depression: A General Equilibrium Analysis' (*Journal of Political Economy*, Vol. 112, No. 4 (August 2004), pp. 779–816) contain a critical analysis and review of the New Deal measures.

Notes

1. Irving Fisher, 'The Debt-Deflation Theory of Great Depressions', *Econometrica*, (Oct. 1933), Vol. 1, No. 4, pp. 337–57.
2. Ben Bernanke, 'Non-Monetary Effects of the Financial Crisis in the Propagation of the Great Depression', *American Economic Review*, (June 1983), Vol. 73, No. 3, pp. 257–76.
3. Antonio Carlo, 'The Crisis of the State in the Thirties', *Telos*, (winter 1980-81), pp. 62–80; Martin J. Sklar, *The United States as a Developing Country: Studies in US History in the Progressive Era and the 1920s* (New York: Cambridge University Press, 1992); Chris Harman, *Zombie Capitalism: Global Crisis and the Relevance of Marx* (London: Bookmarks Publications, 2009).
4. K.A. Manikumar, *A Colonial Economy in the Great Depression, Madras (1929–1937)* (Chennai: Orient Longman, 2003); G. Balachandran, *John Bullion's Empire: Britain's Gold Problem and India Between the Wars* (Richmond Surrey: Curzon Press, 1996).

9

The Rise of America: WWII and After

The chapter begins with the US entry to the WWII followed by Allied victory. America's rise to 'superpower' in the post-WWII period entailed its unique political diplomacy, economic domination and control, and cultural hegemony over the other nations. American role during the Cold War down to the post-Cold War phase of unipolar world scenario is sketched in this chapter. Its deleterious impact, especially upon the decolonized, 'underdeveloped' 'Third World' nations, is noted under global capitalism when America emerged as the biggest power to control and take unanimous decisions in global politics and economy.

'It is a rich tale of the continuing interplay between soaring ideals and gritty reality, aspiration and compromise, accident and purpose, and the will of the United States and the often contrary will of countless other international actors.'[1] The United States' rise to 'superpower' in the aftermath of the WWII in a gradually emerging unipolar world is the saga of its unique political diplomacy, economic domination and control, and cultural hegemony over the other nations.

a. WWII – The Context, Entry of the United States, and Allied Victory

In the mid-1930s, as war clouds began to gather in Europe and Asia, Americans who found themselves in the depths of the Depression did not want to get involved in a world war, and retreated into a deeper position of isolationism. In 1935, under the leadership of Senator Gerald Nye of

North Dakota, the Senate passed the Neutrality Act signed by President Franklin Delano Roosevelt. Further neutrality acts were passed in 1936, and by 1937, on the context of aggravating international tensions, the United States backed off and passed a less restrictive neutrality act, but it was certainly not in a mood to get back into war. In October 1937, Roosevelt called for international co-operation to quarantine aggressor nations and suggested on the modification of the earlier neutral stance of the Congress. Meanwhile Japan attacked China and proposed an *East Asian co-prosperity sphere* that would liberate the Asian nations from the shackles of western imperialism and colonialism and create a self-sufficient economic zone under the leadership of Japan. Circumstances became critical in late 1937 when Japanese planes sank the American gunboat *Panay* which was evacuating Americans from Nanjing. Though the incident set a warning note to the American President, yet apology from Japan in the immediate post-*Panay* incident defused a potential crisis.

German aggression and finally the German invasion of Poland in September 1939 led to the official beginning of WWII. Alarmed at the Nazi surge, Roosevelt pressurized the Congress to take measures to help Britain and France. America took an anti-neutral position and sold military armaments to belligerents in lieu of money, later it initiated a 'lend-lease' policy to sell munitions to the Allies which also included Stalinist Russia. The US began co-ordinating military strategy with Britain, and in August 1941, Roosevelt and British Prime Minister Winston Churchill met and forged a formal wartime alliance agreeing to an eight-point Atlantic Charter that endorsed the creation of a post-War world organization for ensuring international security. It also disavowed territorial expansion and emphasized protection of human rights and self-determination.

The US did not enter into the War in spite of German attacks on US ships as public opinion was against such a move. Japan sparked American involvement in WWII when Japanese bombers attacked Pearl Harbour, Hawaii on 7 December 1941, and caused massive destruction to the US Pacific Fleet in face of its impending economic strangulation when Roosevelt froze all Japanese assets in the US in mid-1941 and brought under his control commercial transactions of the two countries including petroleum. The next day, i.e., on 8 December, the Congress declared war against Japan and mobilized effectively, guided by its 'crash program of mobilization' under new bureaucracies and technologies.[2]

The war in Europe ended with the capture of Berlin by Soviet Union and the subsequent German unconditional surrender in May 1945. During 1944 and 1945, the United States defeated the Japanese Navy and captured the West Pacific islands. The dropping of atomic bombs on Hiroshima and Nagasaki finally made Japan to surrender. The total victory of the Allied powers over the Axis altered the political alignment and social structure of the world. The influence of European great powers started to decline with the power centre gradually shifting towards America leading to the megalomaniac rise of the United States as the 'superpower hegemon'.[3]

The most important factor to understand the rise of US in the immediate post-War period was its tremendous economic expansion since wartime. Unlike Europe, America was not a war-weary nation, and moreover, federal government nearly quadrupled in size during the War. Between 1940 and 1945, the GNP rose by 15 per cent or more year-by-year. New economic agencies like the War Production Board, War Manpower Commission, and the Office of Price Administration proliferated. The Office of Price Administration regulated prices to control inflation and rationed scarce commodities like gasoline, rubber, steel, shoes, coffee, sugar, and meat.[4] The nation also spent a lot on the manufacture of millions of tons of ships, and this huge spending provided a fiscal stimulus that played a major part in liquidising the under-consumption of the Great Depression.

The Roosevelt administration gradually adopted a co-operative stance towards big business, as corporations were essential to run the new wartime agencies and provide financial favour.

The United Nations and Cold War Politics

Even before the end of WWII, the American policymakers were deciding on post-war peace arrangements. In the Atlantic Charter of 1941, and a conference in Moscow in 1943, the Allied Powers thought of creating a new international organization for peace as the League of Nations foundered on many a rock. At the Dumbarton Oaks Conference in Washington in August 1944, and at a meeting of 50 nations in San Francisco, the United Nations was established with the United States playing a major role and becoming one of the five permanent members of the U.N. Security Council.[5]

American policy and attitude towards USSR sharply differed during and after the War. Roosevelt struck a conciliatory tone with Stalin as long as Russian military was imperative to defeat Germany; but in the post-Roosevelt era, the Soviet sphere of influence in Eastern Europe was the germ seed behind bipolar tensions and generation of what historians term as 'cold war' or 'hot peace' between the US and the USSR which went on till the dissolution of the USSR in the late 1980s.

At the Yalta Conference in 1945, Germany was divided into four zones with USSR-dominated zones in the east. Berlin was also divided. The Poland issue enraged the Americans when Russia tried to control it and prevented free election there. After the dropping of atom bombs, Little Boy and Fat Man at Hiroshima and Nagasaki, respectively, and the final defeat of Japan, Japan-controlled Korea was divided into separate zones of operation, establishing US and USSR controls. All these were long-lasting scars in the US-USSR relationship in the next few decades.

The US called for a global stand against communism and concentrated on both economic policies and military strategies at home front and outside. The US actively sought allies, which it subsidized with military and economic foreign aid, and also diplomatic support. The Truman Doctrine, a policy set forth by President Harry S. Truman on 12 March 1947 stating that the US would support Greece and Turkey with economic and military aid to prevent their falling into the Soviet sphere, initiated Cold War politics. The Doctrine was 'the policy of the United States to support free people who are resisting attempted subjugation by armed minorities or by outside pressures'[6] (**Annexure 1**). America sent $400 million, and in 1952, both Greece and Turkey joined North Atlantic Treaty Organization (NATO), the military alliance that guaranteed their protection. In June 1947, in accordance with the Truman Doctrine, the United States enacted the Marshall Plan, a pledge of economic assistance for all European countries willing to participate, including the Soviet Union. Its aim was to rebuild the democratic and economic systems of Europe and to counter perceived threats to Europe's balance of power, such as communist parties seizing control through revolutions or elections.[7] Stalin prevented the Eastern Bloc nations from receiving Marshall Plan aid and involved Soviet subsidies and trade with Eastern Europe, known as the Molotov Plan which was later institutionalized in January 1949 as the Comecon.

Next, the containment policy was developed by US diplomat George Kennan in 1947 that opposed the spread of communism. The Soviet Union was characterized as an aggressive, anti-Western power that necessitated containment, i.e. to match Soviet aggression by US with force wherever it occurred while not using nuclear weapons. The policy created a bipolar, zero-sum world where the ideological conflicts between the Soviet Union and the United States dominated geopolitics. Due to the antagonism on both sides and search for security, a tense worldwide contest developed between the two states as both the nations vied for global supremacy militarily, culturally, and influentially. John M. Murrin argues that, 'containment became a catchphrase for a global anticommunist national security policy.'[8] Confronted with the communist revolution in China, and the end of the American atomic monopoly in 1949, the Truman administration aimed at escalating and expanding the containment policy.

The containment policy was expanded into Asia, Africa, and Latin America in order to counter revolutionary nationalist movements. John Gaddis argues that America was conscious to put an assault on these movements, fighting against the restoration of Europe's colonial empires in South-East Asia and elsewhere, that were often led by communist parties financed by the USSR.[9] The US also formalized a series of alliances and pacts with Japan, Australia, New Zealand, Thailand, and the Philippines, notably the ANZUS (Australia, New Zealand, United States Security) Treaty in 1951, and SEATO (South East Asia Treaty Organization) in 1954, thereby guaranteeing the United States a number of long-term military bases. Hence this phase is often referred to as 'pactomania'.

So far as the 'Third World' was concerned, the nations that went through the process of decolonization and other 'under-developed' nations, the United States and the Soviet Union increasingly competed for influence which included the sell of armaments in the 1950s and 1960s. In 1953, President Eisenhower's Central Intelligence Agency (CIA) implemented Operation Ajax which aimed at the overthrow of the Iranian Prime Minister, Mohammad Mosaddegh who was 'increasingly turning towards communism' and was moving Iran towards the Soviet sphere.[10] Mohammad Reza Pahlavi assumed control as an autocratic monarch and immediately banned the communist Tudeh Party. In

Guatemala, a CIA-backed military coup ousted the left-wing President Jacobo Arbenz Guzmán in 1954 followed by the establishment of a military junta headed by Carlos Castillo Armas. Armas returned nationalized American property, set up a National Committee of Defense Against Communism, and decreed Preventive Penal Law Against Communism at the request of the United States.[11] Peace accords signed in Geneva left Vietnam divided between a pro-Soviet administration in North Vietnam and a pro-Western administration in South Vietnam. Between 1954 and 1961, Eisenhower administration sent economic aid and military advisers to strengthen South Vietnam's pro-Western regime to destabilize the communist efforts. When The Kennedy administration sought ways to oust communist Fidel Castro's government, Russia prepared to install nuclear missiles in Cuba in response. John Gaddis remarks in *The Cold War: A New History* that the Cuban Missile Crisis of 1962 brought the world closer to nuclear war than ever before.[12] In Chile, when the Socialist Party candidate Salvador Allende won the presidential election of 1970, becoming the first democratically elected Marxist to become president of a country in the Americas, General Augusto Pinochet, backed by CIA, carried out a violent coup against the government in September 1973 and quickly consolidated all political power as a military dictator; Allende's economic reforms were rolled back, and leftist opponents were killed or detained in internment camps under the Dirección de Inteligencia Nacional (DINA). The US also backed dictators in Argentina, Brazil, Bolivia, Chile, Uruguay, and Paraguay to suppress leftist dissent. US foreign policy objectives during the Cold War period also involved it her in Yom Kippur War in the Middle East,[13] and later, the policy of aiding anti-Soviet Mujahideen forces in Afghanistan under Operation Cyclone.[14]

However, many emerging decolonized nations of Asia, Africa, and Latin America rejected the pressure to choose sides in the East-West competition, and the 1955 conference at Bandung in Indonesia created the stepping stone for the Non Alignment Movement, transforming the post-War order into a more pluralistic world of decolonized African and Middle Eastern nations and of rising nationalism in Asia and Latin America.[15]

The Cold War ended with the American victory. In 1980, Ronald Reagan defeated Jimmy Carter in the 1980 presidential election and formulated his Doctrine that emphasized increased military spending to confront the Soviets everywhere (**annexure 2**). Reagan and British Prime

Minister Margaret Thatcher denounced the Soviet ideology and labelled the Soviet Union an 'evil empire' predicting that communism would be left on the 'ash heap of history'.[16] The CIA sought to weaken the Soviet Union by promoting political Islam in the majority-Muslim Central Asian Soviet Union. It also encouraged anti-communist Pakistan's Inter-Services Intelligence (ISI) agency to train Muslims from around the world to participate in the *jihad* against USSR.

In 1985, when Mikhail Gorbachev became the General Secretary of the Soviet Union, the economy showed a downward spiral seeking for deeper structural changes. In June 1987, Gorbachev announced an agenda of economic reform called *perestroika* or restructuring that relaxed the production quota system, allowed private ownership of businesses and paved the way for foreign investment, and *glasnost* or openness, which increased freedom of the press and the transparency of state institutions. These measures enabled increased contact between Soviet citizens and the Western world, particularly the United States. Soviets officially declared their will of no further intervention in the affairs of allied states in Eastern Europe. Oil and gas subsidies and the cost of maintaining massive troops represented a substantial economic drain for the Soviet government. Gorbachev and George Bush declared the Cold War to be over at the Malta Summit on 3 December 1989. Soviet forces withdrew from Afghanistan, and by 1990, Gorbachev consented to German reunification. Revolutionary wave swept across Central and Eastern Europe including Poland, Hungary, Czechoslovakia, Bulgaria, Romania, etc., to overthrow the Soviet-led communist regime. A growing number of Soviet republics, particularly Russia threatened to secede from the USSR and the later was severely weakened by a failed coup against the revolutionary states. The Commonwealth of Independent States was created on 21 December 1991 that represented a loose confederation, and the USSR was declared officially dissolved on 25 December 1991, leaving the world unipolar and providing an entire space for American domination and hegemony.

The Post-Cold War Era

During the 1990s, the United States concentrated on scaling back its foreign policy budget and Cold War defence budget which amounted to

6.5 per cent of the GDP and focussed on domestic economic prosperity under President Clinton. The 9/11 attacks on the World Trade Centre and Pentagon gave way to a trend of unilateral action under President Bush to combat what was seen to be the growing trend of fundamentalist terrorism in the Middle East. Reasons for the attacks stated in several sources include the support of Israel by the United States, presence of the US military in the Kingdom of Saudi Arabia, and the US enforcement of sanctions against Iraq.[17] Bush immediately declared 'War on Terrorism' and US foreign policy embarked on two military campaigns in the Middle East, in Afghanistan and Iraq. When no Weapons of Mass Destruction (WMDs) were found after the military conquest of Iraq, there was worldwide scepticism on the actual American purpose that had severe negative public relations consequences for the image of the United States. Bernard Lewis in his 2004 book *The Crisis of Islam: Holy War and Unholy Terror* gives a very interesting analysis within a comprehensive historical backdrop and argues that animosity toward the west has to be understood with the decline of the once powerful Ottoman Empire, compounded by the import of western ideas – Arab socialism, Arab liberalism, and Arab secularism. He remarks,

> During the past three centuries, the Islamic world has lost its dominance and its leadership, and has fallen behind both the modern West and the rapidly modernizing Orient. This widening gap poses increasingly acute problems, both practical and emotional, for which the rulers, thinkers, and rebels of Islam have not yet found effective answers.[18]

In an essay titled 'The spirit of terrorism', Jean Baudrillard described 9/11 as the first global event that 'questions the very process of globalization.'[19]

Conclusion

America dominated the international scene since the WWII and we have seen how it tried to intervene into matters relating to the other states and nations. While there was political intervention through the formulation and imposition of the 'development' discourse, the US deeply intervened into economic, social and cultural, and environmental spheres causing catastrophes and leading to what Andre Gunder Frank calls 'development of underdevelopment' of the decolonized 'Third World'.[20] The International Monetary Fund (IMF) and the International Bank for Reconstruction and Development (IBRD), which later became the World Bank emerged from the Bretton Woods Agreements when 44 Allied nations with US as the leader met at Bretton Woods, New Hampshire, United States in July 1944 to set up a system of rules, institutions, and procedures to regulate the international monetary system. The effect of this for the 'Third World' was deleterious when their economy was tactfully tied up under the Structural Adjustment Programmes (SAPs) launched by the west. In the aftermath of the Cold War, America was the sole power to control and take unanimous decisions in global politics and economy.

Globalization nakedly revealed the dichotomy between rich and poor economies, the later failing to uplift their standards at the cost of more economic prosperity of the former. Along with economic programmes to actually 'recolonize' the so-called 'decolonized' nations there were extra-economic socio-cultural strategies to make space for the ideological justification of imperialist west, imperative for protest management. Yet, in the last few decades the alternative trend is also visible with grassroots movements protesting and contesting against globalization.[21] These movements are still not consolidated, and what is required is the independent initiatives of the non-western, Southern countries; the most challenging task is creating a bridge between anti-imperialist popular struggles in non-west and South with that small (yet active) part of the North which is critical of the excesses of globalization and counters its devastating impact in both the domestic and outer fronts.[22]

Annotated Bibliography

- John M. Murrin, Paul E. Johnson, and James M. Mcpherson's *Liberty, Equality, Power: A History of the American People* (USA: Wadsworth, 2008, 2012; Vol. 2: Since 1863, sixth edition) is the latest and most comprehensive documentation and analysis of American History integrating the best of recent social and cultural scholarship into a political story. It not only discusses the impact of the notions of liberty and equality, which are often associated with the American story, but also how dominant and subordinate groups have affected and been affected by the ever-shifting balance of power.

- In *Russia, the Soviet Union and the United States: An Interpretative History* (New York: McGraw-Hill, 1990) and *The Cold War: A New History* (New York: Penguin Press, 2005) John Gaddis unlocks the events that brought America and the Soviet Union in a deadly stalemate, applies prospographic approach to understand what was going on in the minds of Stalin, Reagan, Gorbachev, and others, and explores the long course of power struggles and its impact among nations.
- George F. Kennan's *American Diplomacy, 1900–1950* (Chicago: University of Chicago Press, 1951) is an evaluation of the diplomatic history of the US. Key themes include: the development and significance of the Cold War, the escalation of the nuclear arms race, and the American involvement in Vietnam, etc.
- Joyce P. Kaufman's *A Concise History of U.S. Foreign Policy* (U.K.: Rowman and Littlefield Publishers, 2009) offers a historical overview of American foreign relations from the founding to the present. With an analysis of the economics of US foreign policy, the book pays particular attention to the Cold War and beyond including the shifts and changes in the direction of American foreign policy in the aftermath of September 11.
- In *The Crisis of Islam: Holy War and Unholy Terror* (New York: Random House, 2004), Bernard Lewis provides explanation behind the 9/11 attacks from Islam's point of view.
- Amiya Bagchi's *The Perilous Passage: Mankind and the Global Ascendancy of Capital* (Lanham, MD: Rowman & Littlefield, 2005), Francis Robert Shor's *Dying Empire: U.S. Imperialism and Global Resistance* (USA, Canada: Routledge, 2010), and Arturo Escobar's 'Reflections on "development": Grassroots Approaches and Alternative Politics in the Third World' (*Futures*, Vol. 24, No. 5 (June 1992), pp. 411–36) are critical interpretations on the northern domination and hegemony of the south and the latter's response and reaction to it.

Annexure 1
Special Message to the Congress on Greece and Turkey: The Truman Doctrine, 12 March 1947

Mr. President, Mr. Speaker, Members of the Congress of the United States,

The gravity of the situation which confronts the world today necessitates my appearance before a joint session of the Congress.

The foreign policy and the national security of this country are involved.

One aspect of the present situation, which I present to you at this time for your consideration and decision, concerns Greece and Turkey.

The United States has received from the Greek Government an urgent appeal for financial and economic assistance. Preliminary reports from the American Economic Mission now in Greece and reports from the American Ambassador in Greece corroborate the statement of the Greek Government that assistance is imperative if Greece is to survive as a free nation.

I do not believe that the American people and the Congress wish to turn a deaf ear to the appeal of the Greek Government.

Greece is not a rich country. Lack of sufficient natural resources has always forced the Greek people to work hard to make both ends meet. Since 1940, this industrious, peace loving country has suffered invasion, four years of cruel enemy occupation, and bitter internal strife.

When forces of liberation entered Greece they found that the retreating Germans had destroyed virtually all the railways, roads, port facilities, communications, and merchant marine. More than a thousand villages had been burned. Eighty-five per cent of the children were tubercular. Livestock, poultry, and draft animals had almost disappeared. Inflation had wiped out practically all savings. As a result of these tragic conditions, a militant minority, exploiting human want and misery, was able to create political chaos which, until now, has made economic recovery impossible.

Greece is today without funds to finance the importation of those goods which are essential to bare subsistence. Under these circumstances the people of Greece cannot make progress in solving their problems of reconstruction. Greece is in desperate need of financial and economic assistance to enable it to resume purchases of food, clothing, fuel and seeds. These are indispensable for the subsistence of its people and are obtainable only from abroad. Greece must have help to import the goods necessary to restore internal order and security so essential for economic and political recovery.

The Greek Government has also asked for the assistance of experienced American administrators, economists and technicians to insure that the financial and other aid given to Greece shall be used effectively in creating a stable and self-sustaining economy and in improving its public administration. The very existence of the Greek state is today threatened by the terrorist activities of several thousand armed men, led by Communists, who defy the government's authority at a number of points, particularly along the northern boundaries. A Commission appointed by the United Nations Security Council is at present investigating disturbed conditions in northern Greece and alleged border violations along the frontier between Greece on the one hand and Albania, Bulgaria, and Yugoslavia on the other.

Meanwhile, the Greek Government is unable to cope with the situation. The Greek army is small and poorly equipped. It needs supplies and equipment if it is to restore authority to the government throughout Greek territory.

Greece must have assistance if it is to become a self-supporting and self-respecting democracy. The United States must supply this assistance. We have already extended to Greece certain types of relief and economic aid but these are inadequate.

There is no other country to which democratic Greece can turn.

No other nation is willing and able to provide the necessary support for a democratic Greek government.

The British Government, which has been helping Greece, can give no further financial or economic aid after March 31. Great Britain finds itself under the necessity of reducing or liquidating its commitments in several parts of the world, including Greece.

We have considered how the United Nations might assist in this crisis. But the situation is an urgent one requiring immediate action, and the United Nations and its related organizations are not in a position to extend help of the kind that is required.

It is important to note that the Greek Government has asked for our aid in utilizing effectively the financial and other assistance we may give to Greece, and in improving its public administration. It is of the utmost importance that we supervise the use of any funds made available to Greece, in such a manner that each dollar spent will count toward making Greece self-supporting, and will help to build an economy in which a healthy democracy can flourish.

No government is perfect. One of the chief virtues of a democracy, however, is that its defects are always visible and under democratic processes can be pointed out and corrected. The government of Greece is not perfect. Nevertheless it represents 85 per cent of the members of the Greek Parliament who were chosen in an election last year. Foreign observers, including 692 Americans, considered this election to be a fair expression of the views of the Greek people.

The Greek Government has been operating in an atmosphere of chaos and extremism. It has made mistakes. The extension of aid by this country does not mean that the United States condones everything that the Greek Government has done or will do. We have condemned in the past, and we condemn now, extremist measures of the right or the left. We have in the past advised tolerance, and we advise tolerance now. Greece's neighbor, Turkey, also deserves our attention.

The future of Turkey as an independent and economically sound state is clearly no less important to the freedom-loving peoples of the world than the future of Greece. The circumstances in which Turkey finds itself today are considerably different from those of Greece. Turkey has been spared the disasters that have beset Greece. And during the war, the United States and Great Britain furnished Turkey with material aid.

Nevertheless, Turkey now needs our support.

Since the war Turkey has sought additional financial assistance from Great Britain and the United States for the purpose of effecting that modernization necessary for the maintenance of its national integrity.

That integrity is essential to the preservation of order in the Middle East.

The British Government has informed us that, owing to its own difficulties, it can no longer extend financial or economic aid to Turkey.

As in the case of Greece, if Turkey is to have the assistance it needs, the United States must supply it. We are the only country able to provide that help.

I am fully aware of the broad implications involved if the United States extends assistance to Greece and Turkey, and I shall discuss these implications with you at this time.

One of the primary objectives of the foreign policy of the United States is the creation of conditions in which we and other nations will be able to work out a way of life free from coercion. This was a fundamental issue in the war with Germany and Japan. Our victory was won over countries which sought to impose their will, and their way of life, upon other nations.

To ensure the peaceful development of nations, free from coercion, the United States has taken a leading part in establishing the United Nations. The United Nations is designed to make possible lasting freedom and independence for all its members. We shall not realize our objectives, however, unless we are willing to help free peoples to maintain their free institutions and their national integrity against aggressive movements that seek to impose upon them totalitarian regimes. This is no more than a frank recognition that totalitarian regimes imposed upon free peoples, by direct or indirect aggression, undermine the foundations of international peace and hence the security of the United States.

The peoples of a number of countries of the world have recently had totalitarian regimes forced upon them against their will. The Government of the United States has made frequent protests against coercion and intimidation, in violation of the Yalta agreement, in Poland, Rumania, and Bulgaria. I must also state that in a number of other countries there have been similar developments. At the present moment in world history nearly every nation must choose between alternative ways of life. The choice is too often not a free one.

One way of life is based upon the will of the majority, and is distinguished by free institutions, representative government, free elections, guarantees of individual liberty, freedom of speech and religion, and freedom from political oppression.

The second way of life is based upon the will of a minority forcibly imposed upon the majority. It relies upon terror and oppression, a controlled press and radio, fixed elections, and the suppression of personal freedoms.

I believe that it must be the policy of the United States to support free peoples who are resisting attempted subjugation by armed minorities or by outside pressures.

I believe that we must assist free peoples to work out their own destinies in their own way. I believe that our help should be primarily through economic and financial aid which is essential to economic stability and orderly political processes.

The world is not static, and the status quo is not sacred. But we cannot allow changes in the status quo in violation of the Charter of the United Nations by such methods as coercion, or by such subterfuges as political infiltration. In helping free and independent nations to maintain their freedom, the United States will be giving effect to the principles of the Charter of the United Nations.

It is necessary only to glance at a map to realize that the survival and integrity of the Greek nation are of grave importance in a much wider situation. If Greece should fall under the control of an armed minority, the effect upon its neighbor, Turkey, would be immediate and serious. Confusion and disorder might well spread throughout the entire Middle East.

Moreover, the disappearance of Greece as an independent state would have a profound effect upon those countries in Europe whose peoples are struggling against great difficulties to maintain their freedoms and their independence while they repair the damages of war.

It would be an unspeakable tragedy if these countries, which have struggled so long against overwhelming odds, should lose that victory for which they sacrificed so much. Collapse of free institutions and loss of independence would be disastrous not only for them but for the world. Discouragement and possibly failure would quickly be the lot of neighboring peoples striving to maintain their freedom and independence.

Should we fail to aid Greece and Turkey in this fateful hour, the effect will be far reaching to the West as well as to the East.

We must take immediate and resolute action.

I therefore ask the Congress to provide authority for assistance to Greece and Turkey in the amount of $400,000,000 for the period ending 30 June 1948. In requesting these funds, I have taken into consideration the maximum amount of relief assistance which would be furnished to Greece out of the $350,000,000 which I recently requested that the Congress authorize for the prevention of starvation and suffering in countries devastated by the war.

In addition to funds, I ask the Congress to authorize the detail of American civilian and military personnel to Greece and Turkey, at the request of those countries, to assist in the tasks of reconstruction, and for the purpose of supervising the use of such financial and material assistance as may be furnished. I recommend that authority also be provided for the instruction and raining of selected Greek and Turkish personnel.

Finally, I ask that the Congress provide authority which will permit the speediest and most effective use, in terms of needed commodities, supplies, and equipment, of such funds as may be authorized. If further funds, or further authority, should be needed for the purposes indicated in this message, I shall not hesitate to bring the situation before the Congress. On this subject the Executive and Legislative branches of the Government must work together.

This is a serious course upon which we embark. I would not recommend it except that the alternative is much more serious.

The United States contributed $341,000,000,000 toward winning World War II. This is an investment in world freedom and world peace.

The assistance that I am recommending for Greece and Turkey amounts to little more than 1/10 of 1 per cent of this investment. It is only common sense that we should safeguard this investment and make sure that it was not in vain.

The seeds of totalitarian regimes are nurtured by misery and want. They spread and grow in the evil soil of poverty and strife. They reach their full growth when the hope of a people for a better life has died.

We must keep that hope alive.

The free peoples of the world look to us for support in maintaining their freedoms.

If we falter in our leadership, we may endanger the peace of the world–and we shall surely endanger the welfare of this Nation.

Great responsibilities have been placed upon us by the swift movement of events.

I am confident that the Congress will face these responsibilities squarely.

Annexure 2
Message on the Observance of Afghanistan Day: The Reagan Doctrine, 21 March 1983

Today, March 21st, is New Years Day in much of the Moslem world. New years, of course, should be an occasion for celebration. But for the Moslem people of Afghanistan, whose country was attacked and is occupied by the Soviet Army, it is a bitter reminder of a national calamity that befell their nation more than 3 years ago. To focus the world's attention on this crime against an innocent and brave nation, we observe today the second annual Afghanistan Day.

In Afghanistan, tens of thousands of people have been killed, millions have lost their homes and their livelihood. Others have been subjected to torture and other atrocities, and many have been victims of the grisly chemical and biological weapons, including yellow rain–weapons the Soviets have used in violation of solemn international agreements. The consequences of this calamity extend to Pakistan, which has assumed the burden of sheltering and feeding nearly 3 million refugees.

Yet, while we condemn what has happened in Afghanistan, we are not without hope. To watch the courageous Afghan freedom fighters battle modern arsenals with simple hand-held weapons is an inspiration to those who love freedom. Their courage teaches us a great lesson–that there are things in this world worth defending.

To the Afghan people, I say on behalf of all Americans that we admire your heroism, your devotion to freedom, and your relentless struggle against your oppressors.

The Soviet people have known great suffering–more than other people. They should be able to sympathize with the terrible suffering of the Afghan people. To the Soviet leaders, I urge you in the name of humanity to end the bloodshed so that an independent Afghanistan can again take its place in the community of nations. The West has no designs upon Afghanistan. We do not threaten you there or anywhere on the globe. All we seek is the restoration of peace and freedom for a noble and brave people whom we remember today.

Note: The President's message was taped at 11:12 a.m. in his study adjoining the Oval Office at the White House.

Notes

1. George C. Herring, *From Colony to Superpower: U.S. Foreign Relations Since 1776* (Oxford: Oxford University Press, 2008), editor's introduction, p. xiv.
2. John M. Murrin, Paul E. Johnson, and James M. Mcpherson, *Liberty, Equality, Power: A History of the American People* (USA: Wadsworth, 2008, 2012), vol. 2: Since 1863, sixth edition, p. 884.
3. George C. Herring, *From Colony Superpower*; Michael Adas,. 'From Settler Colony to Global Hegemon: Integrating the Exceptionalist Narrative of the American Experience into World History', *The American Historical Review*, Vol. 106, No. 6 (December 2001), pp. 1692–1720.

4. George C. Herring, *From Colony Superpower*, p. 892.
5. America donated prime real estate in New York City and provided billions for its budget.
6. Truman Library Public Papers, 12 March 1947; available at: http://www.trumanlibrary.org/publicpapers/index.php?pid=2189&st=&st1= (date of access: 10.05.2012).
7. John Gaddis, *Russia, the Soviet Union and the United States: An Interpretative History* (New York: McGraw-Hill, 1990), p. 186.
8. John M. Murrin, et. al., *Liberty, Equality, Power*, p. 910.
9. John Gaddis, *The Cold War: A New History* (New York: Penguin Press, 2005), p. 212.
10. Mark J. Gasiorowski and Malcolm Byrne, *Mohammad Mosaddegh and the 1953 Coup in Iran* (Syracuse, New York: Syracuse University Press, 2004), p. 125.
11. Thomas Bulmer, *The Political Economy of Central America since 1920* (Cambridge: Cambridge University Press, 1987), p. 142.
12. John Gaddis, *The Cold War*, p. 82.
13. It was fought between Israel and a coalition of Arab states led by Egypt and Syria in 1973. America favoured Israel and under the decision of Secretary of State Kissinger supplied additional arms to Israel.
14. Operation Cyclone was a programme launched by CIA to arm, train, and finance Afghan *mujahideen* during the Soviet war in Afghanistan between 1979 and 1989. From Peter Bergen's *Holy War* (Free Press, 2001, p. 68) we find that it was one of the longest and most expensive covert CIA operations where funding began with $20–30 million per year in 1980 and rose to $630 million per year in 1987.
15. Samir Amin in one of his recent lectures delivered on March 2012 entitled 'The Countries of the South Take Their Own Independent Initiatives' at the seminar on *Marxism: Marx and Beyond* (a joint initiative by the Centre for Marxian Studies, Jadavpur University and the Institute of Development Studies Kolkata) has pointed out that the Bandung Conference of 1955 and the constitution of the Non Aligned Movement 'did not originate in the heads of the nationalist leaders' like Nehru and Sukarno, but 'was the product of a radical leftwing critique' and opened up 'possible socialist advances in the contemporary world'.
16. Gaddis, *The Cold War*, p. 197.
17. Sources included the videos of Ayman al-Zawahiri and Fatawā, interviews and videos and audio recordings of Osama bin Laden.
18. Bernard Lewis, *The Crisis of Islam: Holy War and Unholy Terror* (New York: Random House, 2004).
19. Jean Baudrillard, *The Spirit of Terrorism*, available at: http://homes.chass.utoronto.ca/~ikalmar/illustex/baudriterror.htm (date of access: 10.05.2012).

20. Sing C. Chew and Robert Denemark, eds, *The Development of Underdevelopment: Essays in Honor of Andre Gunder Frank* (California: Sage Publications, 1996).
21. Arturo Escobar, 'Reflections on 'Development': Grassroots Approaches and Alternative Politics in the Third World', *Futures*, Vol. 24, Issue 5 (June 1992), pp. 411–36; Francis Robert Shor, *Dying Empire: U.S. Imperialism and Global Resistance* (USA, Canada: Routledge, 2010).
22. Samir Amin, *Marxism*.

10

The Quest for Equality

The first section of this chapter deals with women's struggle for political rights and provides a detailed account of the entire course of political action from Seneca Falls Convention in 1848 till the ratification of the Nineteenth Amendment to the Constitution that granted women the right to vote. The section ends with a critical evaluation of the movement focussing on the elements of alienations and exclusions in it. The second section traces the quest for equality among the African-Americans, and how long and difficult the entire course had been till their fight brought final success through civil rights and suffrage. It is a detailed depiction from the origin of slavery in colonial America to emancipation through Reconstruction (the fruits of which were limited) to their final victory through legal battles and violent activism in the later part of the Civil Rights Movement.

a. Women Suffrage Movement, 1848–1920

There is a rich history of women's rights movements, especially initiatives pressing for women's political rights in every country against long-held notions of female inferiority. In her article 'Women Suffrage and the Left: An International Socialist-Feminist Perspective', Ellen Dubois rightly points out, 'It is difficult to imagine a richer subject for a comparative history of democracy than the enfranchisement of women… Whereas manhood suffrage, for instance, or the breaking of the political color bar, have occurred more erratically, with limited links between national experiences, woman suffrage has been a self-consciously transnational popular political movement.'[1] The results were hard-won by courageous women who risked ridicule, and even imprisonment, by confronting society's acceptance of gender inequality. There had been strict opposition from the well-educated and politically powerful yet absolutely gender-insensitive male stalwarts. Even the enlightenment thinkers during the days of the French Revolution like Jean Jacques Rousseau took conservative-traditional stance on the women question. Women in every society were viewed as biologically, and therefore, socially different from men, destined to play domestic roles inside the family rather than public, political ones.

The American society, partially influenced by social customs and taboos of Europe, as a part of its colonial legacy,[2] and partially standing on its own codes of ethics and morality, was not exceptional. The result of this time-immemorial exclusion, discrimination, and marginalization was the growing consciousness among the 'object' population that culminated in the American Women Suffrage Movement between the late nineteenth and early twentieth century.

Roots of the Movement: Status of Women in Nineteenth Century America

Like every other societies on the verge of political consolidation in the late eighteenth and early nineteenth centuries, the other face of the inclusiveness of citizenship was exclusion.[3] The American experiment that began as a Republic after ratification of the Constitution created political, social, and economic participation for its citizens, but not for women. Some of the nation's founding principles like the right to representation, in terms of taxation and other governmental issues did not apply to women, who could not participate in elections.[4]

American women faced severe inequality in all sectors including education, political, legal, economic, etc. There were no educational opportunities for women until Emma Hart Willard opened a seminary for girls in Troy, New York in 1821; and before the Civil War, there were only three colleges that women could attend. They were prohibited from the medical and legal professions; married women had to surrender many of their rights, including the right to own property, to their husbands. Between 1800 and 1850, a woman gave up so many rights when she married that lawyers said she entered a state of 'civil death'.[5] Married women had no legal right to their own wages, for they were considered incapable of spending their own or other people's money. In Massachusetts, before

1840, a woman could not, legally, be treasurer of her own sewing society unless some man was responsible for her.[6] If a married couple divorced, unlike most cases today, the husband kept custody over the children. If a woman's husband died without a will, a wife's right to inherit property was restricted to one-third of his estate. 'In New York a widow could inherit only a Bible, pictures, books, and the like under $50 in value, the spinning wheel, stove, loom, 10 sheep and two pigs. Along with clothes, bedding, etc., she received one table, six chairs, six knives and forks, six tea cups and saucers, one sugar dish, one milk-pot and six spoons.'[7]

Care-based ethics, issues of morality, virtue, patience, love, silence, obedience, generosity, perseverance, and purity were attached to womanhood; the ideological constructs being powerful to justify the restriction of women in the private domain. It was determined that the more virtuous women maintained a more stable home life. The private-public divide is very well reflected in Alfred Lord Tennyson's remark, 'Man for the field, woman for the hearth, man for the sword and for the needle she; man with the head and woman with the heart, man to command and woman to obey; all else confusion.'[8] Gender inequality generated multiple repercussions among different classes of white American women. While the poor accepted it as their fate, the middle and upper classes indulged themselves in penning their experiences sharply criticizing the laws and norms of their contemporary parochial society. Elaine Showalter has edited and compiled an interesting volume consisting of short stories of few renowned and less familiar women that reveal a universe of feelings and emotions hidden beneath a sectarian system.[9] Women writers wrote short stories, which became the national genre in the nineteenth century, the most important outlet for their particular experiences.

The public entry of women as workforce and reformers seemed to be the turning points leading to the dawn of political awareness. The rapid spread of the New England textile mills with large-scale manufacturing units in Lowell and Massachusetts led to the absorption of the New England women into labour market. The dual bind of class and gender exploitation was predominant in the mills and factories. Their labour was subjugated; women and children worked long hours in the cotton and woollen mills and they were paid much less from their male counterparts. But the entry of women into the labour market led to the dawn of working-class women consciousness, when out of their father's farms and homes, they found themselves independent, formed a collective, became aware of their claims and rights, and took every opportunity to assert that.[10] The mill owners required women to attend churches which bestowed inferiority on women where they had no voice; they were asked to cultivate silence, obedience, and piety. But the impact was paradoxical and Elizabeth Frost-Knappman and Kathryn Cullen-DuPont rightly interprets that religion became 'a major impediment to the broadening of women's rights.'[11] When working women attended churches, they organized numerous societies that worked for social causes like: fund raising for charity, children's education, anti-liquor demonstrations, etc. These societies (where women learnt how to organize meetings, deliver speeches, raise money on their own, etc.) became the baseline for the later activities of women in the women's rights movement.

Women Suffrage Movement: The Various Phases

Agitation for equal suffrage surfaced with the beginning of the nineteenth century, though it remained restricted among few for the first few decades. Frances Wright, a Scottish woman who came to the United States in 1826, advocated women suffrage in an extensive series of lectures. In 1836 Ernestine Rose, a Polish woman, came to the country and carried on a similar campaign so effectively that she obtained a personal hearing before the New York Legislature. Though her petition bore only five signatures but that was a crucial initiative breaking the traditional portrayal of women. In 1840, Lucretia Mott and Margaret Fuller became active in Boston and Fuller composed an essay entitled *The Great Lawsuit: Man vs. Woman*.[12] Fuller concluded with an apprehension,

> And will not she soon appear? The woman who shall vindicate their birthright for all women; who shall teach them what to claim, and how to use what they obtain? Shall not her name be for her era Victoria, for her country and her life Virginia? Yet predictions are rash; she herself must teach us to give her the fitting name.[13]

'The woman', aware of her own rights and fearless to make claims, soon appeared to change her own destiny and traditional status in the United States.

The nomination of Gerrit Smith as the Liberty Party's presidential candidate on 29 June 1848 in Rochester, New York was a significant development and a prelude to the **Seneca Falls Convention of July 1848** which was a landmark event in the entire movement for women suffrage. In his address at the National Liberty Convention held during 14–15 June in Buffalo, New York, Smith called for a demand for 'universal suffrage in its broadest sense, females as well as males being entitled to vote.'[14] The delegates approved the demand addressing suffrage rights for women. Five votes were placed calling for Lucretia Mott to act as Smith's vice-president; the first time in the United States that a woman was nominated for federal executive office. The addresses, discussions, and speeches promoted for the cause of gender equality,

> Neither here, nor in any other part of the world, is the right of suffrage allowed to extend beyond one of the sexes. This universal exclusion of woman... argues, conclusively, that, not as yet, is there one nation so far emerged from barbarism, and so far practically Christian, as to permit woman to rise up to the one level of the human family.[15]

Between 19 and 20 July 1848, the Seneca Falls Convention on women's rights was hosted by Lucretia Mott, Mary Ann M'Clintock, and Elizabeth Cady Stanton in New York where 300 men and women participated. Many sessions were conducted within the span of these two days which mainly focussed on the role of women in society. Stanton and Mott presented the *Declaration of Sentiments* and an accompanying list of resolutions that demanded women's right to vote (at Stanton's insistence), equal education, equal access to trades and professions, equality in marriage, and the rights to make contracts, to own property, to sue and be sued, to testify in court, and to have guardianship over children.[16] A heated debate followed over the issue of resolution nine that declared, 'That it is the duty of women of this country to secure to themselves their sacred right to the elective franchise,' Mott herself urging the removal of this concept. The resolution was passed by a small margin as many women feared at that time that the demand for vote would work against their other set of demands turning the entire exercise unfruitful. Finally, Frederick Douglass put an end to the inconclusive debate, eloquently arguing for its inclusion; the suffrage resolution was retained. 68 women and 32 men among 300 attendees signed the document.

The convention was not positively looked upon by many, and women participants faced a storm of ridicule especially from the press with few exceptions like Douglass's *The North Star* and Horace Greeley's *Tribune*. The meetings were called 'the most shocking and unnatural incident ever recorded in the history of womanity.'[17] The *Worcester Telegraph* in Massachusetts opined, 'The list of grievances which the Amazons exhibit, concludes by expressing a determination to insist that women shall have 'immediate admission to all rights and privileges which belong to them as citizens of the United States' . . . This is bolting with a vengeance.'[18] As a result of this ill treatment and animosity, many of the 100 people who had signed the declaration eventually withdrew their names.

But in spite of all these, the Seneca Falls Convention can be considered as the revolutionary beginning to the struggle by women for political rights, the *Declaration of Sentiments* being the foundational document in the movement. The Seneca Falls Convention was a huge success in the sense that within months, preparations for conventions began in other states including Massachusetts, Indiana, Pennsylvania, and Ohio. Historian S.G. McMillen rightly remarks that it was a glorious moment when the push for women suffrage first gained national prominence,[19] and Elizabeth Frost-Knappman and Kathryn Cullen-DuPont further add on its significance, 'A program had been put forth and a leadership established. The women's rights movement in America had officially begun.'[20]

In 1850, the National Women's Rights Convention was organized at Worcester that brought together the leading lights of American feminism like Lucretia Mott, Paulina Kellogg Wright Davis, Abby Kelley Foster, William Lloyd Garrison, and Wendell Phillips. It brought together many of those who had been working individually for women's rights and highlighted some of the challenges of unifying strongly opinionated leaders into one movement. It introduced Lucy Stone, the morning star of the woman's movement, to the leaders of Seneca Falls. The deliberations attracted many from the audience to join the cause. From the account of Elinor R. Hays, we find that the stirring speech delivered to 1000 audience by Lucy Stone on the closing day of the convention inspired Susan B. Anthony (later to become one of the greatest proponents of Women Suffrage Movement) to join the cause.[21]

National conventions were held every year mainly under the initiatives of women's rights advocates, and by 1860, few achievements were accomplished. In Indiana, divorces could be granted on the basis not only of adultery but on desertion, drunkenness, and cruelty; in New York, Indiana, Maine, Missouri, and Ohio, women's property rights expanded to allow married women to keep their own wages.

During the Civil War, strategic differences among suffragists appeared within the political context of the time. The Fourteenth Amendment to the Constitution introducing gender restriction and pushing forward suffrage only for American-American males was the germ seed behind such schism.[22] Fearing that this was not 'negro suffrage,' but male suffrage expanded, Anthony and Stanton immediately opposed it and Anthony even travelled throughout the Northeast to convince other women's rights leaders to oppose it as well.[23] In *The Revolution,* published in January 1868, Anthony and Stanton made harsh criticisms of the Republican Party.[24] They prepared a petition which requested a constitutional amendment prohibiting states from disfranchising any of their citizens on the ground of sex. But not many supported it, and 'Even worse, in Stanton's view, was the fact that women themselves were torn.'[25]

In November 1868, in Boston, at the largest women's rights convention, Lucy Stone, her husband Henry Browne Blackwell, Isabella Beecher Hooker, Julia Ward Howe, and Thomas Wentworth Higginson formed a new organization called the **New England Woman Suffrage Association (NEWSA)** which was, according to feminist historian Dubois, the first major political society established for the sole purpose of gaining suffrage for women.[26] NEWSA was a pro-Republican group, with men in important leadership positions, designed to attract an alliance with that political party and this Republican connection pushed it in the direction of advocating voting rights for the African-American male. At the first NEWSA convention, Douglass declared that 'the cause of the negro was more pressing than that of woman's.'[27]

Later in 1869, Lucy Stone, Julia Ward Howe, and Josephine Ruffin formed the **American Woman Suffrage Association (AWSA)** in Boston which was a much larger and more moderate organization including both men and women in its membership. It supported the Fifteenth Amendment and resolved to gain the incremental victory of black men's voting rights before moving forward to achieve women's voting rights. AWSA continued working at the state level to secure women's voting rights after the passage of the Fifteenth Amendment.

In May 1869, the **National Woman Suffrage Association (NWSA)** was formed by Susan B. Anthony and Elizabeth Cady Stanton with the primary object of securing an amendment to the Constitution in favour of women's suffrage. This group, mainly consisting of women, also opposed the passage of the Fifteenth Amendment which declared that the right of citizens of the United States to vote shall not be denied or abridged by the United States or by any state on account of race, colour, or previous condition of servitude, unless it was modified to guarantee to women's right to vote. NWSA disagreed to Stone's position that it was essential that women desiring the franchise for them do not alarm those holding the power to grant it. Again, to Stone, Stanton was 'utterly indiscreet'[28] as She did not even think twice before making radical comments as,

> When I think of all the wrongs that have been heaped upon womankind, I am ashamed that I am not forever in a condition of chronic wrath, stark mad, skin and bone, my eyes a fountain of tears, my lips overflowing with curses, and my hand against every man and brother! Ah, how I do repent me of the male faces I have washed, the mittins I have knit, the trousers mended, the cut fingers and broken toes I have bound up![29]

After nearly 20 years of differences and divergences,[30] which historians Elizabeth Frost-Knappman and Kathryn Cullen-DuPont refer to as 'separate paths to suffrage'[31], the **National American Woman Suffrage Association (NAWSA)** was formed in 1890 uniting the two groups **NWSA** and **AWSA**.

Stanton was elected president; Anthony, vice president; Stone, chair man of the executive committee; and Stone's daughter, Alice Stone Blackwell, corresponding secretary. In 'Beneath the Suffrage Narrative', Grace Farrell remarks that the Anthony faction rewrote history to obscure the roles of Stone and Stanton.[32]

World War I provided the final push for women suffrage in America, and women were up in arms with President Woodrow Wilson's announcement of the inevitability of the war for democracy. Alice Paul and Lucy Burns of the **National Women's Party (NWP)**[33] led a series of protests against the Wilson Administration in Washington, becom ing the first to picket outside the White House. On 20 June 1917, suffragettes unfurled a banner that stated, 'We women of America tell you that America is not a democracy. Twenty million women are denied the right

Table 10.1: Presidents of NAWSA

Women Candidates	Tenure
Elizabeth Cady Stanton	1890–92
Susan B. Anthony	1892–1900
Carrie Chapman Catt	1900–04
Anna Howard Shaw	1904–15
Carrie Chapman Catt	1915–20

Source: Information collected from Ellen C. Dubois's *Woman Suffrage and Women's Rights* (New York and London: New York University Press, 1998); Elizabeth Frost-Knappman and Kathryn Cullen-DuPont's *Women's Suffrage in America* (New York: facts on File Inc., 2005), updated edition.

to vote. President Wilson is the chief opponent of their national enfranchisement.'[34] The women activists faced severe opposition, many were subject to arrests and others jailed.[35] But the flames of revolution did not extinguish. Within these circumstances, Wilson finally changed his position in 1918 to advocate women suffrage as a war measure. The next year, the Congress passed the Nineteenth Amendment giving women the right to vote. On 5 June (Thursday), 1919, *The New York Times* published a report, 'Suffrage Wins in Senate: Now Goes to States' which reflected that in addition to the strategy to obtain full suffrage through a constitutional amendment, reformers pursued state-by-state campaigns to build support for, or to win, residence-based state suffrage.[36]

It was crucial that the amendment passed and made effective before the general elections of 1920. A special session of the Congress and a bill introducing the amendment was brought by the President before the House again. On 21 May 1919, it was passed, 42 votes more than necessary being obtained, and on 4 June 1919, it was brought before the Senate and passed with 56 ayes and 25 nays. Illinois, Wisconsin, and Michigan ratified the amendment, their legislatures being then in session. Other states followed suit until the amendment had been ratified by 35 of the necessary 36 state legislatures. Washington ratified on 22 March 1920, followed by Tennessee on 18 August 1920. On 26 August 1920, the Nineteenth Amendment to the Constitution was finally ratified, making it the law throughout the United States. The National American Woman Suffrage Association was resolved into the National League of Women

Voters. American women were enfranchised, and it was declared for the first time that they, like men, deserve all the rights and responsibilities of citizenship. In an interesting study, Lynn Dumenil depicts how the newly enlarged electorate was taken care of by politicians of both the parties, emphasizing issues of special interest to women like prohibition, child health, public schools, and world peace.[37]

Alienations and Exclusions: A Critical Evaluation of the Movement

'When the woman suffrage movement is given its due, we may begin to understand the process by which democratic hope turned into mass political alienation, which is the history of modern American politics',[38] remarks feminist historian Ellen Carol Dubois, provoking a deeper analysis of the movement that shows that it was not at all inclusive along class and racial lines. The issues that divided the late nineteenth century women's movement in America included religion, sex, and family, and the role of the state in women's liberation.[39]

Political rights for the men of colour found stark opposition from the so-called 'progressive' advocates of women's rights. At the height of tension, some suffragists resorted to crude racism. They issued a poster of a brutish-looking Negro porter sitting next to a refined-looking White lady with a caption that read 'He can vote; why can't I?'[40] However, all suffragists did not think on the same line and there were divergences in views and arguments that led to a split in the movement.

When the Republicans proposed a Fourteenth Amendment to the United States Constitution that would enfranchise the two million newly freed men of colour in 1865, suffragists, in an effort to secure their political rights alongside freedmen, resolved to merge the abolitionist and suffragist movements into one single movement under the umbrella of **American Equal Rights Association (AERA)** whose objective was to 'secure Equal Rights to all American citizens, especially the right of suffrage, irrespective of race, color, or sex.'[41] This was the implementation of an idea, which was officially proposed by female suffrage activists Lucy Stone and Susan B. Anthony at an antislavery meeting in January, 1866 into action. However, the Republicans began to collaborate more closely with the abolitionists during the period of Reconstruction and believed that black suffrage, held far more prospects than women suffrage as a party measure in national politics. The Republican cry, 'This is the negro's hour,'[42] antagonized and alienated many of the women leaders. And it has been already discussed that how this resulted into a bone of contention within the Women Suffrage Movement leading to the formation of Stone- and Blackwell-led AWSA and Stanton- and Anthony-led NWSA. Dubois argues in her book *Feminism and Suffrage* that Stanton and Anthony's steadfast commitment to George Francis Train, a known racist, who however advocated women's suffrage, left suffragists vulnerable to the Republican accusation that the Democratic Party was only using women's suffrage to defeat black suffrage, thus giving black equal rights supporters reason to feel animosity towards suffragists.[43] On the other hand, Anthony severely criticized the Republican stance and reflected in *The Revolution*,

> While the dominant party have with one hand lifted up two million black men and crowned them with the honor and dignity of citizenship, with the other they have dethroned fifteen million white women – their own mothers and sisters, their own wives and daughters – and cast them under the heel of the lowest orders of manhood.[44]

Later in 1890, the AWSA and NWSA united to form the NAWSA that finally earned victory to the cause of women suffrage. But the gains and achievements were accomplished by and for the upper and upper-middle class white women.[45] It is interesting to note that when Susan B. Anthony was leading the New York Woman Suffrage Movement and collecting signatures for a petition and also trying to raise fund as she recognized a great opportunity in the constitutional convention of 1894, elite women did not find it wise to cooperate with her and rather formed their own organization. They get themselves in the movement with an agenda of men of their class that the influence of the wealthy in government had to be strengthened and with their vote they would be able to increase the political power of their class. Philanthropist Olivia (Mrs. Russell) Sage even went to the extent of presenting woman suffrage as an antidote to the growing and dangerous 'idleness' of elite women, who had forgotten their responsibility to set the moral tone for society. The problem for elite suffragists was that woman suffrage meant the enfranchisement of working-class, as well as elite women. The elite women believed that their class would provide political leadership for all women once they had the vote; they guided ignorant working class women (whom they considered too weak, timid, and disorganized) that they could be made to counterbalance, when necessary, with the votes of ignorant and interested men. Stanton was sharply against enfranchising non-educated working class women which was criticized by her daughter Militance Harriot Stanton Blatch who insisted the claims of the working women group. And it is important to mention in this context that the twentieth century was different from nineteenth century-definitions of the unity of women that emphasized their place in the home, their motherhood, and their exclusion from the economy, and instead stressed the unity that productive work provided for all women. The Women's Trade Union League (WTUL) was formed in 1903, a coalition of working-class and elite women to draw wage-earning women into trade unions. In 1907, Blatch formed the Equality League of Self-Supporting Women, a suffrage organization that provided the medium for introducing a new and aggressive style of (militant) activism into the suffrage movement. But the perspectives of the leaders and associations had elitism in it and there was a unique paradox: the women of these organizations could neither repudiate the Socialist support they were attracting and alienate working-class women, nor associate too closely with Socialists, and lose access to the wealthy.[46]

Thus, like all other movements for citizenship, the Women Suffrage Movement in America between 1848 and 1920 was not inclusive. This issue has been theoretically addressed by Immanuel Wallerstein in his article 'Citizens All? Citizens Some! The Making of the Citizen' published in *Comparative Studies in Society and History* in 2003.[47] He points out that as the social/labour movements had great difficulty in accepting the legitimacy of the women's/feminist movements in their demands for the rights of active citizenship, in a similar manner, the women's/feminist movements had great difficulties in accepting the legitimacy of the ethnic/racial movements in the latter's demands for the rights of active citizenship. It was as though there weren't enough room on the ship to accommodate everyone or perhaps there was an unwillingness to accept the idea of a one-class ship – citizens all, citizens equal.[48] It is unfortunate to note that this second organizational conflict in the United States gave rise to African-American Civil Rights Movement that had to take its own separate path.

Annotated Bibliography

- Elizabeth C. Stanton, Susan B. Anthony, and Matilda J. Gage, *History of Woman Suffrage* (NY: Charles Mann, 1887), 3 volumes consist of scattered reports of the Woman Suffrage Movement till the publication of the volume along with some personal reminiscences and brief biographical sketches of the actors in the struggle.
- Elaine Showalter, ed, *Scribbling Women: Short Stories by 19th-Century American Women* (Piscataway, NJ: Rutgers University Press, 1997) is a compilation of essays that shed light on the condition of women in nineteenth century America revealed through personal self-experiences.
- Ellen C. Dubois's *Woman Suffrage and Women's Rights* (New York and London: New York University Press, 1998) is a fascinating account of the long struggle of women for political rights in the United States where the author also tries to explore the relationship between feminism and other political trends like liberalism, Marxism, etc.
- Elizabeth Frost-Knappman and Kathryn Cullen-DuPont's *Women's Suffrage in America* (New York: Facts on File Inc., 2005, p.2, updated edition) offers a chronological guide of the movement from Seneca Falls Convention to the granting of women's right to vote in 1920. In the updated edition, the authors have included biographies of the eminent figures, court decisions regarding property rights, dowry and divorce, several eyewitness testimonies, etc.
- Immanuel Wallerstein's article 'Citizens All? Citizens Some! The Making of the Citizen' (*Comparative Studies in Society and History*, Vol. 45, No. 4 (October 2003), pp. 650–79) explores the dilemma in the concept of citizenship itself and reveals how exclusive claims of citizenship rights had been, especially in the western world, since the days of the French Revolution. Within this broader context, Wallerstein shows how women's struggle for voting rights in America between 1848 and 1920, reflected only on the needs and interests of white women and became thoroughly divisive along class and racial lines. Dorothy Sterling, ed, *We are your Sisters: Black Women in the Nineteenth Century* (New York: Norton and Company, 1984), consisting of letters, oral histories, diary, and autobiography excerpts of black women from the south, portrays the difficulties, hardships, and alienation that they had to undergo and clearly shows how exclusive Women Suffrage Movement had been.

Table 10.2: Timeline of Key Events

Year	Event(s)
1848	The first women's rights convention is held in Seneca Falls, New York. After two days of discussion and debate, 68 women and 32 men sign a *'Declaration of Sentiments'*, which outlines grievances and sets the agenda for the women's rights movement. A set of 12 resolutions is adopted calling for equal treatment of women and men under the law and voting rights for women.
1850	The first National Women's Rights Convention takes place in Massachusetts attracting more than 1,000 participants.
1869	May: Elizabeth Cady Stanton and Susan B. Anthony form the National Women Suffrage Association (NWSA). The primary goal of the organization is to achieve voting rights for women by means of a Congressional amendment to the Constitution. Nov: Lucy Stone, Henry Blackwell, and others form the American Women Suffrage Association (AWSA). This group focuses exclusively on gaining voting rights for women through amendments to individual state constitutions. Dec: The territory of Wyoming passes the first women's suffrage law. The following year, women begin serving on juries in the territory.
1890	The NWSA and AWSA merge to form the National American Woman Suffrage Association (NAWSA). As the movement's mainstream organization, NAWSA wages state-by-state campaigns to obtain voting rights for women.
1893	Colorado adopts an amendment granting women the right to vote. (Utah and Idaho follow suit in 1896, Washington State in 1910, California in 1911, Oregon, Kansas, and Arizona in 1912, Alaska and Illinois in 1913, Montana and Nevada in 1914, New York in 1917; Michigan, South Dakota, and Oklahoma in 1918).
1903	The National Women's Trade Union League (WTUL) is established to advocate for improved wages and working conditions for women.
1913	Alice Paul and Lucy Burns form the Congressional Union to work toward the passage of a federal amendment to give women the vote. This group is later renamed as the National Women's Party (NWP).

(Continued)

(Table 10.2 continued)

Year	Event(s)
1919	The federal woman suffrage amendment, originally written by Susan B. Anthony and introduced in Congress in 1878, is passed by the House of Representatives and the Senate. It is then sent to the states for ratification.
1920	The Women's Bureau of the Department of Labor is formed to collect information about women in the workforce and safeguard good working conditions for women. 26 Aug.: The Nineteenth Amendment to the Constitution, granting women the right to vote, is signed into law by Secretary of State Bainbridge Colby.

b. African-American Civil Rights Movement in America, late-nineteenth–late twentieth century

The African-American Civil Rights Movement between late-nineteenth and late-twentieth century is one of the most significant chapters of disillusionment depicting how inequality, discrimination, exploitation, torture, and alienation went on along racial (and also class) lines in a country that took pride in the declaration of freedom, equality, and liberty as early as the framing of its constitution in 1787. That its political independence was a mere compromise that denied equal rights to the non-whites gains ground if one scrutinizes into the historical context and background of the emergence of Civil Rights Movement in the United States.

The Context: Exploitation and Discrimination in the Pre- and Post-Reconstruction Era

The Civil Rights Movement in America has to be understood within the historical context of the import and settlement of 'black' African people in the continent and the long saga of exploitation, discrimination, and unfulfilled promises of the Reconstruction era.

The first enslaved Africans arrived in the United States in the San Miguel de Gualdape colony (most likely located in the Winyah Bay area of present-day South Carolina), founded by Spanish explorer Lucas Vásquez de Ayllón in 1526. Saint Augustine colony in Florida, founded by Pedro Menéndez de Avilés included an unknown number of free and enslaved Africans that were part of this colonial expedition. With the establishment of Jamestown, Virginia in 1607 and widespread tobacco cultivation,[49] there was a sharp demand for more labour. Initially indentured servants were used as the needed labour,[50] which was followed by the import of African slaves to Jamestown by Dutch traders in 1619.[51] With the founding of Charles Town and South Carolina, from the overpopulated sugar island colony of Barbados in 1670, one of the first major establishments of African slavery colonies occurred. The colonists also practiced Indian (Native American) slavery to meet labour needs, triggered by the difficulty in acquiring enslaved Africans north of the Caribbean. The Carolinians transformed the Indian slave trade during the late seventeenth and early eighteenth centuries by treating slaves as a trade commodity to be exported, mainly to the West Indies. Alan Gallay estimates that between 1670 and 1715, between 24,000 and 51,000 Indian slaves were exported from South Carolina, much more than the number of Africans imported to the colonies of the future United States during the same period.[52]

Table 10.3: Distribution of Slaves

Destination	**Percentage**
Portuguese America	38.5
British America (minus North America)	18.4
Spanish Empire	17.5
French Americas	13.6
British North America	6.45
English Americas	3.25
Dutch West Indies	2.0
Danish West Indies	0.3

Source: Stephen Behrendt, 'Transatlantic Slave Trade', *Africana: The Encyclopedia of the African and African American Experience* (New York: Basic Civitas Books, 1999).

The African and Indian slaves had to undergo a penurious life. Though the treatment of slaves in the United States varied widely across states, it was generally characterized by brutality, degradation, and inhumanity.

Whippings, executions, and rapes were commonplace; sexual abuse of slaves was partially rooted in a patriarchal Southern culture which treated black women as property or chattel. Slaves were denied the opportunity to learn to read or write, to protect against their forming aspirations that could lead to escape or rebellion. During the late seventeenth century and early eighteenth century, newer and harsher slave codes (laws established to demonstrate legal sanctions over slaves) limited their rights and cut off their avenues to freedom.[53] For example, a 1691-Virginia law prohibited slaveholders from emancipating slaves (African) unless they paid for the freedmen's transportation out of Virginia. Moreover, Virginia criminalized interracial marriage in 1691 and subsequent laws abolished their rights to vote, hold office, and bear arms.[54] According to Virginia's 1705 slave code, 'All Negro, mulatto, and Indian slaves within this dominion … shall be held to be real estate. If any slave resist his master … correcting such slave, and shall happen to be killed in such correction … the master shall be free of all punishment … as if such accident never happened.'[55] Some states also prohibited religious gatherings of slaves as planters feared that group meetings would facilitate communication and may lead to rebellion.[56]

Waves of protests against this surfaced as early as the first half of the eighteenth century. African and African-American slaves expressed their opposition to slavery through armed uprisings such as the Stono Rebellion and the New York Slave Insurrection of 1741. These uprisings included strategies and techniques that included malingering and tool-breaking, and most commonly, by running away, either for short periods or permanently. However, it is unfortunate to note that until the Revolutionary era, almost no white American colonists spoke out against slavery; even the Quakers generally tolerated slaveholding and slave-trading until the mid-eighteenth century, although they emerged as vocal opponents of slavery in the Revolutionary era.

Soon after the Revolutionary War, the Northern states began to abolish slavery with New Jersey acting last in 1804. President Thomas Jefferson denounced the international trade as 'violations of human rights which have been so long continued on the unoffending inhabitants of Africa, in which the morality, the reputation, and the best interests of our country have long been eager to proscribe' in 1807 Congress, and by 1808, all states (except South Carolina) banned the international buying or selling of slaves, though domestic slave trade continued.[57] Anti-slavery resistances went on like the German Coast Uprising of 1811 in Orleans and Nat Turner's rebellion in Virginia, etc., and abolitionism (a movement to end slavery grew in strength throughout the United States) started gaining strength. Quakers, Evangelical Methodists, Presbyterians, and Congregationalists, and leaders like Frederick Douglass and William Lloyd Garrison took active part in the anti-slavery resistances and mobilizations. American North took the lead, becoming the hub of abolitionist societies and supporters, and the question of abolition became the bone of contention between North and South culminating into the outbreak of war of 1860s (chapter 4, section 1).

The end of the war with Northern victory resulted in the complete implementation of the Emancipation Proclamation; with the ratification of the Thirteenth Amendment to the Constitution in December 1865, all remaining slaves were officially declared free. Booker T. Washington, a boy of around seven years when the Emancipation Proclamation was read on his plantation in Virginia, later recalled in his 1901 memoir,

> As the great day drew nearer, there was more singing in the slave quarters than usual. It was bolder, had more ring, and lasted later into the night. Most of the verses of the plantation songs had some reference to freedom.... Some man who seemed to be a stranger (a United States officer, I presume) made a little speech and then read a rather long paper—the Emancipation Proclamation, I think. After the reading we were told that we were all free, and could go when and where we pleased. My mother, who was standing by my side, leaned over and kissed her children, while tears of joy ran down her cheeks. She explained to us what it all meant, that this was the day for which she had been so long praying, but fearing that she would never live to see.[58]

But the greatest limitation of the Thirteenth Amendment was that it only outlawed slavery and provided neither citizenship nor equal rights. In 1868, the Fourteenth Amendment was ratified by the states, granting African-Americans citizenship, and the Fifteenth Amendment (ratified in 1870) stated that race could not be used as a condition to deprive men of the ability to vote.

During the era of Reconstruction (1865–77), Northern troops occupied the South and tried to administer and enforce the new constitutional amendments. During this period, many black leaders were elected to local and state offices. But the end of the era following the Compromise of 1877 between Northern and Southern white elites drew a black curtain on the fate of these freed slaves. In exchange for deciding the contentious Presidential election in favour of Rutherford B. Hayes, supported by Northern states, over his opponent, Samuel J. Tilden, the compromise called for the withdrawal of Northern troops from the South that caused violence and fraud in southern elections from 1868–76, reducing black voter turnout on one hand and enabling Southern white Democrats to regain power in state legislatures across the South on the other. That effort of the Radical Republicans to eliminate both governmental and private discrimination by legislation was largely ended by the Supreme Court's decision of 1883, in which the Court held that that Congress lacked the constitutional authority under the enforcement provisions of the Fourteenth Amendment to outlaw racial discrimination by private individuals and organizations, rather than state and local governments. United States also legalized racial segregation in the Supreme Court's decision in *Plessy v. Ferguson* case (1896) that upheld state-mandated discrimination in public transportation under the 'separate but equal' doctrine and extended it all other spheres of private and public lives.

Racial segregation (which was known as 'Jim Crow' system),[59] disfranchisement,[60] increased exploitation (that included denial of economic opportunities, etc.), and mass racial violence against blacks (through lynching, race riots, etc.) in the Reconstruction and immediate post-Reconstruction period paved the way towards the African-American Civil Rights Movement in America between late nineteenth and twentieth century.

Civil Rights Movement: Events and Nature

The men of colour implemented various tactics and strategies to ameliorate their condition; while some, led by Booker T. Washington focussed on economic development, others, including most prominently the leading scholar and intellectual William Edward Burghardt (W.E.B.) Du Bois, insisted upon an uncompromising effort to achieve the voting and other civil rights promised by the Constitution and its post-War amendments.

Realizing that practical skills and economic independence were the keys to black advancement, Washington established the Tuskegee Normal and Industrial Institute (now Tuskegee University) in industrial education (carpentry and blacksmithing for male students and nursing or dressmaking for girls) which also trained schoolteachers to staff African-American schools throughout the South.[61] In September 1895, in his Atlanta Compromise speech he argued, that the greatest danger facing African Americans,

> '...is that in the great leap from slavery to freedom we may overlook the fact that the masses of us are to live by the productions of our hands, and fail to keep in mind that we shall prosper in proportion as we learn to dignify and glorify common labor, and put brains and skill into the common occupations of life. ... It is at the bottom of life we must begin, and not at the top. Nor should we permit our grievances to overshadow our opportunities.'[62]

Though Washington remained the nation's leading African-American figure for many years, his gradualist posture was unacceptable to blacks unwilling to defer to some unspecified future their claims for full and equal civil rights.

W.E.B. Du Bois was highly admired by many as he sharply reacted against legal segregation and other forms of discrimination and exploitation against the blacks and looked at political agitation and protests as the only means to assert rights and power. He criticized Washington's policies and highlighted its limitations in his *The Souls of Black Folk* (1903),

> '...his doctrine has tended to make the whites, North and South, shift the burden of the Negro problem to the Negro's shoulders and stand aside as critical and rather pessimistic spectators; when in fact the burden belongs to the nation, and the hands of none of us are clean if we bend not our energies to righting these great wrongs.'[63]

In 1905, Du Bois and other leading black intellectuals formed the Niagara Movement which is often considered as the inconsequential precursor of the National Association for the Advancement of Colored People (NAACP) in 1909. The Niagara group held a notable 1906 conference at Harpers Ferry, West Virginia, site of John Brown's rebellion. But with poor funding and internal conflicts it was disbanded in 1910 with a new and stronger organization (NAACP) ready to take its place by then. In a very recent study, Angela Jones has divided the Civil Rights Movement into four phases: i. black publics (initial dialogue), legal phase (legal attempts at reform), direct action (physical protest), and revolutionary movement (rise of black power). She argues that the Niagara Movement is not only to be remembered for playing a major role in the development of the larger Civil Rights Movement, but for creating 'black publics', i.e., groups of concerned citizens that met publicly to challenge hegemonic discourses and shift public opinion which was crucial to social change and social movements.[64]

The NAACP was established in February 1909 with the initiative of Du Bois and black leaders, and white activists, such as Mary White Ovington, Oswald Garrison Villard, William English Walling, Henry Moskowitz, Julius Rosenthal, Stephen Wise, and others. It used the court to attack Jim Crow laws in its early years.[65] In 1913, NAACP lobbied against President Woodrow Wilson's introduction of racial segregation into Federal government employment and offices, and demanded for commissioning of African Americans as officers in World War I. In 1915, it organized public education and protests in cities across the nation against D.W. Griffith's silent film *Birth of a Nation* which glamorized the *Ku Klux Klan*.[66] It is important to note that the NAACP consisted of many members from the American Jewish community who also felt the brunt of discrimination with the blacks.

The participation of men of colour in World War I, despite the fact that the military was segregated, and organized on the basis of Jim Crowism, exposed them to the different racial mores of Europe, and influenced the black veterans who then created a widespread demand for freedom and equality. The unique feature of this generation of black activists was that they responded with a far more militant spirit, urging blacks to fight back when whites attacked them. A. Philip Randolph introduced the term the 'New Negro' in 1917 which became the catchphrase to describe the new spirit of militancy and impatience of the post-War era. In the meantime NAACP's membership rose from 9,000 to almost 90,000 in 1920 under the brilliant leadership of James Weldon Johnson who was appointed field secretary in 1916 and was elected head of the organization in 1920. Over the next 10 years, NAACP escalated its lobbying and litigation efforts, becoming internationally known for its advocacy of equal rights and equal protection for the American 'Negro'.

By 1920s, the 'Great Migration' that started before WWI expanded rapidly when hundreds of thousands of African Americans moved from rural South to Northern industrial cities.[67] Marcus Garvey's Universal Negro Improvement Association (UNIA) made great strides in organizing these new communities in the North in the early 1920s. Garveyism was on the lines of Washington's dreams, i.e., far away from mainstream civil rights organizations such as the NAACP, and instead of striving for integration into white-dominated society, it promoted *Pan Africanism* that encouraged economic independence within the system of racial segregation in the United States and urged African Americans to 'return to Africa', if not physically, at least in spirit. The UNIA attracted thousands of supporters, both in the United States and in the African diaspora in the Caribbean, claimed 11 million members, and was broadly popular in Northern black communities.

The economic nightmares of the Great Depression of the 1930s took their toll on blacks throughout the country as 'the fall of the economy pushed many black Americans to the edge of starvation.'[68] Severe discrimination and exclusion continued; even government programmes such as the US Employment Service (USES) hired only whites as defense workers. A. Phillip Randolph, a member of the Socialist Party of America and Brotherhood of Sleeping Car Porters (BSCP), established in 1925, gave effective leadership in the movement in the late 1930s and 1940s and played crucial role in bridging the gap between labour movement and Civil Rights Movement in America. The BSCP became the only black-led union within the American Federation of Labor (AFL) in 1935 and Randolph remained within the AFL when the Congress of Industrial Organizations (CIO) split from it. Though the CIO was much more committed to organizing African-American workers and made strenuous efforts to persuade the BSCP to join it, Randolph believed more could be done to advance black workers' rights, particularly in the railway industry, by remaining in the AFL, to which the other railway brotherhoods belonged. Randolph remained the voice for black workers within the labour movement, raising demands for elimination of Jim Crow unions within the AFL at every opportunity.

While many of the CIO unions made advocacy of civil rights part of their organizing strategy and bargaining priorities and remained vocal in calling for elimination of racial discrimination by defense industries during World War II, Randolph and the BSCP took the battle against employment discrimination and organized a march in Washington in 1942 so that government take steps to outlaw racial discrimination by defense contractors. The March on Washington Movement (MoWM) was restricted to black organizations to maintain black leadership which led to harsh criticism of other leftist members. However, the plan was dropped as BSCP managed to win substantial concessions from the Roosevelt administration.[69]

Throughout the WWII, the US military maintained a policy of 'separate but equal,' continuing to segregate blacks and other minorities in their own units. One million black Americans were assigned to auxiliary units (transportation and engineering corps). Black organizations such as BSCP, NAACP, the National Urban League, and other secondary groups (the National Association of Colored Graduate Nurses, etc.) protested against these racist discriminatory policies; editorials appeared in the NAACP and the National Urban League published *The Crisis* and *Opportunity*. These pressures from below caused the War Department to gradually respond in a positive way. It is interesting to note that the War Department along with black leaders produced a training film titled *The Negro Soldier* (directed by Frank Capra) in 1943 that emphasized the contributions of black soldiers in the nation's wars since the American Revolution.[70] The WWII created a new generation of black Americans, more conscious of their own rights and claims. Tim McNeese argues in *The Civil Rights Movement: Striving for Justice* that many of them returned to their homes different than when they had put on their uniforms for the first time; they returned to civilian life with an enhanced sense of themselves and a commitment to the fight for black equality.[71]

A number of legal battles were fought against segregation during 1930s, 1940s, and 1950s, and the NAACP was instrumental in this. In 1936, through one of his cases, *Pearson v. Murray*, Charles Houston, dean of Howard University Law School and chief legal advocate of NAACP, succeeded in getting the US Supreme Court to declare the student acceptance program at the University of Maryland to be unconstitutional on the ground that it only accepted white students which was a clear violation of the concept of 'separate but equal'. Houston was followed by Thurgood Marshall, and during the next few years a number of legal battles were won in favour of the men of colour which included *Lane v. Wilson* (1939; Supreme Court decided to strike down Oklahoma law that restricted black voting), *Mitchell v. United States* (1941; Supreme Court decided to strike down Arkansas law that required blacks to ride on segregated railroad cars), *Smith v. Allwright* (1944; a Texas law that denied blacks the vote in primary elections was effective no longer), *Morgan v. Virginia* (1946; a Virginia law that had denied a black woman the right to sit on the seat of her choice on an interstate bus was struck down), *Sweatt v. Painter* and *McLaurin v. Oklahoma State Regents for Higher Education* (1950; blacks were no longer to be denied entry to professional schools, including the University of Texas School of Law in Austin). However, the decision of the Supreme Court in the *Brown v. Board of Education of Topeka* was one of the greatest victories achieved when the court overturned *Plessy v. Ferguson* and put an end to the 60-year mandate of 'separate but equal'. Public schools throughout the country could no longer be kept segregated. But segregation, which by then was more a social and psychological phenomenon, continued and desegregation could not be achieved rapidly. There were resistances against the ruling of the court, and though a second ruling came out by 1955 to make the law effective, desegregation in America's schools did not take place overnight.[72]

The reaction to the continued resistances in the the South by proponents of racial segregation and voter suppression (which included filing lawsuits to disband NAACP on the ground that it was a part of the communist conspiracy) was the adoption of a combined strategy of direct mass action (boycotts, sit-ins, Freedom Rides, marches, etc.) with nonviolent resistance known as civil disobedience by the African Americans that characterized the movement between mid-1950s and late-1960s.

One common discriminatory practice that still went was segregation in public buses. In a recent study by Juan Williams the indignity gets sharply reflected,

> The city buses were a microcosm of this segregated society. Black passengers, after paying their fares at the front of the bus, had to leave it and reenter through the back door. They were allowed to sit only in the rear, and had to give up their seats whenever a white rider was left standing.... Day by

day blacks stood together in the rear of crowded buses while the agents of their indignity sat comfortably right in front of them.[73]

Though protest against this first started in Louisiana in 1953 when a petition was submitted to the city council to end this form of discrimination, soon Montgomery became the epicenter of movement surrounding the issue.

Edgar Daniel Nixon, a former leader of the Montgomery chapter of the NAACP and other protesters like Jo Ann Robinson were already considering the possibility of a Montgomery Bus Boycott when the Rosa Parks' incident added fuel to fire. On 1 December 1955, when Rosa Parks refused to give up her seat on a public bus to make room for a white passenger, she was arrested, tried, and convicted for disorderly conduct and violating a local ordinance. Once the news of this incident reached the black community, 50 African-American leaders gathered and organized the Montgomery Bus Boycott to demand a more humane bus transportation system. With the support the most of Montgomery's 50,000 African Americans, the boycott lasted for 381 days until a federal court ordered Montgomery's buses desegregated in November 1956. The movement provided huge exposure to Martin Luther King, Jr., President of the Montgomery Improvement Association, the organization that directed the boycott and his eloquent appeals to Christian brotherhood, and American idealism created a positive impression on people both inside and outside the South.

The movement spread to epidemic proportions in the 1960s. To explain the causes behind such eruption, demographic changes, political realignments, and exigent foreign policy needs coalesced to break the shackles of segregation and to spark militant protest.[74] The movement Rosa Parks sparked and Martin Luther King kindled into flame blazed more brightly in February 1960 when four black students (Ezell A. Blair, Jr., David Richmond, Joseph McNeil, and Franklin McCain) from North Carolina Agricultural and Technical College sat down at a Woolworth's lunch counter in Greensboro to demand equal service.[75] It soon inspired other sit-ins, and despite being spat on, beaten, burned, and insulted, black students continued the tactic; they won at the lunch counters of more than 126 Southern cities by the end of 1960.[76] In April 1960 King called a conference at Shaw University in Raleigh, North Carolina where activists who had led these sit-ins joined hands to form the Student Nonviolent Coordinating Committee (SNCC).[77] SNCC became the spearhead for the civil rights revolt for the subsequent years, taking tactics of nonviolent confrontation further, to the freedom rides.[78] These 'New Abolitionists',[79] paying heed to King's singular synthesis of Christian and Gandhian ideals, achieved one milestone after another and did not stop in spite of jail sentences for their leader in Birmingham and Atlanta, resistance to classroom integration by the governor (George Wallace) of Alabama himself, Sheriff Bull Connor's police dogs in Birmingham, and the violence of Alabama state troopers at Selma.[80]

The more difficult the path of struggle, the more the protesters affirmed to their goals and the more encouragement they received from other communities including many white people from the Northern cities. This was evident in the second march on Washington, D.C. (after the first march of 1941) where over 200,000 blacks and whites gathered on 28 August 1963 to demand meaningful civil rights laws, a massive federal works program, full and fair employment, decent housing, adequate integrated education and most importantly, the right to vote. King delivered his famous *I Have a Dream* speech where he revealed his dream of a day, 'when the sons of former slaves and the sons of former slave-owners will be able to sit together at the table of brotherhood.'[81] And the dream seemed not to be distant as President Kennedy issued executive orders desegregating interstate transport and proposed civil rights legislation. On 6 August 1965, President Johnson signed the Civil Rights Act that banned discrimination based on 'race, color, religion, sex or national origin' in employment practices and public accommodations. And with the passage of the Civil Rights Act of 1965, the movement accomplished one of its most significant successes. 'On paper, at least, a revolution, a second Reconstruction, had been consummated.'[82]

Limitations and Achievements in the Post-1965 Period

To render legal rights meaningful, did the nation offer African-Americans the economic and social opportunities? In 1966, black activist Bayard Rustin pointed out that Negroes today are in worse economic shape, live in worse slums, and attend more highly segregated schools than in the previous decades. The day-to-day lot of the ghetto has not been improved by the various judicial and legislative measures of the past decade. Statistics buttressed his indictment: black unemployment was double that of whites (32 per cent among youths), the gap between black and white wages widened, and ghetto housing deteriorated even in northern open occupancy cities and states.[83] These material conditions caused a number of race riots in the impoverished areas including the Harlem Riot of 1964 in New York and the Watts Riot of 1965 in Los Angeles. The riots spread to New Jersey and Detroit by 1967; in April 1968, after the assassination of Martin Luther King, Jr. in Memphis, Tennessee, rioting broke out in Cleveland, Baltimore, Washington, D.C., Chicago, New York City, and Louisville, Kentucky from frustration and despair.

The terminal phase of the Civil Rights Movement is often associated with what historians term as 'Black Power' to capture the final transition of the movement from passivity to resistance, protest to politics, and integration to cultural nationalism.[84] And power, political power was the crucial need of the hour to influence government to the economic and social advantages of the blacks. Stokely Carmichael, who became the leader of SNCC in 1966, was one of the most articulate spokespersons for 'Black Power' Movement that brought the charge of 'reverse racism' on him. In this way, the Civil Rights Movement was infused with a self-interest ideology that defined and shaped the concepts of welfare of the men of colour on the basis of their own belief and not imposed from above. Black votes for black candidates serving black needs gained concrete grounds at the conceptual level. The sense of cultural identity also surfaced when blacks started to wear loosely fit dashikis, started to grow their hair naturally (which became popular as the Afro style) instead of straightening it, and proclaimed that to be black is to be beautiful. However, 'Black Power' was made most public by the Black Panther Party, founded by Huey Newton and Bobby Seale in Oakland, California, in 1966. This group followed the ideology of Malcolm X, a former member of the Nation of Islam, using a 'by-any-means necessary' approach against inequality. They sought to rid African-American neighbourhoods of police brutality, referring to police officers as 'pigs', displayed shotguns and raised the clarion cry 'Power to the people'.

As King was not happy with the 'Black Power' Movement, and it appeared separatist and anti-integrationist to him, SNCC activists continued embracing the non-violent right to self-defense in response to attacks from white authorities. When King was murdered in 1968, Carmichael stated that whites murdered the one person who would prevent rampant rioting and that blacks would burn every major city to the ground. With King's assassination, racial riots broke out in the black community in every major city from Boston to San Francisco often leading to 'White Flight'.

However, the 'Promised Land' that King dreamt was not in vain, and from the historical perspective, the movement was successful to a great extent as the right to vote equipped black Americans with the tools that immigrants and other minority groups long have used to pursue. In the post-1965 period, blacks were adept to cast their ballots throughout the country and elect many of their own races to public offices that ranged from mayor to legislator to congressional representative. Though Americans still wrestle with racial issues but these differ from the pre-1965 scenario. The victory of Barack Obama, the son of a black man from Kenya and a white woman from Kansas, in the presidential election and his speech on the night of his electoral triumph is one of the greatest measures to indicate the emancipation of the men of colour and the progress of the nation over the decades that followed the Civil Rights Movement:

> If there is anyone out there who still doubts that America is a place where all things are possible; who still wonders if the dream of our founders is alive in our time; who still questions the power of our democracy, tonight is your answer.[85]

Annotated Bibliography

- While Alan Gallay's *The Indian Slave Trade: The Rise of the English Empire in the American South 1670–1717* (New York: Yale University Press, 2002) is a historical narrative of the origin and expansion of slavery in colonial America. William Goodell's *The American Slave Code in Theory and Practice: Its Distinctive Features Shown by Its Statutes, Judicial Decisions, and Illustrative Face* (London: Clarke, Beeton, Sc Co., 1853) focuses on slave code, the chief instrument to control and tame their lives and how these codes were devised as more exploitative strategies to torture blacks in both colonial America and its Southern states in the post-Revolutionary period.

Thomas D. Morris's *Southern Slavery and the Law, 1619–1860*, (Chapel Hill, NC: University of North Carolina Press, 1996) depicts the legal norms by which slavery was justified and slaves ruthlessly exploited in the agrarian states of South.

- Tim McNeese's *The Civil Rights Movement: Striving for Justice* (New York: Chelsea House, 2008) is a phase-by-phase chronological account of the movement, following the empirical approach. C. Carson's *In Struggle: SNCC and the Black Awakening of the 1960s* is a fascinating account of the activities of SNCC including sit-ins, freedom ridings, etc., in the last phase of the movement when it gradually took a violent turn; Howard Zinn's *SNCC: The New Abolitionists* (Boston, Massachusetts: Beacon Press, 1964) is an 'on-the-spot' reportage in several parts of the country including southwest Georgia, Selma, Alabama, and Hattiesburg, Mississippi in the 1960s.

Notes

1. Ellen C. Dubois, *Woman Suffrage and Women's Rights* (New York and London: New York University Press, 1998), ch. 13, pp. 252–82.
2. The English common law regulated the relation of husband and wife in the colonies. It gave the 'custody' of the wife's person to the husband.
3. Immanuel Wallerstein, 'Citizens All? Citizens Some! The Making of the Citizen', *Comparative Studies in Society and History*, Vol. 45, No. 4 (October 2003), pp. 650–79.
4. New Jersey was an exception. On 2 July 1776, the state adopted a constitution that gave the vote to all free inhabitants who met legal age, property, and residency standards. But by 1800, local politicians were condemning the practice of women voting, arguing that soon the legislature would be 'filled with petticoats'. Men claimed that married women had no independent income and thus should not be allowed to vote. By 1807, the legislature passed a law restricting the right to vote to white propertied males, declaring, 'Whereas doubts have been raised and great diversities in practice obtained throughout the state in regard to the admission of aliens, females and persons of color, or negroes to vote in elections . . . it is highly necessary to the safety, quiet, good order and dignity of the state, to clear up said doubts by an act of the representatives of the people . . .'. Catherine Clinton, *The Other Civil War: American Women in the Nineteenth Century* (New York: Hill and Wang, 1984), pp. 14–16.
5. Elizabeth Frost-Knappman and Kathryn Cullen-DuPont, *Women's Suffrage in America* (New York: Facts on File Inc., 2005), p. 2, updated edition.
6. Harriet Robinson, *Loom and Spindle: Or Life Among the Early Mill Girls* (New York: Crowell, 1898), p. 55.

7. Eleanor Flexner, *Century of Struggle: The Women's Rights Movement in the United States* (Cambridge, Massachusetts: Harvard University Press, 1975), p. 63.
8. http://web.clark.edu/afisher/HIST253/lecture_text/WomenMiddleClass_19c_Europe.pdf (date of access: 12.10.2012).
9. Elaine Showalter, ed, *Scribbling Women: Short Stories by 19th-Century American Women* (Piscataway, NJ: Rutgers University Press, 1997).
10. During the wage cuts and speed-ups of the 1830s, women workers in mills started protesting against these injustices. In 1824, the first female factory workers strike broke out at Pawtucket, Rhode Island which was followed by another strike in Dover, New Hampshire in 1828, where 300 to 400 women joined hands together. Elizabeth Frost-Knappman and Kathryn Cullen-DuPont, ibid., p. 5.
11. Ibid.
12. Margaret Fuller, 'The Great Lawsuit: Man vs. Woman', *Dial* 4 (July, 1843).
13. Ibid., Text by Ann Woodlief; available at: http://transcendentalism.tamu.edu/authors/fuller/debate.html (date of access: 13.10.2012).
14. Judith Wellman, *The Road to Seneca Falls* (Urbana and Chicago: University of Illinois Press, 2004), p. 176.
15. Ibid.
16. Elizabeth C. Stanton, Susan B. Anthony, and Matilda J. Gage, *History of Woman Suffrage* (NY: Charles Mann, 1887), Vol. 1, p. 68.
17. Miriam Gurko, *The Ladies of Seneca Falls: The Birth of the Women's Rights Movement* (New York: Schocken Books, 1974), p.103.
18. Elizabeth C. Stanton, Susan B. Anthony, and Matilda J. Gage, *History of Woman Suffrage*, p. 73.
19. S.G. McMillen, *Seneca Falls and the Origins of the Women's Rights Movement* (New York: Oxford University Press, 2008), p. 102.
20. Elizabeth Frost-Knappman and Kathryn Cullen-DuPont, *Woman's Suffrage in America*, p. 74.
21. Elinor R. Hays, *Morning Star: A Biography of Lucy Stone 1818–1893* (New York: Harcourt, Brace & World, 1961), p. 88.
22. As one of the Reconstruction Amendments in 1868, it was ratified by the states, granting African Americans citizenship.
23. Elizabeth C. Stanton, Susan B. Anthony, and Matilda J. Gage, *History of Woman Suffrage*, Vol. 2, p. 92.
24. *The Revolution* was a weekly women's rights newspaper published between 8 January 1868 and February 1872.
25. Elizabeth Frost-Knappman and Kathryn Cullen-DuPont, *Woman's Suffrage in America*, p. 166.
26. Ellen C. Dubois, *Feminism and Suffrage: The Emergence of an Independent Women's Movement in America, 1848–1869* (New York and London: New York University Press, 1998), p. 168.

27. Ibid., p. 167.
28. Elizabeth Cady Stanton, *Eighty Years and More: Reminiscences 1815–1897* (New York: Schocken Books, 1971), p. 254.
29. Elizabeth C. Stanton, Susan B. Anthony, and Matilda J. Gage, *History of Woman Suffrage*, Vol. 2, pp. 91–92.
30. Rachel Davidson, 'The Split in the 19th Century Woman Suffrage Movement', *The Concord Review*, available at: http://www.tcr.org/tcr/essays/Web_Suffrage.pdf (date of access: 13.10.2012).
31. Elizabeth Frost-Knappman, Kathryn Cullen-DuPont, *Woman's Suffrage in America*, chapter 9.
32. Grace Farrell, 'Beneath the Suffrage Narrative', *Canadian Review of American Studies*, Vol. 36, No. 1 (2006), pp. 45–65.
33. A faction led by Alice Paul and Lucy Burns split from the NWSA and formed NWP in 1917. Instead of focusing on lobbying individual states, the NWP emphasized on the passage of a constitutional amendment ensuring women's suffrage. It was originally under the name the Congressional Union for Woman Suffrage in 1913; by 1917, the name had been changed to the National Women's Party, and Alva Belmont was appointed as its President.
34. James Ciment and Thaddeus Russell, *The Home Front Encyclopedia: United States, Britain, and Canada in World Wars I and II*, Vol. 1 (Santa Barbara: ABC-CLIO, 2007), Vol. 1, p. 163.
35. Doris Stevens et al., *Jailed for Freedom: American Women Win the Vote*, (Troutdale, Ore: New Sage Press, 1995); J.S. Lemons, *The Woman Citizen: Social Feminism in the 1920s* (Charlottesville, VA: University of Virginia Press, 1973).
36. Available at: http://www.fordham.edu/halsall/mod/1920womensvote.html (date of access: 13.10.2012).
37. Lynn Dumenil, *The Modern Temper: American Culture and Society in the 1920s* (New York: Hill and Wang, 1995), pp. 98–144.
38. Ellen C. Dubois, *Feminism Suffrage*, p. 177.
39. Ibid., p. 161.
40. Aileen S. Kraditor, *The Ideas of the Woman Suffrage Movement, 1890–1920* (New York: Columbia University Press, 1965), p. 31.
41. Elizabeth C. Stanton, Susan B. Anthony, and Matilda J. Gage, *History of Woman Suffrage*, Vol. 2, p. 173.
42. Ellen C. Dubois, *Feminism and Suffrage*, pp. 74–75.
43. Ibid., p. 95.
44. Dorothy Sterling, ed, *We are Your Sisters: Black Women in the Nineteenth Century* (New York: Norton and Company, 1984), p. 66.
45. Though there is a dispute among contemporary feminist historians on the 'class' question and 'the complex relationship between paid labor, marital status, and

women's place in the class structure was a fundamental puzzle', Ellen C. Dubois, ibid., p. 178.

46. *Working Women, Class Relations, and Suffrage* by Militance Harriot Stanton Blatch and the *New York Woman Suffrage Movement, 1894–1909*, Ellen C. Dubois, *Feminism and Suffrage*, pp. 176–209.
47. Immanuel Wallerstein, 'Citizens' all?'
48. Ibid.
49. One has to remember the efforts of one of the early English settlers John Rolfe, who is credited with the first successful cultivation of tobacco as an export crop in the Colony of Virginia.
50. These servants provided up to seven years of free service and had their trip to Jamestown paid for by someone in Jamestown. Once the seven years was over, the indentured servant was free to live in Jamestown as a regular citizen. But gradually it became an expensive affair for the colonists.
51. Rolfe's account of 31 August 1619 reveals the incidental introduction of African servants to Virginia from a passing ship, 'there came in a Dutch man-of-war that sold us twenty negars', Francis E. Lutz, *The Prince George-Hopewell Story* (Richmond: William Byrd Press, 1957), p. 21.
52. Alan Gallay, *The Indian Slave Trade: The Rise of the English Empire in the American South 1670–1717* (New York: Yale University Press, 2002), p. 299.
53. William Goodell, *The American Slave Code in Theory and Practice: Its Distinctive Features Shown by Its Statutes, Judicial Decisions, and Illustrative Face* (London: Clarke, Beeton, Sc Co., 1853).
54. Alan Taylor, *American Colonies* (New York: Viking, 2001), p. 156.
55. Larry Huch, *Free at Last: The U.S. Civil Rights Movement* (Pennsylvania: Whitaker House, 2004), p. 5.
56. Thomas D. Morris, *Southern Slavery and the Law, 1619–1860*, (Chapel Hill, NC: University of North Carolina Press, 1996), p. 347.
57. Dumas Malone, *Jefferson and the President: Second Term, 1805-1809* (Boston, MA, USA: Little, Brown, 1974), pp. 543–44.
58. Booker T. Washington, *Up from Slavery: An Autobiography* (New York: Penguin Books, 1901), pp. 19–21; available at: http://www.alcyone.com/max/lit/slavery/ (date of access: 14.12.2012).
59. The system became known informally as 'Jim Crow', from the 1828 minstrel show song 'Jump Jim Crow', which was typically performed by white performers in blackface as a caricature of the unlettered, inferior black man. Larry Huch, *Free at Last*, p. 21.
60. When white Democrats regained power, they passed laws that made voter registration more inaccessible to blacks. Black voters were forced off the voting rolls. The number of African-American voters dropped dramatically, and they no longer were able to elect representatives. From 1890 to 1908, Southern states of

the former Confederacy created constitutions with provisions that disfranchised tens of thousands of African Americans.

61. A number of leading philanthropists, such as the oil magnate John D. Rockefeller, steel producer Andrew Carnegie, and Sears, Roebuck head Julius Rosenwald, all raised funds for Tuskegee.
62. Larry Huch, ibid., p. 22.
63. Ibid., p. 23.
64. Angela Jonnes, African American Civil Rights: Early Activism and the Niagara Movement (Santa Barbara, California: ABC-CLIO, LLC, 2011), pp. 1–2.
65. It gained a Supreme Court ruling striking down Oklahoma's 'grandfather clause' that exempted most illiterate white voters from a law that disfranchised African-American citizens in *Guinn v. United States* (1915). It successfully challenged the Louisville, Kentucky ordinance that required residential segregation in *Buchanan v. Warley* (1917).
66. *Ku Klux Klan* (gv. 3 phases) is the name of organizations in the United States which advocated extremist reactionary currents such as white supremacy, white nationalism, and anti-immigration, historically expressed through terrorism. It opposed the Civil Rights Movement and minorities' claims. Charles Quarles, *The Ku Klux Klan and Related American Racialist and Anti-Semitic Organizations: A History and Analysis* (Jefferson, NC: McFarland, 1999).
67. The 'Great Migration' was the movement of six million African Americans out of the rural Southern United States to the Northeast, Midwest, and West from 1910 to 1970. It occurred in two phases: the First Great Migration (1910–30), numbering about 1.6 million migrants who left mostly rural areas to migrate to Northern and Midwestern industrial cities, and, as an aftermath of Great Depression, a Second Great Migration (1940–70), in which five million or more people moved, including many to California and various western cities. William H. Frey, *The New Great Migration: Black Americans' Return to the South, 1965–2000* (The Brookings Institution, May 2004), pp. 1–3.
68. Darlene Clark Hine, *The African-American Odyssey* (N.J.: Prentice Hall, 2005), p. 429.
69. In June 1941, Roosevelt gave in to Randolph's demands and issued Executive Order 8802, which stated, 'I do hereby affirm the policy of the United States that there shall be no discrimination in the employment of workers in the defense industry or government because of race, creed, color, or national origin.' Darlene Clark Hine, ibid., p. 485.
70. Darlene Clark Hine, ibid., p. 489.
71. Tim McNeese, *The Civil Rights Movement: Striving for Justice* (New York: Chelsea House, 2008), p. 42.
72. Ibid., Chapter 4: 'The Fight in the Courts', pp. 44–58.

73. Juan Williams, *Eyes on the Prize: America's Civil Rights Years, 1954–1965* (New York: Penguin Books, 2002), p. 60.
74. M. Dubofsky, A. Theoharis, and D. Smith, *The United States in the Twentieth Century* (N.J.: Prentice-Hall, 1978), p. 439.
75. William H. Chafe, *Civilities and Civil Rights: Greensboro, North Carolina, and the Black Struggle for Freedom* (New York: Oxford University Press, 1980), p. 81.
76. M. Dubofsky, A. Theoharis, and D. Smith, *The United States in the Twentieth Century*, p. 440.
77. C. Carson, *In Struggle: SNCC and the Black Awakening of the 1960s* (Cambridge: Harvard University Press), p. 311
78. Freedom Rides were journeys by Civil Rights activists on interstate buses into the segregated southern United States to test the United States Supreme Court decision in *Boynton v. Virginia*, (1960) 364 US that ended segregation for passengers engaged in interstate travel. Organized by Congress of Racial Equality (CORE), the first Freedom Ride of the 1960s left Washington D.C. on 4 May 1961 and was scheduled to arrive in New Orleans on 17 May.
79. Howard Zinn, *SNCC: The New Abolitionists* (Boston, Massachusetts: Beacon Press, 1964).
80. M. Dubofsky, A. Theoharis, and D. Smith, *The United States in the Twentieth Century*, p. 441.
81. D.D. Hansen, *The Dream: Martin Luther King, Jr., and the Speech that Inspired a Nation* (NY: Harper Collins, 2003).
82. M. Dubofsky, A. Theoharis, and D. Smith, *The United States in the Twentieth Century*, p. 443.
83. Ibid.
84. 'Black Power' is a political slogan (coined by activist and organizer Willie Ricks, in Greenwood, Mississippi on 17 June 1966) and a name for various associated ideologies aimed at promoting the Black racial group. James W. Scott, *The Black Revolts: Racial Stratification in the U.S.A* (Cambridge, Mass: Schenkman Pub., 1973)
85. Larry Huch, *Free at Last*, p. 67.

11

American Environmentalism and Environmental History

This chapter provides a historical account of the emergence of American environmental history mainly from American environmentalism in the 1960s, traces the transformation of the field to a mature subject asserting how America became the pioneer and trend-setter in the birth of environmental history as a separate discipline within history. The works of environmental historians from early thinkers like Walter Prescott Webb to recent scholars like Donald Worster have been incorporated with an analytical treatment. It captures the South-Asian perspective of looking into and understanding American environmental history bringing out the sharp lines of bifurcation between 'ecology of affluence' and 'environmentalism of the poor'. The chapter finally ends with theorizing what it calls the 'World Environment History'.

Environmental history as a separate sub-set or sub-discipline of history actually emerged out of the growing environmental crisis due to massive industrialization and urbanization that paved the way towards preservationist, conservationist approaches, and environmental movement or environmentalism in the United States. Concern for nature reflected much earlier in the writings of scholars like Thucydides and Herodotus and also in the narratives of Fernand Braudel (Braudel was perhaps the first historian of the Annales school who wrote the history of the Mediterranean world beginning it with a chapter on 'The Role of Environment' in 1939), Le Roy Ladurie, Bodin, Machiavelli, Montesquieu, More and Bacon, but there is a need to understand the bifurcatory line between environmental consciousness and environmental history as a discipline. The US was the pioneer and trend-setter in the birth of environmental history as a separate discipline of history with its well-sketched out methodological canon.

Historians argue that the emergence of the field occurred with the writings of Frederick Jackson Turner and Walter Prescott Webb. Alfred Crosby dates the origin of the American environmental history to the 1926-publication of Avery Odell Craven's *Soil Exhaustion as a Factor in the Agricultural History of Virginia: 1606–1860*, a work that appeared just two decades before Aldo Leopold's path-breaking study.[1] In these works like Turner's *The Significance of the Frontier in American History* and Webb's *The Great Plains* and few other writings that came out in the nineteenth and early twentieth centuries, nature was the central point of analysis.[2] Physical aspects of the environment were emphasized with lesser understanding on the relationship between human and nature or ecology and human social institutions. It was James Malin, the founder of modern environmental history who brought out the complex, interdependent, and intertwined relationship between nature and societal institutions.[3] In *The Grassland of North America: Prolegomena to Its History*, Malin carried out a deeper ecological analysis and was critical of the crude environmental determinism of his predecessors.[4]

The discipline of the US environmental history concretized itself since the 1960s with the outgrowth of American environmentalism; the various rationales of this environmentalism in the following decades shaped the then American environmental history. Richard White argues that the post-1960 period saw the emergence of two parallel trends and the dichotomy between these two approaches – conservationist and preservationist.[5] While Samuel Hays's *Conservation and the Gospel of Efficiency* represented the conservationist approach, Roderick Nash's *Wilderness and the American Mind* stressed the importance of wilderness in American society and the immense importance of its preservation.[6] Both these approaches drew from mainstream political and intellectual history and analyzed environmental factors as shaped within this background, the approach that was completely missing in the works of the first generation of environmental historians in the pre-1960 era. Hay's work contextualized within the backdrop of the American Progressive Movement where conservation was looked into as a revealing example of the larger political structure of the Progressive era, the conservationists being trained experts concerned with the country's scientific development. Hence, the political economy of conservation found an early interpretation in the work of Hays. Like Hays, Nash reflected on American conceptions of nature, with wilderness as one of the most significant elements, to interpret the American mind. Importance was not given to the impact of the government policies on nature but on what socio-economic and cultural conditions actually set those policies to work.

With the emergence of such studies that addressed issues relating to the contemporary environmental crisis and environmentalism as its response to that, the early emphasis on nature–society relationship started to disappear, and while the current studies represented the emerging field of environmental history, the former works were included within the realm of historical geography.

The conservationist trend set by Hays was later taken up by a number of environmental historians like Elmo Richardson, George Michael McCarthy, and James Penick. Along with Hays's managerial analysis, they provided detailed description of political battles and controversies regarding the implementation of conservation policies in the Progressive era.[7] These works, however, became a more inward study of the bits and pieces of the internal affairs of government organizations rather than having a broad interpretative synthesis that Hays once put forward. But again in the 1980s, more studies came up that sought to provide a deeper analysis of political economy to explain the environmental contour. These include William G. Robbins's *Lumberjacks and Legislators: Political Economy of the U.S. Lumber Industry, 1890–1941*, Abraham Hoffman's *Vision or Villainy: Origins of the Owens Valley-Los Angeles Water Controversy*, and William L. Kahrl's *Water and Power: The Conflict over Los Angeles' Water Supply in the Owens Valley.*[8] Robbins work is a critical account of initiatives by the early twentieth-century lumbermen to use conservation to create a stable and orderly market by eliminating competition in the New Deal era. Hoffman's and Kahrl's accounts have been brilliantly posited within the historical context of the rapid economic development of the mid-twentieth-century California.

While Hays's conservationist framework proved itself adept to continue a renewed interest among the historians, Nash's preservationist approach was also not lagging behind. Barbara Novak's *Nature and Culture: American Landscape and Painting, 1825–1875* dealt with a variety of landscapes and did justice to the Nash paradigm.[9] An area of research where the preservationists like Gifford Pinchot, Michael Cohen, and Stephen Fox seem to enjoy their monopoly is the portrayal of biographies of eminent naturalists, transcendentalists, and preservationists of the earlier generation including John Muir, Henry David Thoreau, Ernest Thompson Seton, and Aldo Leopold.[10] But these works suffer from certain pitfalls. The spatial-temporal context is often blurred, and White argues, 'Instead of a search for historical context, there is an attempt to find a universal language shared by author and subject.'[11] Another serious weakness is that these reflect the concerns of the people who lived within it, rather than the concerns of the present period. The opposite trend is also notable among the followers of Nash, i.e., scholars who concentrated on particular environments and local contexts rather than dwelling upon the universal framework. Roderick Nash was the first chief exponent to speak on the importance of preservation of national parks which became an important agenda of American environmental movement. On his line of argument, studies of particular parks continue to appear in abundance.[12]

In the 1970s, the preservationist/conservationist approach and dichotomy found stark criticism on the ground that these were unable to incorporate newer environmental concerns within their purview of research. The prominent figures in the New Conservation Movement, Rachel Carson, Barry Commoner, and Garrett Hardin differed from the early conservationists and preservationists like Muir and Thoreau in exploring the concepts of scientific ecology. It had been accepted since the 1970s that environmentalism did not evolve as a cohesive, monolithic whole but as distinguished phase of movement and activism at distinct points of time. Joseph Petulla has pointed out in *American Environmental History: The Exploitation and Conservation of Natural Resources* about the separate influence of ecology by adopting a new tripartite division of the movement into biocentric (preservationist)/economic (conservationist)/ecological components. In the third category people forms the basis of leadership of current environmentalism.[13] Thus, the philosophical rationale of environmentalism shifted from scientific to popular ecology.

The difference between the scientific and popular rationale has been very well interpreted by Donald Worster in *Nature's Economy*.[14] In the post-World War II scenario, beneficence of technological progress and human mastery of nature became inevitable replacing Muir's ideas of nature and alike. Schrepfer argued a two-way paradigm in which she pointed out that while once science was used by environmentalists to attack the idea of universal progress, in the next phase the inefficiency of science and the scientists were understood as mere reductionist and arrogant to supply the society with necessary and humanitarian goals, leading them to move back to pagan animism and other initiatives that the tribal, pre-colonial communities practiced.[15]

Donald Worster is one of the greatest environmental historians who laid stress on specific socio-cultural conditions to understand how environmental policies were shaped and tackled. The ethical question gradually came to be added. With the understanding that imperialism provided the greatest onslaught on nature, the pre-colonial Indian Arcadian approach towards nature (which advocated greater harmony between nature and human beings) was revered, and more researches came up in this field including the path-breaking study of J. Donald Hughes's *American Indian Ecology*.[16] In this way, the ghost of Malin was resurrected to understand the deeper connections between social institutions and the environment. Richard White remarks, 'Malin sometimes seems the Lazarus of American historians; for the last decade so many scholars have been trying to resurrect his scholarly reputation that it is perhaps time for someone to point out that the tomb is empty.'[17] Donald Worster in *Dust Bowl: The Southern Plains in the 1930s* followed Malin's legacy in carrying out the interdisciplinary study resting on society-nature relationship where he attacked capitalism as the main evil.[18] Newer studies started to take shape providing detailed account and analysis of the consequences on the environment due to human activities in regional and local contexts. William Cronon's *Changes in the Land*, Richard White's *Land Use, Environment, and Social Change*, and Albert Cowdrey's *This Land, This South* fall within this ambit.[19]

The impact of European colonization on the North American environment has been studied with the capitalist/imperialist counter on environment framework. Pioneering works in this field has been done by Alfred Crosby in *The Columbian Exchange: Biological and Cultural Consequences of 1492* and *Ecological Imperialism: The Biological Exchange of Europe, 900–1900*.[20] Crosby has explored the severe ecological impact of the entry of the Europeans from the Old World into the New World on the later. The introduction of *portmanteau biota* (the Europeans and their accompanying organisms) caused demographic disaster and environmental upheaval in the New World. The demographic disaster through the annihilation of indigenous populations in the Americas was the outcome of large-scale ecological alterations. The massive transformation or reworking of the ecological landscapes had a cultural element to it; the Europeans wanted to establish a cultural familiarity in the newly conquered environment.

Finally, there has been a development of a recent group of environmental historians who study the issues relating to the contemporary environmental crisis in America surrounding deforestation, decline of pastures, intervention to water resources, and the response that it generates among the conscious activists. It also deals with the politics of resource scarcity. While Tim Palmer's *Stanislaus: The Struggle for a River* is a journalistic account of the controversy over the eventual damming of the Stanislaus River in California,[21] Richard H.K. Vietor's *Environmental Politics and the Coal Coalition* explains how changing economic organization has contributed to the ability of coal producers and their allies to blunt the impact of environmental regulations which pressurizes producers to assume the social costs of energy production.[22]

From the South-Asian Perspective

It is important to understand that the environmental movement that gave birth to the US environmental history was a product of post-material or post-industrial society when the mass consumer society enlarged the opportunities for leisure. According to John C. Pierce, Nicholas P. Lovrich, Takematsu Tsurutani, and Takematsu Abe, the period between 1945–95 can be referred to as 'post-industrialist' that marked an economic advancement of the service sector, the development of complex nationwide communication networks, expansion of the knowledge industry, the growth of the public sector, widespread affluence, etc. Post-industrialism brought value changes giving rise to a new set of beliefs concerning the relationship of humans to nature. Thus, 'NEP' (New Environmental Paradigm) directly challenged 'DSP' (Dominant Social Paradigm) that traditionally reflected belief in abundance and industrial progress, devotion to growth and prosperity, faith in science and technology, commitment to laissez-faire economy, limited governmental planning, and private property rights.[23] When car becomes almost everyone's possession, in a sharp contradiction this most modern creation of industry becomes the vehicle of anti-industrial impulses, taking one to 'homey little towns, enchanting fairy tale forests, far from stale routine, functional ugliness, or the dictates of the clock.'[24]

The US environmentalism relies more heavily on the social movement organizations like the Sierra Club or the Friends of the Earth 'with its own cadre, leadership, and properly audited sources or funds.'[25] It has an insular approach and there is a lack of American engagement with the rest of the world.[26] Ramachandra Guha writes in *Movement Scholarship*,

> American environmentalists are notably insular in their concerns–seriously worried about the threats to the American wilderness and waters, but somewhat unconcerned about the global consequences of the consumer society, the impact on land, soil, forests, and climate elsewhere. The US environmentalism seems to be a single-issue movement demanding for attitudinal changes rather than thinking of alteration in the mode of production and distribution.[27]

This argument can have a clearer understanding if we look into the South-Asian context. Like the US, the emergence of South-Asian environmental history as a separate and a distinct field can be linked to the growth of vigorous environmentalism (environmental activism) in this region. Indian environmentalism is a wide connotation consisting of numerous local conflicts and struggles. Its origins can be traced back to the Chipko movement in the Garhwal Himalaya in 1973. Between 1973 and 1980, country-wide resistances in defence of community rights pitting the rich against the poor; the state against the common people; and the trans-national corporations against the sons of the soil prompted a thorough criticism of forest policy of modern India. This in turn led historians to delve deep into the relation between forest, forest products and local communities, and the colonial and post-colonial forestry perception of the state. The discourse on water also emerged out of environmental activism. One can think about the Narmada Bachao Andolan against the Sardar Sarovar project of building dam in the Narmada River and the rise of scholarship regarding this issue, criticizing the *big is beautiful* model leading to ecological destruction along with massive displacement and livelihood crisis of the common people.[28]

Contradictory to wilderness cult that mainly emphasize the preservation of nature for nature's sake, Indian environmentalism emerges out of access to habitat, natural resource, etc., which is linked to the question of livelihood. Here the urge to save and protect ecology comes not from nature for nature's sake but from nature for the sake of the human beings, for whom without environmental conservation sustenance is not possible. American environmentalism emerged out of its 'post-material' pursuits of an urge of having a clean environment, breathing pure air, and ferrying in the transparent water of the canals. This is true for the countries of the North (in general). This is what Guha and Martinez Alier regard as 'ecology of affluence'.[29] On the other hand, South-Asian environmentalism has its own distinct characteristics, its own flow, and dimension. It is more intrinsically linked with the questions of livelihood, distributive justice, human rights, etc. This is what Guha and Alier regard as 'environmentalism of the poor' which originates as 'a clash over productive resources... one with deep ecological implications....Red on the outside, but green on the inside.'[30]

The divergences in the two approaches can be best illustrated by the Dudois/Patkar comparison.[31] Both Mark Dubois and Medha Patkar intended to offer their lives to stop dam construction in the Stanislaus River in California and the Narmada River, respectively. Dubois chained himself to a boulder, and Medha Patkar decided to drown herself in the river. Though the strategy of protest was similar, but the goal was not absolutely the same. Mark Dubois's protest was to save the Stanislaus canyon as the last remaining example and icon of virgin and unspoilt American wilderness. Medha Patkar was massively fighting for the cause not only to save the Narmada River but also the huge number of inhabitants of the area who would be displaced with the construction of the dam with the completion of the Sardar Sarovar Project.

The southern variety of environmentalism, i.e., the 'environmentalism of the poor' or liberation ecologics[32] can be compared to a third strand in American environmentalism which is known as the Environmental Justice Movement. It was a movement against environmental racism uniting environmentalism and social justice where the 'people of colour' residing in poverty pockets with depressed economies actively participated. The pioneer in this field Robert D. Bullard writes, 'Grassroots groups challenge the 'business-as-usual' environmentalism that is generally practiced by the more privileged wild-life and conservation-oriented groups.'[33] In this regard, a convergence between 'environmentalism of the poor' of the south and the environmental justice movement of the US can be drawn. But there is a difference too. Alier rightly argues that if a book is written on US environmental justice movement, it can easily be entitled as 'The environmentalism of the poor and the minorities' as the movement mainly fights for the minority groups in the US; on the contrary southern 'environmentalism of the poor' encompasses the majority of the people.[34]

'World Environment History' – Beyond the 'Insular Approach'

In recent times, with the thrust moving away from local to global, the limits of environmental history has expanded to incorporate within its purview global topics of global concern rather than only concentrating on ecological sustainability and growth at the home front, neglecting environmental degradation beyond the border. The North American environmental historians had already entered into the phase of evolving a world environmental history that can more broadly explain human activities which are 'less often circumscribed by specific ecosystems (although even these cross borders) and more often extend throughout the bio-sphere, transcending every national frontier.'[35] During the first formal conference of the American Society for Environmental History, held at the University of California at Irvine in January 1982, Donald Worster gave an eloquent lecture entitled *World Without Borders: The Internationalizing of Environmental History* in which he called for a 'post-nationalist synthesis' in environmental history that would take account of predicaments forced on historians by several transitions in modern culture away from the vernacular and local toward the professional and global.[36]

Two trends that can be overtly seen in the writings of the American environmental historians are – an understanding and perceiving the ecology of the American continents as a Melting Pot, the landscape being the central stage of cross-fertilization and cross-cultural influences among multiple nationalities, races, ethnicities, etc. and a broader approach of formulating the World Environmental History. While the former trend is brilliantly reflected in Crosby's compilations, the later had surfaced in the works of Donald Worster (*The Ends of the Earth: Perspectives on Modern Environmental History*), J. Donald Hughes (*The Face of the Earth: Environment and World History*), and John R. McNeill, (*Something*

New Under the Sun: An Environmental History of the Twentieth-Century World).[37]

Annotated Bibliography

- Louis S. Warren ed, *American Environmental History* (New York: Blackwell Publishing, 2003), Richard White's 'American Environmental History: The Development of a New Historical Field', (*Pacific Historical Review*, Vol. 54, No. 3 (Aug. 1985), pp. 297–335), and Alfred W. Crosby, 'The Past and the Present of Environmental History' (*The American Historical Review*, Vol. 100, No. 4 (October 1995), pp. 1181–85) contain detailed historiography of the American Environmental History.
- While Wolfang Sachs's *For Love of the Automobile: Looking Back Into the History of Our Desires* (Berkeley: University of California Press, 1992) deals with the isolationist approach in American Environmental History in *Varieties of Environmentalism: Essays North and South* (Delhi: Oxford University Press, 1998), Ramachandra Guha and Joan Martinez Alier bring out the varying trends in Northern and Southern environmental activism and hence environmental history.
- Donald Worster, 'World without Borders: The Internationalizing of Environmental History' (*Environmental Review*, Vol. 6 (Fall 1982), pp. 8–13) and J. Donald Hughes, 'Global Dimensions of Environmental History' (*Pacific Historical Review*, Vol. 70, No. 1 (February 2001), pp. 91–101) propound for the internationalization of environmental history or what is called 'world environment history', and after drawing relevance of the concept in the present world scenario, suggest methods and approaches for it.

Notes

1. Alfred W. Crosby, 'The Past and the Present of Environmental History', *The American Historical Review*, Vol. 100, No. 4 (October 1995), pp. 1181–85.
2. Frederick Jackson Turner, 'The Significance of the Frontier in American History', *Annual Report of the American Historical Association for 1893* (Washington, D.C., 1894), pp. 197–227; Walter Prescott Webb, *The Great Plains* (Boston: Ginn, 1931).
3. Richard White, 'American Environmental History: The Development of a New Historical Field', *Pacific Historical Review*, Vol. 54, No. 3 (August 1985), pp. 297–335.

4. James C. Malin, *The Grassland of North America: Prolegomena to Its History* (1947; Gloucester, Mass.: Peter Smith, 1967).
5. Richard White, 'American Environmental History'.
6. Samuel P. Hays, *Conservation and the Gospel of Efficiency: The Progressive Conservation Movement, 1890–1920* (1959; New York: Atheneum, 1975); Roderick Nash, *Wilderness and the American Mind* (New Haven: Yale University Press, 1982), 3rd edition.
7. Elmo R. Richardson, *The Politics of Conservation: Crusades and Controversies, 1897–1913* (Berkeley: University of California Press, 1962); *Dams, Parks, and Politics: Re-source Development and Preservation in the Truman-Eisenhower Era* (Lexington: University Press of Kentucky, 1973); George Michael McCarthy, *Hour of Trail: The Conservation Conflict in Colorado and the West, 1891–1907* (Norman: University of Oklahoma Press, 1977); James Penick, Jr., *Progressive Politics and Conservation: The Ballinger-Pinchot Affair* (Chicago: University of Chicago Press, 1968).
8. William G. Robbins, *Lumberjacks and Legislators: Political Economy of the U.S. Lumber Industry, 1890–1941* (College Station: Texas A & M University Press, 1982); Abraham Hoffman, *Vision or Villainy: Origins of the Owens Valley-Los Angeles Water Controversy* (College Station: Texas A & M University Press, 1981); William L. Kahrl, *Water and Power: The Conflict over Los Angeles' Water Supply in the Owens Valley* (Berkeley and Los Angeles: University of California Press, 1982).
9. Barbara Novak's *Nature and Culture: American Landscape and Painting, 1825–1875* (New York: Oxford University Press, 1980).
10. Brian Balogh, 'Scientific Forestry and the Roots of the Modern American State: Gifford Pinchot's Path to Progressive Reform', *Environmental History*, Vol. 7, No. 2, (2002), pp. 198–225; Michael P. Cohen, *The Pathless Way: John Muir and American Wilderness* (Madison: University of Wisconsin Press, 1984); Stephen Fox, *John Muir and His Legacy: The American Conservation Movement* (Boston: Little Brown and Co., 1981).
11. Richard White, 'American Environmental History'.
12. Gregory Thompson, *Parks in the West and American Culture* (Sun Valley, Idaho: Institute of the American West, 1984); Susan R. Schrepfer, *The Fight to Save the Redwoods: A History of Environmental Reform, 1917–1978* (Madison: University of Wisconsin Press, 1983); C.W. Buchholtz, *Rocky Mountain National Park: A History* (Boulder: Colorado Associated University Press, 1983); Frank Graham, Jr., *The Adirondack Park: A Political History* (New York: Alfred A. Knopf, 1978).
13. Joseph M. Petulla, *American Environmental History: The Exploitation and Conservation of Natural Resources* (San Francisco: Boyd & Fraser Publishing Co., 1977).
14. Donald E. Worster, *Nature's Economy: The Roots of Ecology* (San Francisco: Sierra Club Books, 1977).

15. Susan Schrepfer, *The Fight to Save the Redwood.*
16. J. Donald Hughes, *American Indian Ecology* (El Paso: Texas Western Press, 1983).
17. Richard White, 'American Environmental History'.
18. Donald Worster, *Dust Bowl: The Southern Plains in the 1930s* (New York: Oxford University Press, 1979).
19. William Cronon's *Changes in the Land: Indians, Colonists, and the Ecology of New England* (New York: Hill and Wang, 1983); Richard White, *Land Use, Environment, and Social Change: The Shaping of Island County, Washington* (Seattle: University of Washington, 1980); Albert E. Cowdrey, *This Land, This South: An Environmental History* (Lexington: University of Kentucky Press, 1983).
20. Alfred Crosby, *The Columbian Exchange: Biological* (Westport: Greenwood Press, 1972); *Cultural Consequences of 1492* and *Ecological Imperialism: The Biological Exchange of Europe, 900–1900* (Cambridge, New York: Cambridge University Press, 1986).
21. Tim Palmer, *Stanislaus: The Struggle for a River* (Berkeley and Los Angeles: University of California Press, 1982).
22. Richard H.K. Vietor, *Environmental Politics and the Coal Coalition* (College Station: Texas A & M University, 1980).
23. John C. Pierce, Nicholas. P. Lovrich, Takematsu Tsurutani and Takematsu Abe, 'Culture, Politics and Mass Publics: Traditional and Modern Supporters of the New Environmental Paradigm in Japan and the United States', *The Journal of Politics*, Vol. 49, No. 1 (February 1987), pp. 54–79.
24. Wolfang Sachs, *For love of the Automobile: Looking Back Into the History of Our Desires* (Berkeley: University of California Press, 1992), pp. 150–51.
25. Ramachandra Guha and Joan Martinez Alier, *Varieties of Environmentalism: Essays North and South* (Delhi: Oxford University Press, 1998), p. 7.
26. Ranjan Chakrabarti, ed, *Situating Environmental History* (New Delhi: Manohar, 2007), p. 14.
27. Ramachandra Guha, 'Movement Scholarship', *Environmental History,* Vol. 10, No. 1 (January 2005), available at: http://www.historycooperative.org/journals/eh/10.1/guha.html (date of access: 30.11.2010).
28. Patrick McCully, *Silenced Rivers: The Ecology and Politics of Large Dams,* (London and New Jersey: Zed Books, 1996); Sanjay Sangvai, *The River and Life,* (Mumbai and Calcutta: Earthcare Books, 2000); Amita Baviskar, *In the Belly of the River: Tribal Conflicts over Development in the Narmada Valley* (Delhi: Oxford University Press, 1997).
29. Ramachandra Guha, 'Movement Scholarship'.
30. Ibid.
31. Ibid.

32. Richard Peet and Michael Watts, eds, *Liberation Ecologies: Environment, Development, Social Movements* (London and New York: Routledge, 1996).
33. Robert. D. Bullard, ed, *Confronting Environmental Racism: Voices from the Grassroots,* Introduction (Boston, Massachusetts: South End Press, 1993).
34. Joan Martinez Alier, *The Environmentalism of the Poor: A Case Study of Ecological Conflicts and Valuation* (New Delhi: Oxford University Press, 2004), p. 13.
35. J. Donald Hughes, 'Global Dimensions of Environmental History', *Pacific Historical Review,* Vol. 70, No. 1 (February 2001), pp. 91–101.
36. It was later published in *Environmental Review,* Vol. 6 (Fall 1982), pp. 8–13.
37. Donald Worster, ed, *The Ends of the Earth: Perspectives on Modern Environmental History* (New York: Cambridge University Press, 1988); J. Donald Hughes, ed, *The Face of the Earth: Environment and World History* (New York: Armonk, 2000); J. R. McNeill, *Something New Under the Sun: An Environmental History of the Twentieth-Century World* (New York: W.W. Norton, 2000).

Epilogue: Perceiving American History Beyond the 'Exceptionalist' Framework

The book ends with an epilogue that engages the readers with the conceptual and methodological questions in American historical research. With the argument that American History has been long perceived within the 'exceptionalist' framework, it sketches its problems as a historical approach and explicates how it had its roots to the politico-economic interests of the country. It then moves on to discuss the origin and limitations of the latest trend of looking into American History from the 'post-exceptionalist' framework sharply recognizing that it is also a culmination of America's very own national and economic interests in the era of globalization and internationalism. Finally, it suggests directions and conviction through which the objective realities of American History can be taken up and studied.

American 'exceptionalism' refers to the belief 'that the United States differs qualitatively from other developed nations, because of its unique origins, national credo, historical evolution, and distinctive political and religious institutions.'[1] The theory that the United States is different from other countries, its 'exceptionalism' stemming from its emergence from the Revolution, becoming the first new nation,[2] and developing a uniquely American ideology based on liberty, egalitarianism, individualism, populism, and laissez-faire first surfaced in the writing of Alexis de Tocqueville who described the United States as 'exceptional' as early as the first half of the nineteenth century. He remarked, 'The position of the Americans is therefore quite exceptional, and it may be believed that no other democratic people will ever be placed in a similar one.'[3] This trend went on, and in one of the recent works published in 2011 entitled *Idea of America: Reflections on the Birth of the United States*, historian Gordon Wood said, 'Our (American) beliefs in liberty, equality, constitutionalism, and the well-being of ordinary people came out of the Revolutionary era. So too did our idea that we Americans are a special people with a special destiny to lead the world toward liberty and democracy.'[4]

The idea originated from a number of groundings. Tocqueville wrote,

> Their strictly Puritanical origin, their exclusively commercial habits, even the country they inhabit, which seems to divert their minds from the pursuit of science, literature, and the arts, the proximity of Europe, which allows them to neglect these pursuits without relapsing into barbarism, a thousand special causes, of which I have only been able to point out the most important, have singularly concurred to fix the mind of the American upon purely practical objects. His passions, his wants, his education, and everything about him seem to unite in drawing the native of the United States earthward; his religion alone bids him turn, from time to time, a transient and distracted glance to heaven. Let us cease, then, to view all democratic nations under the example of the American people.[5]

Scholars have explored possible justifications for the notion of American 'exceptionalism' which include:

- Absence of feudalism;
- Puritan roots;
- American Revolution and Republicanism;
- Democracy;
- Immigration;
- Frontier spirit and American mobility; and
- American variety of communism

Louis Hartz in *The Liberal Tradition in America* argued that due to the absence of feudal traditions in colonial America such as established churches, landed estates, and hereditary nobility, American political tradition lacked the left-wing socialist and right-wing aristocratic elements that dominated in most other lands. Hartz remarks, 'The analysis which this book contains is based on what might be called the storybook truth about American history: that America was settled by men who fled from the feudal and clerical oppressions of the Old World.'[6] The 'liberal consensus' school including David Potter, Daniel Boorstein, and Richard Hofstadter followed Hartz in emphasizing that political conflicts in American History remained within the watertight boundaries of a liberal consensus regarding private property, individual rights, and representative government; and the national government emerged as far less centralized or nationalized as the European counterparts.[7]

Some scholars have traced American 'exceptionalism' to Puritan roots. The Puritans migrated to New England with the aim of building a utopian community that transcended history, a New Zion that was free from the corruption and oppression they sought to leave behind in Europe.[8] From the early years of settlement along the North Atlantic coast, the Puritans embraced a middle ground between strict Calvinist predestination and a less restricting theology of Divine Providence, and believed in the dictum that God had made a covenant with their people and had chosen them to lead the other nations of the Earth. In his metaphor of 'a city upon the hill,' John Winthrop, the Governor of Massachusetts captured the Puritans' sense of the exceptional nature, divinely ordained and without precedent, at least since biblical times.[9] So, we find that the discourse goes a long way, much before the birth of the US as a nation-state.

The intellectual foundations for the Revolutionary concept of American 'exceptionalism' was laid by Thomas Paine when he pointed out in *Common Sense* that America was not a mere extension of Europe, but a new land with unlimited potential and opportunity that had outgrown the British mother country.[10] American Republicanism that prompted and injected the idea that sovereignty belonged to the people and not to the hereditary ruling class, supplemented American uniqueness in governance. The advanced nature of democracy infusing every aspect of society and culture and America's openness to immigration and the immigrants' attraction to this land because of its perceived economic and political opportunities were important arguments justifying the 'exceptionalism' discourse. Finally, 'additional images and beliefs such as the rugged individualism exemplified by the frontiersman (the Turner thesis), the rags-to-riches ascent of the hardworking entrepreneur, and the non-imperialist nature of American expansion–subsequently reinforced exceptionalist formulations of the American experience and national identity on the part of historians and politicians alike.'[11] John Higham in his article 'The Future of American History' has tried to answer the pertinent question that why did the historians encapsulated American History within a national framework for long, relying on the idea of American uniqueness. After a deep-rooted analysis, he answers that this trend continued due to a virtually unchallengeable national myth that identified America as a country created by removal from the corruptions and confinement of Europe.[12]

The impact of this discourse has been deleterious mainly for other (non-American) peoples, other nations, and other cultures since its birth till the Cold War and the post-Cold War era; the concept played a significant role and provided the ideological justification for American policies (especially foreign policy) aimed at promoting the Americanization of non-Western peoples and societies. It had been used in denigrating non-Western cultures which is manifested in early Anglo-American policies toward the Indian peoples of coastal North America leading to the American expansion or internal colonization of the westward dispossession at the cost of Indian dispossession. Since the late 1890s, it had been deployed in encounters with overseas peoples and cultures. In the Cold War period, America's appearance as a messiah for the ravaged nations and in the post-Cold War period, the formulation of the Western/American 'development' discourse and its imposition on the decolonized 'underdeveloped' through the 'Unholy Trinity',[13] World bank, International Monetary Fund (IMF), and World Trade Organization (WTO) for eradicating 'poverty', 'uncertainty', and 'ignorance' in the Third World had its root laid in the 'exceptionalism' discourse which provided that America was the only nation capable of 'uplifting' and 'improving' others through its 'civilizing mission' and 'spread of democracy'. The non-Western peoples were considered as 'savage' and 'barbaric'. While Chinese or Japanese leaders who resisted US inroads into their societies in the late 1800s were caricatured as effete, reactionary, or xenophobic, in the post-Cold War era, Muslim revivalists have been stranded as irrational fanatics bent on fomenting violent opposition to American-inspired efforts to promote economic and cultural globalization.[14]

The 'exceptionalist' framework has drawn scepticism worldwide and also among host of American historians, who since the last few decades have become conscious of the limitations of the insular approach in American History that provides an ideological justification and legitimization of the superiority of American culture and identity; which is false and creates divisive tendencies among peoples and nations making way towards hyper-criticism of American approach in these days of globalization and strong transnational forces.

Ian Tyrell in his 1991 article 'American Exceptionalism in an Age of International History' published in *The American Historical Review*, has criticized the 'exceptionalism' approach in American history and urged for a methodology that would study US history in contrast 'with other histories that conform to fixed patterns of historical development.'[15] Though Tyrell argues in favour of comparative history, but he is conscious of the fact that what is important is the choice of countries for comparison. He remarks, 'It should be clear by now that the critics of exceptionalism cannot defeat the notion by exposing its illogicalities or by using the methodology of comparative history.'[16] To him, the 'New Transnational History' should be constructed in several complementary ways like regional analysis drawing on the footprints of the French *Annales* school and also the earlier local and regional historiography in the United States, to strike out in the direction of a global focus more attentive to historical specificity and variety, the development of a transnational project using an American base, the study of the interaction of the American colonies and republic with the international economic system, etc.

John Higham shows that long before the recent decades, some of the best historians of the United States, even as early as the 1840s onward, consciously turned away from the parochialism of their national history and identified themselves increasingly with a transatlantic world. Nineteenth century American scholars like William H. Prescott, Henry C. Lea, Charles Homer Haskins, and Alfred T. Mahan created a tradition of cosmopolitan scholarship drawing on common Anglo-American value. Though one should acknowledge C.V. Woodward edited *The Comparative Approach in American History* that consisted of a number of essays which addressed various issues from slavery, immigration, mobility to industrialization, urbanization, and Great Depression from the comparative framework,[17] Higham is more comfortable with the transatlantic approach than comparative history as the former could make a place for transatlantic perspective, but without altering the core of American History. Higham finds the best possible solution in 'the reconstruction of a genuinely national history, a history of the connections through which state and society have defined one another and dealt with change' which would entail some venturing beyond the American arena as a natural corollary.[18]

In the recent decades, it is however clear that there has been a shift in history (politics, bureaucracy, etc.) from the 'exceptionalist' to the trans-atlantic paradigm. The reason behind this finds the best expression in Michael Adas's argument,

> By the last half of the twentieth century, transnational exchanges had become so routinized and pervasive that they impinged on virtually all aspects of American life, hence literally globalizing contemporary U.S. history. As early as the oil crisis of 1973, it was clear to all who were willing to see that what had been long been presumed to be American corporations had in fact metamorphosed into international conglomerates with bottom-line priorities that often had little to do with the national interest. New waves of immigration–more likely in post-1960s decades to flow from Latin America, the Caribbean, and Asia rather than Europe–have complicated and increased the ethnic and cultural diversity of the United States to the point where the majority status of peoples of European descent is challenged, or has already been eclipsed, in the fastest-growing and most dynamic areas of the country. The resources this polyglot population consumes, the products it produces, and the environmental consequences of both are now calibrated in terms of international capital flows and market exchanges as well as ecological agendas that are premised on visions of the earth as a single entity.[19]

But the new approach and the waning away of the American 'exceptionalism' has its own problem, and like the earlier period, is a culmination of America's very own politico-economic interests in the era of globalization and internationalism. Donald Pease's work reveals a brilliant analysis of this fact.[20] Pease argues that during the Cold War, American 'exceptionalism' had legitimated America's dominance within a bipolar world order by supplying the rationale for its moral superiority to Russian communism. With the dismantling of the Soviet Union and the formation of the European Union (EU), when the US lost its threatening, socialist, totalitarian enemy Russia, 'the historical conditions that had formerly undergirded its assumptions faded into the historical past,' and the 'exceptional' ideology had every logic to wane away. 'With the loss of the geopolitical rationale for the representation of the US as an exception to the laws of nations, the US also lost the putative right to establish the rules for the global order.' The demands of a newly globalized world order solicited an understanding of the US's embeddedness within transnational forces rather than the reaffirmation of its unique position and isolation from them. Pease argues that in the post-Cold War era, two interrelated dimensions of the disavowed underside of American exceptionalism – US imperialism and US global interdependencies emerged simultaneously. The state's assimilationist paradigm emerged as the new trend of study. But one needs to think deeply 'whether transnational American studies has (really) moved beyond the discourse of exceptionalism or refurbished the other side of its Janus face: the exemplary civic nationalist dimension of American exceptionalism that, during the Cold War, had been all but effaced by the national security state.' 'Does not post-exceptionalist American studies also simply ignore the ways in which two of the core tenets of the discourse of American exceptionalism–the rule of law and neoliberal market ideology–have saturated the global processes in which America is embedded?'[21]

After 9/11, America's interconnectedness seemed delusory and the American state's response to the terrorist attacks supplanted and replaced transnational Americanists' descriptions of the US mobile localizations of global processes with prodigious reassertions of US global dominance. Strong currents of unilateralism emerged in the international arena and in new rules of citizenship and belonging within the borderlands of the newly circumscribed state of exception.[22]

We can conclude by saying that one needs to understand concepts and discourses as per the ideological justifications and legitimizations of a state's action. Laura Ann Stoler rightly remarks that all 'imperial states operate as states of exception that vigilantly produce exceptions to their principles and exceptions to their laws.'[23] The American case is not an exception to this. Comparative history, only for the sake of application of its methodology, as evident in numerous of works by Carl N. Degler, George M. Fredrickson, Peter Kolchin, and others, is a fruitful exercise.[24] But there is a dire need to move ahead and perceive American history within the broader framework of studying historical transformations from one mode of production to the other with emphasis on both internal and external frontiers, bringing out and asserting the often unaddressed tension between America's self-perception and the actual reality which can be mapped through crisis in the domestic front as well as impact on and response by 'others' (non-American/non-western peoples, nations and cultures).

Annotated Bibliography

- Johannes Thimm's *American Exceptionalism–Conceptual Thoughts and Empirical Evidence* (available at: http://www.jukkarannila.fi/docs/American_Exceptionalism_Thimm-American_exceptionalism.pdf, date of access: 14.07.2012) is on the evolution of the concept of American 'exceptionalism' towards multilateral regimes.
- Ian Tyrell talks in favour of and suggest methodologies to pursue comparative history in 'American Exceptionalism in an Age of International History' (*The American Historical Review,* Vol. 96, No. 4 (October 1991), pp. 1031–55) and criticizes the exceptionalist approach in American History.
- John Higham bolsters the reconstruction of a genuinely national history as the need of the hour in 'The Future of American History' (*The Journal of American History*, Vol. 80, No. 4 (March 1994), pp. 1289–1309).
- In 'From Settler Colony to Global Hegemon: Integrating the Exceptionalist Narrative of the American Experience into World History' (*The American Historical Review*, Vol. 106, No. 6 (December 2001), pp. 1692–1720), Michael Adas argues that there has been a shift in history writing from the 'exceptionalist' to the transatlantic paradigm.
- Donald Pease explores the politico-economic context of US post-exceptionalism in the era of globalization and internationalism in 'Re-thinking "American Studies after US Exceptionalism"' (*American Literary History*, Vo. 21, No. 1 (2009), pp. 19–27).

Notes

1. Harold Hongju Koh, 'America's Jekyll and Hyde Exceptionalism', Michael Ignatieff, ed, *American Exceptionalism and Human Rights* (Princeton: Princeton University Press, 2005), pp. 111–44.
2. Seymour Martin Lipset, *American Exceptionalism: A Double-Edged Sword* (New York: W.W. Norton & Company, 1996).
3. Alexis de Tocqueville, *Democracy in America* (New York: Langley, 1840), part 2, p. 36.
4. Gordon Wood, *Idea of America: Reflections on the Birth of the United States* (USA: Penguin Group, 2011), introduction.
5. Alexis de Tocqueville, *Democracy in America* (London: Saunders and Otley, 1831).
6. Louis Hartz, *The Liberal Tradition in America: An Interpretation of American Political Thought since the Revolution* (New York: Harcourt Brace & Company, 1955), p. 3.

7. Gary Cross, 'Comparative Exceptionalism: Rethinking the Hartz Thesis in the Settler Societies of Nineteenth-Century United States and Australia', *Australasian Journal of American Studies*, Vol. 14, No. 1 (1995), pp. 15–41.
8. Michael Adas, 'From Settler Colony to Global Hegemon: Integrating the Exceptionalist Narrative of the American Experience into World History', *The American Historical Review*, Vol. 106, No. 6 (December 2001), pp. 1692–1720.
9. Ibid.
10. Thomas Paine *Common Sense* (Rockville, Maryland: Arc Manor, 2008), originally published as a series of pamphlets in 1776.
11. Michael Adas, 'From Settler Colony to Global Hegemon'.
12. John Higham, 'The Future of American History', *The Journal of American History*, Vol. 80, No. 4 (March 1994), pp. 1289–1309.
13. Richard Peet, *Unholy Trinity: The IMF, World Bank and WTO* (New York, London: Zed Books Ltd, 2003).
14. Michael Adas, 'From Settler Colony to Global Hegemon'.
15. Ian Tyrell, 'American Exceptionalism in an Age of International History', *The American Historical Review,* Vol. 96, No. 4 (October 1991), pp. 1031–55.
16. Ibid.
17. C.V. Woodward, ed, *The Comparative Approach in American History* (New York: Basic Books, 1968).
18. John Higham, 'The Future of American History'.
19. Michael Adas, 'From Settler Colony to Global Hegemon'.
20. Donald Pease, 'Re-thinking "American Studies after US Exceptionalism"', *American Literary History*, Vol. 21, No. 1 (2009), pp. 19–27.
21. Ibid.
22. Ibid.
23. Ibid.
24. Carl N. Degler, *Neither Black Nor White: Slavery and Race Relations in Brazil and the United States* (New York: Macmillan, 1971); George M. Fredrickson, *White Supremacy: A Comparative Study of American and South African History* (New York: Oxford University Press, 1981); Peter Kolchin, *Unfree Labor: American Slavery and Russian Serfdom* (Belknap Press, 1987).

Index